REDEFINING
Christianity

UNDERSTANDING THE
PURPOSE DRIVEN® MOVEMENT

BOB DEWAAY

21ST CENTURY
PRESS
PUBLISHING WITH PURPOSE
WWW.21STCENTURYPRESS.COM

REDEFINING Christianity

Understanding the Purpose Driven Movement

Copyright © 2006 By Bob DeWaay

Published by 21st Century Press
2131 W. Republic Rd.
PMB 41
Springfield, MO 65807

For more information about 21st Century Press visit our website:

www.21stcenturypress.com

ISBN 0-9771964-3-7

Cover Design: Lee Fredrickson
Book Design: Terry White

21ST CENTURY PRESS
PUBLISHING WITH PURPOSE
WWW.21STCENTURYPRESS.COM

Dedication

To my beloved wife, Diane, whose stand for the gospel led me to faith in Christ thirty-four years ago and whose love and support are invaluable in the work of the ministry.

Acknowledgements

Dick Kuffel has been my closest co-worker in the ministry for twenty years. Without Dick's efforts, *Critical Issues Commentary* in both print and radio format would not be possible. Dick consistently challenges me to be the best pastor, speaker and writer that I can be and helps me to that end.

Keith Jentoft continually challenges my thinking and helps me understand the issues about which I write in a deeper manner. Keith cares very deeply about the gospel and its integrity, and has made a significant contribution in helping me finish this book.

The elders of Twin City Fellowship have made it possible for me to devote the necessary time to write this book while carrying on the work of pastoral ministry.

Table of Contents

Foreword

Jan Markell introduced me to Bob DeWaay when we were both being interviewed on her radio program, "Understanding the Times." It was then that I learned of our parallel ministries. Not only were we both pastors of Bible-centered churches, but each of us also had writing ministries dealing with theological issues facing the church today. Since that time I have made it a practice to read Bob's excellent bimonthly positional papers in *Critical Issues Commentary*. More than that, when people write me about subjects that I have not yet addressed, I always refer them to *Critical Issues Commentary* (and I often do so even if I have written on the subject). In reading his work, I have found Bob to be a careful researcher who is gracious yet clear and not afraid to speak the truth in love. But most of all, I have been delighted to confirm time after time that Bob is biblical.

When I learned that he was writing a book on Rick Warren and his ministry, I was excited. Here would be a book, I was sure, which would shine the light of Scripture on what Warren taught and would do so in a way which honored God and edified the church. I was not disappointed. This is the best overall examination of Rick Warren and his "Purpose Driven" ministry that I have read. Pastor DeWaay has done a great service for the church of Christ.

Several times each year I visit the worship services of other evangelical churches. In recent years I have noticed a commonality about most of them. It seems as if they are all reading from the same menu when it comes to philosophy of ministry, worship style, preaching content, and use of Scripture (or, should I say, non-use?). While I was aware of the influence some of the flagship seeker-sensitive churches were having (especially Willow Creek and Saddleback), I was nevertheless mystified at the level of cloning that I saw in the smaller churches that I visited. I had numerous bits and pieces of information, but I still could not comprehend some of the things I was experiencing. Bob connected the dots for me when he documented Warren's successful efforts at franchising his own church, Saddleback Valley Community Church

(Warren calls this his "church-in-a-box" approach).

Bob painstakingly shows that Rick Warren has done for the church what McDonald's has done for the restaurant industry. Unfortunately, the church is not in the hamburger flipping business. Applying franchising principles to Christ's church may result in outward success, but true success cannot be measured by simply reading the bottom line of "nickels and noses," buildings and programs.

But there is a bottom line with which to measure the church – it is doctrinal integrity. The church is the pillar and support of the truth (1 Timothy 3:15). If the church fails in its God-given mission of upholding, defending and propagating the truth then it fails. Period.

It is on this level that Bob DeWaay challenges Rick Warren's "Purpose Driven" agenda. Is the Warren franchise successful? By every criteria that a retail franchise can be measured, the answer is a clear yes. But how is the Warren franchise doing with the all-important commodity of truth? This is the question with which *Redefining Christianity* is concerned. The answer will be hard for some to take. Then again, we are talking about truth. DeWaay demonstrates that Warren strips the faith of key doctrines, accessorizes it with human wisdom, turns it into a journey of self-discovery and sells it to the unsuspecting world as "Christianity."

Some will decry Bob's efforts in this volume. Why expose Rick Warren? After all, he is surely doing some good and his motives seem to be pure. What these people miss is that God has called the elders of the church to not only exhort in sound doctrine, but to also refute those who contradict sound doctrine (Titus 1:9). These two things all elders of every local church are to do, but only a few godly leaders are equipped to exhort and refute in such a manner that the church at large is edified. Pastor DeWaay is one of those few. Provided by God with an analytical mind, willing to do the hard work of careful research, knowledgeable of Scripture, gifted to write and possessing the heart of a pastor, Bob DeWaay is the right man to give us the insight we need into the Purpose Driven movement.

Dr. Gary E. Gilley, Th.D
Senior Pastor of Southern View Chapel, Springfield, Illinois.

Introduction

On September 29, 2005 Rick Warren addressed the Religion Newswriters Association's annual conference.[1] There he announced his bold new agenda to solve the world's five largest problems. He told these writers, "What I am about to tell you is going to change the American church," and went on to tell them about his P.E.A.C.E. plan—an ambitious project to mobilize 2 billion Christians to wipe out the world's biggest problems scheduled for release in 2006. He told the newswriters, "We are going to release it to those 400,000 congregations we have trained, and I believe it will change the world."[2]

The secular press has noticed. *Fortune Magazine's* extensive article by Marc Gunther offers this analysis of Warren: "America's new superstar pastor wants to re-brand evangelical Christianity.[3] He's got the management genius to do it." Gunther cites a businessman who says: "Forget any opinions you have about religion and just look at the guy as a CEO, and you've got to be impressed." Writes Gunther, "And his ambitions are so vast that they practically invite scorn—uniting liberal and conservative Protestants, fixing Africa, transforming the very nature of American culture." Warren plans to change the church, and having changed it, use the church as a vehicle to solve the world's biggest problems.[4]

Should evangelicals be alarmed, or should they join? I am alarmed. The entire forty-minute speech before a mixed group of writers could be summarized as Rick Warren talking about Rick Warren. He presented no mention of the gospel, no description of the Person and work of Christ, and nothing that would lead one to believe that conversions from dead works to faith in the resurrected Christ have a place in this plan. Apparently re-branded evangelicalism is a new form of the old, liberal social gospel.

Warren told his listeners that he has spoken before the United Nations and the Council on Foreign Relations. The apostle Paul likewise was able to speak to kings and dignitaries. His message reached the highest levels of the Roman Empire, but there is a vast difference in content. Paul always preached about the Person and work of Christ, including His resurrection from the dead. He preached the gospel. Never did Paul tell kings or rulers that he could help them solve social problems in their kingdom. He preached Christ—a message which ultimately cost Paul his life.

The version of Christianity that Rick Warren presents to world leaders redefines the message of the first century apostles. The key difference is that the biblical version did not appeal to the world; it appealed only to those who were converted. Warren's version is popular with the world.

Rick Warren has designed a message that appeals to religious consumers whether or not the Holy Spirit has convicted them of their sins. He has devised a business system to mass-market this message to the world. Through his system, he has created a way for pastors to share his success. The sheer effectiveness of this system is rapidly transforming evangelicalism. This transformation is not just a transformation of practice; it is a transformation of message. The change in the practice makes it transferable across a wide spectrum of denominational and theological affiliations. The change in the message makes it acceptable to a wide range of religious consumers.

In this book, we shall examine *The Purpose Driven Church, The Purpose Driven Life*, and the business system that Rick Warren has developed to promote it around the world. We shall look carefully at his claims, his use of Scripture, his integration of human wisdom with Scripture, and his ability to get thousands of pastors to convert from expository Bible preaching to being Purpose Driven. In the end, we shall compare Rick Warren's version of church health with that of Jesus Christ. We shall see how he has redefined Christianity. The world may indeed love this new version and listen, but what it is hearing is something substantially different from biblical Christianity that the world hates and rejects.

Jesus said, *"If you were of the world, the world would love its own; but because you are not of the world, but I chose you out of the world, therefore the world hates you"* (John 15:19). Not even the greatest marketing genius can change this without redefining the church. Seeking the approval of the world is precisely what the Purpose Driven movement is all about.

Rick Warren's Ministry Philosophy

When Rick Warren was a young man, he was profoundly influenced by the church growth writings of Donald McGavran,[1] a visionary who used sociological studies to determine how people could be better enticed to become Christians. This simple idea turned into what is now called "missiology." McGavran later founded The Fuller School of World Mission and Institute of Church Growth, an organization further expanded by C. Peter Wagner.[2] In the preface of the third edition of *Understanding Church Growth*, C. Peter Wagner calls McGavran "The father of the Church Growth movement."[3] One would be accurate calling McGavran the academic founder of the movement and Robert Schuller the popular founder. Both men influenced Warren.

McGavran's ideas changed how many evangelicals view missions and church growth. One idea was that mission efforts should be held accountable for results: churches that are not growing are failing, and any reasons the leaders of such churches give (such as working amongst a resistant people) are merely rationalizations for their own failure.[4] This thinking has taken root so deeply in American evangelicalism that pastors have become desperate for anything that promises church growth. This thinking provides fertile ground for someone like Rick Warren to market a plan that promises growth.

Another of McGavran's key ideas is that people need to be reached as a group rather than as individuals. He came to this conclusion through his sociological studies of people groups and what he called "people movements." One term that came out of

McGavran's mission theory was "homogeneous unit."[5] The significance of this concept is that people are less resistant to attending
church if they can go as a group to a church where everyone else is
like them. Warren's application of this was to identify "Saddleback
Sam."[6] McGavran understood the Great Commission to mean that
the church should "disciple nations" in the sense of "people groups"
or "tribes" rather than individuals. The traditional understanding
was that God would save individuals from the various tribes, and
these were to be brought into the church as a new people of God
made up of persons from diverse backgrounds. McGavran claimed
that individual people groups would become their own distinct
Christian tribes like the Jewish tribes of the Old Testament were a
people."[7] Along with this was the idea of group conversion.[8]

This thinking is reflected in Warren's teaching of defining a
target group for a particular church to reach. Having defined the
target, the church must devise a service that is relevant to the "felt
needs" of that demographic profile.[9] It is easy to see McGavran's
homogeneous unit thinking at work here. Warren discusses his key
idea about how to attract a crowd: "The answer is quite simple:
Create a service that is intentionally designed for your members to
bring their friends to. And make the service so attractive, appealing, and relevant to the unchurched that your members are eager
to share it with the lost people they care about."[10] This means that
the felt needs of a particular target group of the unregenerate
determine what happens in the church.

However noble-minded McGavran, Wagner, Schuller, Warren,
and other church growth advocates may be, the movement has
changed the teaching and practice of the church in ways that have
been detrimental to the gospel. Hearing the gospel is not a felt need
of any demographic of sinners. But, pastors are intimidated into
producing results under threat of losing their jobs or professional
reputation. McGavran claimed that resources should only be directed to those efforts that are producing measurable results in terms of
church growth. Though these people all deny that they are only trying to fill pews with bodies, that is precisely what individual pastors

feel an urgent need to do.

The literature for the *40 Days of Purpose* campaign (which I receive regularly) states: "What were the results in other churches"? The answers: Attendance grew 20%; new groups grew 59%; tithing increased 20%.[11] Pleas from concerned church members who disagree with Rick Warren's teachings fall on deaf ears as church leaders, desperate for church growth, latch on to the promise of just that. Furthermore, the campaign comes pre-packaged so that church leaders do not have to rely on their own talents to create a popular Christian message. Warren has done all the work.

I can personally attest to how hard it is to be characterized a failure. When I was in seminary classes being forced to study the principles of the Church Growth movement, our church was declining in attendance and had been doing so for several years. It was declining for a variety of reasons, not the least of which was increased gang violence, including a couple of murders within yards of our church. Some families no longer felt safe attending church there. One person, who was a new Christian and whose wife had just left him, had his car stolen by a drug dealer while he was in Sunday School with his children. He soon left our church to attend one in a safer neighborhood—and he was someone who came to the Lord in our church. Week after week I was being told that I was failing (by the definitions that they affirmed), no matter what my practice or teaching may have been.

Occasionally, I would speak up in class and tell them that it was not right to compare someone in a situation like mine with the successful role models they paraded before us. I once said, "Last Sunday, I had to get a passed out drunk removed from the front steps before people started showing up to church. Do you suppose that the hot shot pastor from the suburbs has that problem?" I felt more pathetic trying to defend myself than if I just said nothing. But the situation helped me clarify my resolve: I pledged to the Lord to preach the gospel and feed whatever flock He gave us (and we have been faithful in that). Imagine, however, how tempting it would be if someone offered you 20 percent more people and 20 percent more money if you adopted his program.

During the years I was at seminary, the seminary shifted its focus from theological education to promoting the agenda of the therapeutic and seeker sensitive approaches to ministry. In one class, Rick Warren and Stephen Covey (the Mormon who wrote the famous *Seven Habits* series of books) were required reading. The seminary was committed to helping us become pastors of healthy, growing churches, using all the current means available.

Once the leaders of the seminary accepted the principles of the Church Growth movement, the outcome was already determined. Too often, people in today's culture do not care about theology, so why train leaders in theology if your goal is to get more people to come to your services?[12] During this transition, the seminary adopted a therapeutic program called "Marriage and Family Therapy." It exploded in popularity, while many who came would only go to theology classes if forced. There was little demand for theology classes. This has not changed since I graduated—it has only gotten worse. A friend of mine recently went back to finish his degree work and found that they had two June class offerings—one on Luke and the other studying the life and teachings of the Catholic mystic Henri Nouwen. The Nouwen class was full, but there were many openings for Luke.[13]

The key idea of this new "paradigm," as they call it, is that the church needs to change its entire focus of ministry so that it becomes "relevant" to the perceived needs of the "unchurched" of the community. An evangelical infrastructure is now available to help transition churches from the traditional model to the seeker model. Everything from demographic studies to focus groups are utilized to best understand the desires and needs of the unchurched. Every possible tool is being put into the hands of pastors to accomplish this transition.

Rick Warren is now the most prominent person in this movement, having (by the sheer volume of book sales and prominence gained through the mass media) eclipsed other luminaries such as Robert Schuller and Bill Hybels. The momentum of the Purpose

Driven movement shows no signs of slowing down. Many pastors feel like they need to either join the movement or be left behind as this new revival sweeps the nation. Later, we will see how Rick Warren's marketing savvy is helping church leaders succeed without their having the skills or assets normally required of most popular megachurch pastors.

Unbelievers Determine the Church's Message

The key idea behind Warren's Purpose Driven church movement is not new—Robert Schuller invented it when he began his ministry in California in the 1950s. Schuller's idea was to make a church that unchurched people would find appealing. He consulted his good friend Norman Vincent Peale to find an answer. Schuller writes, "Hoping to impress unchurched people, I wrote to Dr. Norman Vincent Peale, who wrote back a marvelous statement with his permission to quote extensively. So I grabbed hold of his coattails."[14] In 1957, Schuller persuaded Peale to speak at his drive-in church.[15] From Peale he learned a key lesson about appealing to the unchurched. The lesson was, "Jesus never called a person a sinner."[16] This insight led to Schuller's philosophy of possibility thinking and self-esteem.[17] Schuller developed and perfected this non-offensive message and eventually turned it into the Crystal Cathedral and the "Hour of Power." His Institute for Successful Church Leadership has trained many of the key leaders that are currently promoting the seeker model within evangelicalism, including Bill Hybels and Rick Warren.[18]

The key idea is very simple: Change the Sunday Morning church service so that non-Christians will not only attend it, but enjoy it and keep coming back. Using a fishing analogy, Warren says, "Catching fish on their terms means letting your target determine your approach."[19] The way to do this is to begin with the felt needs of the unchurched.[20] One felt need that unbelievers (unchurched is a euphemism for sinners) do not have, according to Warren, is for the truth. Warren reasons, "While most unbelievers aren't looking for truth, they *are* looking for relief."[21] Since, in our post-modern milieu, most people are more interested in what works for them (in terms of their own wants and priorities), making a church service designed to appeal to the general public means not making truth claims a prominent part of the message of the church. Warren knows the culture of the age:

> Because preachers are called to communicate truth, we often mistakenly assume that unbelievers are eager to hear it. But unbelievers aren't that interested in truth these days. In fact, surveys show that the majority of Americans reject the idea of absolute truth.[22]

The bottom line for Warren is that the church must meet people's felt needs and not expect them to listen to sermons that proclaim the truth.

Some of us protest that this seems very unbiblical, but not according to Warren. He uses this passage to support his practice: "Ephesians 4:29 says, 'Speak *only* what is helpful for building up others according to their needs, that it may benefit those who listen.'"[23] He interprets this as follows: "Notice what we say should be determined by the needs of the people to whom we are speaking."[24] Both his translation and his application are faulty. Here is the passage from the NASB: *"Let no unwholesome word proceed from your mouth, but only such a word as is good for edification according to the need of the moment, that it may give grace to those who hear"* (Ephesians 4:29). The passage sets up a contrast between speaking "unwholesome" (or "corrupt") words versus those that would edify. The context is that of general admonitions about Christian living. Paul goes on to say, *"Let all bitterness and wrath and anger and clamor and slander be put away from you, along with all malice. And be kind to one another, tender-hearted, forgiving each other, just as God in Christ also has forgiven you"* (Ephesians 4:31, 32). The issue is how Christians speak to one another. There is no ground in the text for Warren's claim that the message of the church, as preached from the pulpit on Sunday morning, should be determined by the needs (he means felt needs not real needs as he has made clear) of unbelievers. Yet this is exactly what Warren claims: "It stands to reason that if this is God's will for our conversations, it must also be God's will for our sermons."[25]

Warren is very wrong about this. Jesus commissioned the church to teach *"all that I commanded you"* (see Matthew 28:20). He did not tell us to study the ideas of pagans to determine what they were willing to hear. This passage also bears heavily on this matter:

> *I solemnly charge you in the presence of God and of Christ Jesus, who is to judge the living and the dead, and by His appearing and His kingdom: preach the word; be ready in season and out of season; reprove, rebuke, exhort, with great patience and instruction. For the time will come when they will not endure sound doctrine; but wanting to have their ears tickled, they will accumulate for themselves teachers in accordance to their own desires; and will turn away their ears from the truth, and will turn aside to myths* (2 Timothy 4:1-4).

Paul, predicting that people would not endure sound doctrine, prescribed exactly what they did **not** want to hear. Far from the felt needs of the sinner determining the message of the pastor, the doctrines of the Bible were to be preached. Not only that, Paul chastises those whose desires determined which teachers they would listen to! They turn away from the truth because they do not want the truth; it does not feed their carnal appetites. Rick Warren has misused Ephesians 4:29 in order to promote a practice that is diametrically opposed to what Paul taught in 2 Timothy 4:1-4.

So we have a decision to make. Shall we preach the whole counsel of God, including the key issues of the gospel such as the blood atonement, or shall we determine the felt needs of a target group, and preach a message that is relevant to those needs? What we decide will determine if we need the services of Warren and other Church Growth advocates.

If one decides to adopt the Warren approach, then the self perceived needs of the unregenerate audience determine the message
of the church. There are lots of other trappings such as the pastor's
attire, the music style, the order of service, décor, etc.; but none of
these is ultimately as crucial as the message. If one took all of the
other advice found in the *Purpose Driven Church* and other seeker
approaches, but still preached biblical doctrine right from the
Bible, and preached the gospel as preached by Christ and His apostles, one would not have a Purpose Driven church. The offensive
message of the cross would thwart everything else in the program.

Consider this crucial passage: *"For indeed Jews ask for signs, and
Greeks search for wisdom; but we preach Christ crucified, to Jews a stumbling
block, and to Gentiles foolishness"* (1 Corinthians 1:22, 23). Neither Jew
nor Greek (by this Paul means "Gentile") had the felt need for a crucified, Jewish Messiah. So why would Paul purposely preach a gospel
he knew would offend his unregenerate audience? He tells us why:
*"but to those who are the called, both Jews and Greeks, Christ the power of God
and the wisdom of God"* (1 Corinthians 1:24).

Rick Warren has a different understanding than Paul. He makes
this amazing claim: "It is my deep conviction that anybody can be
won to Christ if you discover the key to his or her heart. . . . The most
likely place to start is with the person's felt needs."[26] The "called," in
Paul's inspired teaching, are those God has chosen: *"and whom He
predestined, these He also called; and whom He called, these He also justified;
and whom He justified, these He also glorified"* (Romans 8:30). Since no
one knows who these people are, the gospel is to be preached faithfully to all, though we know it is a perpetually offensive message. But
God will use it to save those whom He has called from all eternity:
*"For this reason I endure all things for the sake of those who are chosen, that
they also may obtain the salvation which is in Christ Jesus and with it eternal
glory"* (2 Timothy 2:10). It is impossible to reconcile Paul's teaching
on this with Warren's idea that anyone can be won to Christ if we
just figure out the right key to his or her heart.

This is very important. If one sincerely believed that Rick
Warren is right and that there is no person who could not be

turned Christian if we just had the right information to present to them, then it would make sense to preach and teach whatever works to bring them to Christ. On the other hand, if we believe that only the called respond to the gospel and that the called are those God has chosen and predestined, then it would make no sense to preach any message BUT the gospel to the lost. We do not know who the called are, but we do know they will respond to the gospel if it is preached in a biblical manner.

Furthermore, according to the biblical pattern, **God** determines the message of the church. According to the Purpose Driven pattern, unbelieving man determines the message of the church. The different patterns result in two different paths with two different destinies. The different approaches will also create two distinctively different churches—one made up mostly of the elect, the other made of mostly of religious consumers getting their religious appetites fed. One is the church Jesus Christ is building on the rock (Matthew 16:16-19); the other is the church man is building using human wisdom and abilities.

Defining Man's Need

Rick Warren does not deny the need for the Bible. Biblical truths are to be taught, Warren says, but in a manner that shows unbelievers that the Bible has answers to their own perceived needs: "By starting with a topic that interests the unchurched and then showing what the Bible says about it, you grab their attention, disarm prejudices, and create an interest in the Bible that wasn't there before."[27] What are these needs? "People feel the same emotional and relational needs. These include the need for love, acceptance, forgiveness, meaning, self-expression, and a purpose for living. People are also looking for freedom from fear, guilt, worry, resentment, discouragement and loneliness."[28]

This may be what people feel, but the unbelieving masses are deceived and are living according to wrong motivations. The Bible says, *"For all that is in the world, the lust of the flesh and the lust of the eyes and the boastful pride of life, is not from the Father, but is from the world. The world is passing away, and also its lusts; but the one who does the will of God lives forever*" (1 John 2:16, 17). This is a comprehensive summary of what motivates those in the world. Accordingly, if one were truly going to meet their felt needs one would have to figure out how to offer fulfillment to these lusts. Warren's version sounds innocuous—nothing seems wrong with looking for love, meaning, self-expression and purpose. But this soft-pedals the sin nature and suggests that by nature we are not rebellious sinners abiding under God's wrath; just honest people trying to find our purpose in life.

Given this view of man, it is not surprising how Warren characterizes the Bible. He says, "Jesus began the Sermon on the Mount by sharing eight secrets of genuine happiness."[29] This mischaracterization of Jesus' teaching echoes Robert Schuller's *Be Happy Attitudes*[30] and may show Schuller's influence on Warren. Jesus was not teaching prescriptions for happiness, but descriptions of the citizens of the Kingdom of God. The first and last of the Beatitudes (this term comes from the Latin term for "blessings"[31] and has nothing to do with our English term "attitudes") end with, "for theirs is the kingdom of God." Those between the first and last beatitudes are promised future blessings such as, "they shall inherit the earth." Far from "secrets to happiness" or "be happy attitudes," these blessings are for people who appear to be far from blessed in the eyes of the world, but have by faith seen that the kingdom has drawn near. They have "hungered and thirsted for righteousness" and are "persecuted for righteousness." Righteousness only comes through faith in the Person and work of Christ.

Though Warren finds secrets to happiness in the Sermon on the Mount, there is an underlying theme of God's law which pulls the rug out from under the self-righteousness of religious man. There are many things that make people happy in this life. One does not need to be religious to be happy. Of much weightier concern is how one can gain true righteousness and thus inherit the kingdom of God. Jesus also said in the Sermon on the Mount, "*For I say to you that unless your righteousness surpasses that of the scribes and Pharisees, you will not enter the kingdom of Heaven*" (Matthew 5:20).

This shows us that we have a desperate need for Christ's righteousness that we cannot achieve by religious works. To hammer home this point, Jesus said,

> *"You have heard that the ancients were told, 'You shall not commit murder' and 'Whoever commits murder shall be liable to the court.' But I say to you that everyone who is angry with his brother shall be guilty before the court; and whoever says to his brother, 'You good-for-nothing,' shall be guilty before the supreme court; and whoever says, 'You fool,' shall be guilty enough to go into the fiery hell"* (Matthew 5:21, 22).

This could have no other effect than to convince every one of Jesus' hearers that he or she was "guilty enough to go into the fiery hell." Jesus was not giving secrets to a better life, and He was not meeting "felt needs." He was showing people that they were far needier than they could ever have imagined.

Rick Warren consistently neglects or ignores the issue of God's law that shows the need for the gospel and finds "how-to" messages for "changed lives." He continues in his characterization of the Sermon on the Mount:

> Then he talked about living an exemplary lifestyle, controlling anger, restoring relationships, and avoiding adultery and divorce. . . . After that, he moved on to other practical life issues like how to give with the right attitude, how to pray, how to store up treasure in heaven, and how to overcome worry.[32]

He then concludes, "This is the kind of preaching we need in churches today—preaching that not only attracts crowds—it changes lives!"[33] There is a problem with the "how to" approach—it assumes that people already have the power, motivation and ability to do what is pleasing to God, but are lacking the proper techniques to implement righteous living. But this is **not** the case.

As sinners, humans have two major problems: 1) they have no ability to do what is pleasing to God and 2) they have no desire to do what is pleasing to God. Jesus was not teaching a "how-to class" for better living, but describing the righteousness of the kingdom of God that cannot possibly be attained by human effort. In the Sermon on the Mount, Jesus said, *"Therefore you are to be perfect, as your heavenly Father is perfect"* (Matthew 5:48). Rick Warren's approach—having the perceived needs of the sinner determine the message of the church—falls on its face at precisely this point. The needs of the sinner are infinitely greater than he or she could imagine. The standard Jesus set is unattainable. It destroys the self-righteousness of man-made religion and shows the need for the gospel. Rick Warren's "how-to" approach fails to address either of the sinner's greatest needs: to be made aware of their lost and sinful condition through the Law and then to find forgiveness and Christ's perfect righteousness through the gospel.

This fatal flaw is shown by this statement: "What people need today are fewer "ought-to" sermons and more "how-to" sermons."[34] The part he wants most to remove (the "ought-to") is the law of God that shows people their need for the gospel. This "ought-to" is lacking in Rick Warren's approach, both in the *Purpose Driven Church*, and the *Purpose Driven Life*. He assumes that people will be motivated to be Christian if the preacher can show them how Christianity will benefit them in terms of needs and desires that they already have. Teaching "how-to" classes to the unregenerate is *"casting pearls before swine"* (Matthew 7:6). It is teaching how to please God when the person's motivation is not to please God, but to find self-fulfillment in this life.

The Christian life is not like using an assembly manual: "Here is the diagram, here are the tools and the parts, and here is a step-by-step process for putting this device together." Such an approach is a **huge** understatement of the depth of human depravity. Even if we had a perfect prescription, we would hate it and reject it; if we had the tools, we would not be motivated to use them; and if we actually were motivated, we would lack the power to put it all together. Paul said, *"The mind set on the flesh is hostile toward God; for it does not subject itself to the law of God, for it is not even able to do so, and those who are in the flesh cannot please God"* (Romans 8:7, 8).

The weak "how-to" approach of Rick Warren fails to address these matters. A manual of "how to put together a happy life as a Christian" would be worthless in the hands of those whose minds Paul says are "hostile toward God." Yet Warren consults such people to determine the message of the church. In *The Purpose Driven Life*, Warren perpetuates the "how to" manual understanding: "It [the Bible] is our Owner's Manual, explaining why we are alive, how life works, what to avoid, and what to expect in the future."[35]

The Bible is not merely a manual about having a happy, meaningful life. The Bible's theme is about redemption and atonement, not finding meaning and solving problems. Paul told Timothy, *"and that from childhood you have known the sacred writings which are able to give you the wisdom that leads to salvation through faith which is in Christ Jesus"* (2 Timothy 3:15). The Bible begins with Creation and the Fall (Genesis 1-3) and ends with Judgment and the New Creation (Revelation 20-22). At the center of this message is the cross where Jesus bore God's wrath against sin and shed His blood for our sins. The seekers in any given neighborhood are not going to tell you that this is what they want to hear in church. They want to find solutions to problems, which makes Warren's owners manual misrepresentation of the Bible seem attractive. Warren knows that the unchurched are not interested in eternal things. Warren writes, "He's [the unchurched person] not interested in the afterlife. He's consumed with finding out if there is any meaning or purpose to this life. One national survey showed that less than one percent of Americans were interested in the answer to the question, 'How can I get to Heaven?'"[36] However, it is wrong to turn the Bible into a "how-to" book to help the unregenerate find happiness, when it is no such thing.

How the Purpose Driven Approach Attracts Crowds

Rick Warren strongly emphasizes the need for the Sunday church service to be entertaining and relevant to unbelievers. As we just discussed, this starts with tailoring a message to the needs, desires, and sensibilities of unbelievers. It does not end there. If the service is designed for the crowds, it must be more exciting than whatever else they could be doing on Sunday morning.

Rick Warren warns of the danger of boring people: "I believe it is a sin to bore people with the Bible. When God's Word is taught in an uninteresting way, people don't just think the pastor is boring, they think *God* is boring."[37] It is true that being bored is a common complaint of modern Americans. Interestingly, the terms bored or boring used in this manner are not found in literal translations of the Bible. I searched the NASB, KJV, NKJV, and even the NIV and could not find anything about being bored or boring. I also searched the same translations looking for the words entertain and entertaining. Other than the word "entertain" used to "entertain" (show hospitality) strangers in Hebrews 13:2, these words did not show up either, with one exception. The exception is this passage in the NIV: *"While they were in high spirits, they shouted, 'Bring out Samson to entertain us.' So they called Samson out of the prison, and he performed for them'"* (Judges 16:25). This was a description of the Philistines having a pagan party for their god Dagon.

The problem of being bored and needing to be entertained as an antidote is the result of American prosperity and sloth. About ten years ago, I was walking with my father and he observed some children playing. One said to the other, "I am bored." Dad shook his head saying, "When I was a kid I never heard anyone say they were bored." Dad grew up during the Great Depression and used to tell the story that as a kid the only toy he had was a discarded barrel hoop he would roll down the road with a stick. Yet the idea of being bored never occurred to him because he was too busy trying to survive the poverty of his family. Today with houses full of toys, video games, and every manner of high tech entertainment, people still complain of being bored.

Now this problem translates into the church. Over-stimulated unbelievers who have spent their lives enjoying entertainment to a degree that was unknown through most of human history, who have the best of everything at their fingertips, cannot tolerate a moment of being bored. Woe to the pastor who is not inspiring and relevant enough to satisfy their sensibilities. Warren writes, "We slander God's character if we preach with an uninspiring style or tone."[38]

This thinking, if it were held in the times of the Bible, would have put Paul in a very bad light. He preached so long someone literally died:

> *And on the first day of the week, when we were gathered together to break bread, Paul began talking to them, intending to depart the next day, and he prolonged his message until midnight. And there were many lamps in the upper room where we were gathered together. And there was a certain young man named Eutychus sitting on the window sill, sinking into a deep sleep; and as Paul kept on talking, he was overcome by sleep and fell down from the third floor, and was picked up dead* (Acts 20:7-9).

Paul evidently missed the seminar on how to preach short, lively, entertaining messages! Elsewhere, Paul cites what others were saying about him: *"For they say, 'His letters are weighty and strong, but his personal presence is unimpressive, and his speech contemptible'"* (2 Corinthians 10:10). This, however, did not concern the apostle: *"And my message and my preaching were not in persuasive words of wisdom, but in demonstration of the Spirit and of power, that your faith should not rest on the wisdom of men, but on the power of God"* (1 Corinthians 2:4, 5). The content of the message, which centered about the cross, was how God's power changed lives. It was neither the presentation style nor its apparent relevance to the minds of the unregenerate, but the power of the Holy Spirit that made the message of the cross effective: *"And when I came to you, brethren, I did not come with superiority of speech or of wisdom, proclaiming to you the testimony of God. For I determined to know nothing among you except Jesus Christ, and*

Him crucified" (1 Corinthians 2:1, 2). It is safe to say that none of the pagan Corinthians, prior to their conversion, saw the relevance of a crucified Jewish Messiah, nor that they thought hearing such a message would be entertaining.

Rick Warren, however, points to Jesus as proof of the need for creative, inspiring, techniques. He says, "Jesus captured the interest of large crowds with techniques that you and I can use. . . . Jesus was a master story teller. . . . In fact, the Bible shows that storytelling was Jesus' favorite technique when speaking to the crowd."[39] This reference to Jesus' parables as proof that we should use storytelling as a key technique to reach the crowds ignores Jesus' own teaching about why He used parables. Here is what Jesus said:

> *And the disciples came and said to Him, "Why do You speak to them in parables?" And He answered and said to them, "To you it has been granted to know the mysteries of the kingdom of heaven, but to them it has not been granted. For whoever has, to him shall more be given, and he shall have an abundance; but whoever does not have, even what he has shall be taken away from him. Therefore I speak to them in parables; because while seeing they do not see, and while hearing they do not hear, nor do they understand. And in their case the prophecy of Isaiah is being fulfilled, which says, 'You will keep on hearing, but will not understand; And you will keep on seeing, but will not perceive; For the heart of this people has become dull, And with their ears they scarcely hear, And they have closed their eyes Lest they should see with their eyes, And hear with their ears, And understand with their heart and return, And I should heal them"* (Matthew 13:10-15).

The parables did not make Jesus' message easier to understand or more entertaining; they hid the message from all but those to whom the Father chose to reveal it (see Matthew 11:25, 26).

Even the disciples had to privately ask Jesus the meaning of His parables. To this day many of the parables are difficult to interpret, even by advanced Bible scholars. Rick Warren however says this:

"Jesus used simple language, not technical or theological jargon. He spoke in terms that normal people could understand."[40] Actually, Jesus offered very profound interpretations of the Old Testament and arguments that confounded the wisest scribes. Rick Warren mischaracterizes the content and technique of Jesus' teaching to make us think that He serves as a role model for the seeker-sensitive pastor. The facts do not bear out Warren's claims.

Neither Jesus nor Paul was guilty of dumbing down God's message in order to make it entertaining and appealing to the unregenerate mind. Warren says this: "The apostle Paul worried that 'your minds would be led astray from the *simplicity* and purity *of devotion* to Christ' (2 Corinthians 11:3 NASB, his italics)."[41] Warren is misusing the passage because the term "simplicity" does not mean, "easy to be understood," but "singleness" or "sincerity." Lenski says the word means "single-mindedness" and says, "Its opposite is duplicity."[42] It has to do with motives, not the relative complexity—or lack thereof—of the message. Rick Warren has mischaracterized the teachings of Jesus and of Paul in order to promote his concept that preachers should not preach theologically complex messages that are unappealing to the minds of the unregenerate.

In Warren's version of Church Growth theory, not only the message, but the entire Sunday morning service needs to be changed to make it appealing to unbelievers. Warren advises, "Create a service that is intentionally designed for your members to bring their friends to. And make the service so attractive, appealing, and relevant to the unchurched that your members are eager to share it with lost people they care about."[43] He gives dozens of suggestions about how to do this. The key issue, however, is that the Purpose Driven Sunday morning worship service is designed for unbelievers, not for Christians.[44] The role of believers is to bring unsaved friends to the service. The service for believers happens at another time, if there is one at all.

This is not the New Testament pattern. The service where Paul preached so long that a man fell asleep was on Sunday: "on the first day of the week when we gathered to break bread" (Acts 20:7). This was obviously a believer's service. When Paul preached to the lost, he went to their meetings, such as to the synagogue. For example, *"And according to Paul's custom, he went to them, and for three Sabbaths reasoned with them from the Scriptures, explaining and giving evidence that the Christ had to suffer and rise again from the dead, and saying, 'This Jesus whom I am proclaiming to you is the Christ'"* (Acts 17:2,3). The whole concept of church is about people called out of the world and into God's kingdom. The gathering of believers is called "fellowship," which means, "the sharing of a common life together." Paul asks, *"What fellowship does light have with darkness?"* (2 Corinthians 6:14). Yet in the seeker scheme of things, the sensibilities of those in darkness determine the message and practice of the Christian gathering.

I would agree that we should remove needless offenses and show love and hospitality to all who come (1 Corinthians 10:32; 2 Corinthians 6:3). The Bible does anticipate that an unbeliever might come to a Christian gathering (1 Corinthians 14:23). But nowhere do we have teaching that the church service is to be a gathering designed for unbelievers.

How to Pull it Off

The biggest drawback, historically, to the broad scale implementation of the seeker model of ministry has been the talent and resources it takes to pull it off. Traditional churches existed because God saved people and added them to the church—the church itself provided the means of grace. Pastors taught the Bible to the flock so that they would be fed spiritually. People who came worshipped God from the heart, whether with great musical skill or with nothing but an old piano and a joyous noise.

How amazing it was to me when I became a Christian in July 1971, that I actually enjoyed joining a group of older Christians around a piano on Sunday nights and singing old time gospel songs (most of which I had never heard before). The joy of it was that now I REALLY knew the Lord and was so excited to praise Him and sing songs of redemption, the cross, and atonement. I was a product of the rock and roll 1960s. I did not expect the church people to play "my kind of music." I was excited to learn their kind of music because they were so full of love for Christ, in stark contrast to those I saw at rock concerts who were mostly wasted. I still love old gospel hymns!

Today, with a few highly successful and highly publicized churches in the limelight, the bar has been raised. Some churches have Christmas programs with budgets worth hundreds of thousands of dollars. There are professional actors doing drama, professional musicians doing concerts, and professional orators preaching homilies that inspire the audience. The Crystal Cathedral was the first highly successful example of this. Now we have Bill Hybels' Willow Creek Church in Illinois and Rick Warren's Saddleback Church in California and others.

The following is from one of the many e-mails I have received from people whose church has converted to this new approach:

There have been major changes at the church. When you walk in, you will now find a MAC machine, a coffee shop where you can purchase donuts, croissants, coffee, you name it. There are also about a hundred tables with chairs to sit and eat. When service starts there is smoke, lights, lasers, and music so loud my ears ring after church is over. This week there was a 10 minute service. Then, our pastor demonstrated a soccer move he learned that week. He did a flip and kicked a soccer ball. Then, he set up a table and him and his wife talked to each other about their trip to Africa. On top of all this, we no longer use the Bible. We use 'Purpose Driven Life.' I've read your articles and it has been a blessing. Although I do not attend the church any longer, I am very concerned for those who do attend the church. It is a feel good church. They do not talk about the 'Hard Truth.' I'm very afraid for those who are sitting there having a 'blast' while thinking they are going to Heaven but are dead wrong in most cases.

Many others have e-mailed me and said that the Bible itself has been removed from the pulpits of their churches and that entertainment is the new order of the day.

Changing the church to make it attractive to the non-Christian masses is not new. Robert Schuller has been doing it since the 50's. What is new about Warren's Purpose Driven program is that he has convinced evangelicals that they can do this and fulfill the Great Commission in the process. He assures us that we can keep all of our current doctrines. He also assures us that his whole program is based on biblical principles and God's five purposes for the church which he says are worship, evangelism, fellowship, discipleship and ministry.

If the church is going to be attractive to the world, it could never be so by fulfilling these five purposes. The world is deceived and has no desire to worship God on His terms: *"We know that we are of God, and the whole world lies in the power of the evil one"* (1 John 5:19). So how has Rick Warren created a situation in which the world loves the things of God and is attracted to the church because of these five purposes? The answer is redefinition. Rick Warren has redefined the church and redefined many biblical terms to make it seem that his program is biblical when it is not. The result is that his hybrid version of the church is appealing to the world. I will show in the coming chapters how this redefinition process works.

There is another question: "How does an ordinary pastor with a small budget, limited skills, and little access to anything professional create a church that is so relevant, exciting, and attractive that the average, potential religious consumer would want to attend?" The answer is provided by Rick Warren and is the same answer that many successful businesses have used to replicate themselves. It involves developing a franchise where the talent of the franchise founder can be replicated many times over by people of lesser talent who are willing to buy into the benefits of owning a franchise. How Warren makes this work will be addressed later after we have examined his "product."

Redefining the Church

"He is also head of the body, the church; and He is the beginning, the first-born from the dead; so that He Himself might come to have first place in everything" (Colossians 1:18).

A Church that the Unregenerate See as Attractive

The Purpose Driven church designs its church service to attract a target audience in the church's community—on purpose. The plan is not just to get them to walk through the door, but also to make the service so appealing they will come back. Once they become regular attendees, the goal is then to get them involved with membership, service, giving, and helping the church fulfill its mission. The problem is that the underlying assumptions of the Church Growth movement require redefining the church.

The biblical concept of church is that the church is Christ's "little flock" (Luke 12:32) that has been called out of the world (the term "church" means "called out ones") and consists of those who have entered through the narrow gate (Matthew 7:13). Those who enter have heard the voice of the Shepherd of the sheep (John 10:3) and followed Him. Those who enter are those the Father gave to the Son (John 6:37). That is the biblical concept.

Warren's idea is different. Rather than clearly preaching the gospel to all, knowing that God promised to use it in spite of its inherent offense to call forth His sheep from the midst of the world, Warren would like to change the nature of the church and its message so it appears attractive to people as they are in their unregenerate state. In Jesus' teaching, His message is often rejected because those who reject it are not His sheep and are not the ones the Father gave Him. As a matter of fact, when He gave His teaching on the Shepherd and the sheep, this is the reaction of His Jewish contemporaries: *"There arose a division again among the Jews because of these words. And many of them were saying, 'He has a demon and is insane. Why do you listen to Him?'"* (John 10:19, 20). The teaching about the nature of Christ's true flock hardly proved attractive to the masses.

Warren and other Church Growth teachers make a similar error applying the Great Commission. They rightly see Matthew 28:18-20 as a command to "disciple the nations." But what they miss, again, is the intent of the Scripture. As we saw in the last chapter, Donald McGavran, whom Warren praised as an early influence in his life, takes this to mean "disciple people groups" as social units. This thinking creates a need to make the church attractive to people as they are culturally. However, the passage also says "baptizing them." One does not baptize a culture, people group, geopolitical entity, or anything but an individual. So the passage actually means that individuals from every tribe would hear the gospel, and those who respond will be discipled, baptized, and taught. Importantly, what they should be taught is "everything I have commanded you." The various programs Rick Warren has devised such as *Celebrate Recovery* and SHAPE contain mostly the wisdom of man and small parts of what Christ commanded to be taught. So even the Great Commission has been redefined to make it appear that the underlying premises of various Church Growth teachings are true.

Furthermore, if we compare other passages where Christ commissions the church it becomes clear what He had in mind. For example: *"And He said to them, 'Thus it is written, that the Christ should suffer and rise again from the dead the third day; and that repentance for forgiveness of sins should be proclaimed in His name to all the nations, beginning from Jerusalem. You are witnesses of these things'"* (Luke 24:46-48). The Luke version is to proclaim repentance to the nations, using the same Greek word for *nations* as the passage in Matthew. Proclaiming repentance through the work of the resurrected Christ is totally different from trying to make the church attractive to the unregenerate. The book of Acts shows that the disciples understood this commission and carried it out. Peter preached repentance on Pentecost (Acts 2:38). Paul preached repentance to Athenian philosophers, causing them to mock him (Acts 17:30-32).

Another problem is that Church Growth advocates use Christ's promise to build His church and Old Testament prophecy that His kingdom would continually increase as proof that Church Growth (as they define it) is God's will. They are making a category error. It is true that Christ's church and His Kingdom will continually grow until He returns. This is true because every time a soul is converted through the gospel, the church universal and militant (all those truly converted and alive on the earth), the church universal and triumphant (all those truly converted including those who have died in faith) and the kingdom (whose citizens are those submitted to Christ's Kingship) grow. But McGavran, Wagner, Warren and others are not speaking of the church in any of those senses. They are speaking about local congregations wherever they may be, whatever their doctrine may be, and whatever their composition may be.

Christ never promised "church growth" according to the terms that Church Growth advocates use (i.e., that there will be ever more local congregations and that those local congregations shall be growing in membership). Later we will study the seven churches in Revelation and see that Christ never mentions "growth," its absence in His rebukes or in His commendations of local churches. In fact, the two most praised churches were very small and persecuted. They were likely shrinking because their members were being killed or imprisoned. Had these churches being growing in membership throughout their existence, they would not have been small by the time John wrote Revelation.

One further definition is essential and important enough that the rest of this chapter is devoted to it. This is the distinction between the visible and invisible church. Warren, and others of his ilk, rarely, if ever, discuss this distinction. Their concept of growth primarily concerns the visible church—all those who attend whose numbers can be counted. The invisible church, on the other hand, are all those who are truly regenerate and whose names are written in the Lamb's Book of Life.

How Christ Builds His Church

God puts people into His invisible church; man does not. Paul said to the Ephesian elders: *"Be on guard for yourselves and for all the flock, among which the Holy Spirit has made you overseers, to shepherd the church of God which He purchased with His own blood"* (Acts 20:28). Those who are redeemed are redeemed by the blood of Christ, and they have had their sins washed away. This atonement is announced through the gospel. God uses gospel preaching to save people and add them to the church. A few verses earlier, Paul said this about his preaching that had resulted in the formation of a church in Ephesus: *"how I did not shrink from declaring to you anything that was profitable, and teaching you publicly and from house to house, solemnly testifying to both Jews and Greeks of repentance toward God and faith in our Lord Jesus Christ"* (Acts 20:20, 21). Paul was using the keys of the kingdom that Jesus gave to Peter and the other disciples according to Matthew 16:18, 19. He preached the gospel that included the Person and work of Christ, and the need for repentance and faith.

Paul did not stop with preaching the gospel in Ephesus and seeing God add people to the church. He told the Ephesian elders: *"And now, behold, I know that all of you, among whom I went about preaching the kingdom, will see my face no more. Therefore I testify to you this day, that I am innocent of the blood of all men. For I did not shrink from declaring to you the whole purpose of God"* (Acts 20:25-27). Having preached the gospel and taught the whole counsel of God, Paul had discharged his duty. He was turning the church over to the guidance of these elders. It was their duty to nurture and preserve this flock through being on guard and caring for them as pastors (the word "shepherd" in verse 28 is the verb form of the noun translated "pastor"). Paul explained why their solemn duty was so important: *"I know that after my departure savage wolves will come in among you, not sparing the flock; and from among your own selves men will arise, speaking perverse things, to draw away the disciples after them"* (Acts 20:29, 30). False teachers were sure to arise and those who have the duty of shepherding the flock must protect the blood-bought church from them. This duty is often neglected today and the Purpose Driven movement is making things worse.

Christ builds His church through gospel preaching that God uses to graciously grant repentance and faith in those He has chosen (see Acts 11:18; Philippians 1:29; 2 Timothy 2:25). The invisible church grows through conversions: *"And the Lord was adding to their number day by day those who were being saved"* (Acts 2:47b). Paul wrote this: *"For since in the wisdom of God the world through its wisdom did not come to know God, God was well-pleased through the foolishness of the message preached to save those who believe"* (1 Corinthians 1:21). Every time a person is regenerated by the grace and power of God, the invisible church grows.

Therefore, those who are concerned with the growth of the invisible church—the one that ultimately will be assembled for the marriage supper of the Lamb—will preach the gospel clearly and boldly. They will declare the terms of entrance into the kingdom of God. This includes the message of the cross: *"But we preach Christ crucified, to Jews a stumbling block, and to Gentiles foolishness, but to those who are the called, both Jews and Greeks, Christ the power of God and the wisdom of God"* (1 Corinthians 1:23, 24). The message is universally unpopular to the unregenerate mind, but Christ uses it to build His church. We cannot know who the called are. We must faithfully preach the gospel knowing that the called, whoever they are, will respond to it. They respond because of God's supernatural grace, not because of human wisdom.

The saving of souls through the gospel leads to the formation of visible congregations where God's means of grace[1] are provided. I have provided more extensive theological justification for the visible/invisible distinction in Appendix 1. Those who want a better understanding of the nature of the relationship between the invisible church and visible church should consult Appendix 1.

Understanding the difference between the visible church and the invisible church will lay groundwork for the practices and policies that are necessary for a church to be biblical and honoring to God. To summarize, the visible church includes all who attend, whether or not they are truly regenerate. The invisible church consists only of the truly redeemed. At issue in this debate is whether the practices and policies of the church should be geared toward growing the visible church by whatever means work, or nurturing the invisible one by the means laid down in Scripture.

Growing the Visible Church

Prior to the Reformation, the Roman Catholic Church did not distinguish between the invisible and visible church. Salvation was considered to be found within the church; Rome with its papacy was considered the church. Failure to make a proper distinction between the invisible and visible church led to horrible practices— before the Reformation and after, on both sides of the division. Let us look at one example of what can happen when expanding the visible church by any means available is viewed as building Christ's church. This will show the ultimate absurdity of the Church Growth agenda.

In A.D. 770, Christendom had suffered greatly. The former Christian strongholds of northern Egypt and the near east had been overrun by Islam. The pagan Saxons of Germany despised Christianity. They murdered the missionaries sent to them and were enemies of the Franks. At this point in history Charlemagne arose as the great king of the Franks. Through a bloody, thirty-year series of wars, he subjugated the Saxons and forced them to convert to Christianity.[2] Historian Justo Gonzalez writes, "Charlemagne resolved to drown the rebellion in blood and in the waters of baptism. Those who proved intractable were slaughtered. The rest were forced to accept baptism."[3] In A.D. 800, Pope Leo II crowned Charlemagne the emperor in a move to revive the Roman Empire.[4]

Charlemagne's policy of forced conversions (he also forced tithing on the church through civil law[5]) became a new way to enlarge the visible church. The practice continued for many centuries. The result was that the Saxons actually became civilized and accustomed to Christian culture and Christianity became established in a previously pagan land.

Let us consider the consequences of means. We grant that if some light of the gospel is present in a particular visible church, God can use that light to convert people, even if the practices of that church are far from the type of gospel preaching and Bible teaching Christ has ordained. That much would be true of the church that Charlemagne expanded. If we agree that Charlemagne's means were wicked and cannot be justified, then we agree that the practice of expanding the visible church without regard for the means is not valid. Therefore at least SOME means of growing the visible church are wrong. The question then becomes: How do we determine which means are valid and which invalid?

We have to rule out pragmatic tests (i.e., the means that work are thereby valid) because Charlemagne's practice worked, and we agree it was not valid. The only reasonable test of the validity of means is to compare the means to the teachings and practices of Christ and His apostles, since they are the cornerstone and foundation of the church. The church was instituted by Christ, and He is the head of the church. Surely His teachings, as found in the New Testament, must define the church. This means that those teachings and practices that are ordained in the Bible are valid, and those that are not are invalid. This is true even if following the biblical pattern means that in some cases certain churches do not attract large numbers of people. A further implication is that wrong practices are not justified even if they help the church grow.

The failure of pragmatic tests for validity in church growth shows a major problem for Rick Warren and other Church Growth teachers. Their idea is that we must get unchurched people into the church if they are going to be helped. The Scriptural means of getting them into the church (preaching the law to convict them of their sin and the gospel to show them how to escape God's wrath) are not working as proven by statistics. Therefore the means must be changed to something that works or else these people will continue outside of the church.

The underlying assumption in popular church growth thinking is that once people join the visible church (however dim the light of the gospel might be in a given visible church), some will likely be converted. The rest will live better Christian lives, influenced by Christian ethics and teachings. Their children will be raised in the church rather than in the pagan world. As Christendom grows, everyone is better off. This, to be sure, is firmly believed by those joining the Purpose Driven reformation.

What is the difference between the methods of successful Church Growth leaders today and those of Charlemagne? Besides the obvious difference between coercion and persuasion, the differences are cultural. In A.D. 800, religion was often spread through warfare. Islam had proven this method very effective. Today this is not acceptable to any but the most radical religious fanatics. Religion is now spread through marketing. The church, as a visible external institution, can be made attractive to potential religious consumers. There is nothing culturally unacceptable about this.

Donald McGavran very much promoted a pragmatic approach of judging the results of efforts to cause church growth. He wrote, "Jesus Christ, our Lord, came to seek and save the lost. The lost are always persons. They always have countable bodies."[6] His conclusion is that searching or preaching should be judged by numerical results, not in faithfulness in the act of searching and preaching. McGavran wrote, "To God, as He has thus revealed Himself, proclamation is not the main thing. The proclamation of the gospel is a means. It must not be confused with the end, which is that men and women—multitudes of them—be reconciled to God in Christ."[7] It was important to McGavran to judge mission efforts by their outcome in terms of numbers and not accept various excuses like people being hardened. C Peter Wagner wrote in the 1990 foreword to *Understanding Church Growth*, "McGavran demanded more accountability in Christian stewardship. He wanted efforts evaluated by their results."[8] Here are McGavran's words:

> In view of all this and much more evidence, must we not consider mission in intention *a vast and purposeful finding*? Is it possible biblically to maintain that only "search" is the thing, motives are what matter, and the finding of multitudes of persons is something rather shabbily mechanical and "success ridden?" Can we believe it theologically tenable to be uninterested in the numbers of the redeemed?[9]

Results in terms of numbers were the bottom line for McGavran and mission efforts are to be judged accordingly.

The problem with this approach is that it promotes getting countable bodies into the visible church in large numbers and assumes they are redeemed because they came. If one couples McGavran's Church Growth pragmatic theory with Rick Warren's practice of making the church entertaining to a target audience, the likely result is a visible church with a smaller percentage of people in it who are regenerate. The visible church becomes more of a social institution and less of a gathering of the "called out ones." It looks more like the world.

Robert Schuller's Crystal Cathedral is a good example of a church that has grown very large through modern, pragmatic means. Let us consider it in light of the categories of the visible and invisible church. Luther said that there was some invisible church even in Roman Catholicism of his day. It is probable also that some became part of the invisible church after Charlemagne forced them into the visible one. God is merciful, and if some light of the truth of Christ and His work is there some will believe in spite of the fact that the light is diffused through a translucent window. I would argue that some people have likely met Christ at the Crystal Cathedral since Schuller occasionally invites an evangelical as a guest speaker or allows a testimony from someone who does know the Lord. Also, the hymns they sing may have enough of the gospel for someone to believe.

Taking this analysis further, let us consider newer Church Growth leaders Bill Hybels and Rick Warren who were influenced by Schuller. Both of them are more evangelical than Schuller. Their terminology often includes parts of the gospel. This being the case, by God's grace and mercy, there are conversions through their approach. So, in their churches, there exists an invisible church. Perhaps there are many true Christians within.

This, however, does not justify the theory that one ought to use whatever means work best to grow the visible church simply because people are better off churched, and some may actually be saved. That rationale assumes that Christ has not told us what the church is to be and do. It assumes that we have the liberty to adopt any plan that gets people to come to the visible church and stay there (as Charlemagne did). I deny that we have that liberty. It opens the door to unacceptable options.

The Efficient, Market Driven Church

Those churches that have adopted Schuller's strategy (and others like it) are committed to using the latest proven systems to gather the largest possible group. The system that works best is one that is focused and efficient and seeks measurable results (outcome-based). Rick Warren uses these principles in *The Purpose Driven Church*.[10] In this approach, everything starts with a mission statement. Everything the church does has to be justified vis-à-vis the mission statement. The mission statement (Warren uses the term "purpose") is necessary to produce focus and eliminate programs or processes that are not contributing to the stated mission. Warren says, "A narrow mission is a clear mission."[11] This is how corporations keep every aspect of their operation focused and working with "synergy of energy."[12]

The defining mission statement, according to Rick Warren, must be stated in terms of results.[13] Warren also says, "Make it measurable."[14] This is the idea of being "outcome based." If the outcome is not being achieved, then the hindrances must be identified and removed.

The outcome that such churches seek is a growing visible church with dedicated, committed members who work in unity to achieve the mission of the church. The church must be portrayed to the unchurched as desirable and likely to meet their needs in order to gain a maximum number of new members. Rick Warren suggests that since unbelievers are not looking for truth, something else needs to be offered.[15] In his words, "While most unbelievers aren't looking for truth, they *are* looking for relief."[16] Therefore he teaches pastors to teach only what people see as benefiting their needs. He claims that Jesus used the approach of meeting their felt needs,[17] and "Jesus was a life-application preacher."[18] We discussed this in the last chapter.

But Jesus was not creating a pragmatic, outcome based system. For example, Jesus met the felt needs of the crowd in John 6 by multiplying bread. However, He later confronted them with the need for a blood atonement which resulted in the crowd leaving and refusing to follow Jesus.[19] Likewise, Jesus told Pilate that He came to bear witness to the truth, an answer that seemed irrelevant to Pilate.[20] What sinner ever saw a need for a crucified Jewish Messiah without first having been confronted with their sin and the need for atonement? Churches that exist to maximize the size and efficiency of the visible church are forced to change the gospel because the gospel is a narrow gate with few entering.

In the efficient, market driven church, people come in because the church is appealing to them. They get motivated and committed because of the excitement and unity that exists around the church's mission statement. People are asked to make commitments to the church and promise to support the church's programs.[21] People enjoy being a part of a committed community, unified, working together, and achieving measurable results. The ability to make that happen is the key to the success of the religious corporation.

The unity of the church in this contemporary model is determined by the mission statement. Every member must agree to put his or her effort fully into achieving the stated purpose of the church. Evangelical versions of this approach use biblical concepts in their statement. To gain this unity of purpose the pastor has to become a "vision caster." I will explain that concept more fully in the next chapter, but for now, in summary, this means selling his plan and getting everyone excited about it. Rick Warren says that the purpose statement must be continually repeated. He says, "Once you have defined the purposes of your church, you must continually clarify and communicate the purpose to everyone in your congregation."[22] This helps create the "synergy of energy" that makes the combined talents and enthusiasm of a group of people multiply in effectiveness. The resultant excitement is contagious as the group grows and sees the measurable outcome of their mission happen before their eyes.

Rick Warren demands unity of every member and requires that they sign a covenant in which they promise unity.[23] They are led through a series of classes that require entering covenants.[24] These are designed to create deeper commitment. I will show in a later chapter that these are unbiblical. People who do not support the unity of the church are warned and disciplined. This is Warren's interpretation of how he sees the Bible's teaching on dealing with divisive people: "They are to . . . warn those who are argumentative, plead for harmony and unity, rebuke those who are disrespectful of leadership, and remove divisive people from church if they ignore two warnings."[25] We will now compare how a biblically defined church differs from a corporate mission-defined church in how various aspects of the life of the church are handled.

Contrasts Between a Biblical Church and Seeker Church

Let us consider the topic that was just raised—church discipline. The Lord spoke about this in Matthew 18:

> *And if your brother sins, go and reprove him in private; if he listens to you, you have won your brother. But if he does not listen to you, take one or two more with you, so that by the mouth of two or three witnesses every fact may be confirmed. And if he refuses to listen to them, tell it to the church; and if he refuses to listen even to the church, let him be to you as a Gentile and a tax-gatherer.* (Matthew 18:15-17).

Elsewhere the Bible teaches to remove unrepentant sinners from fellowship (for example 1 Corinthians 5). In a biblically defined church, unrepentant sin breaks fellowship. In Matthew 18 Jesus taught about how important every believer is to Him, particularly those who were "little ones" who might be overlooked. They are so important that the ninety nine sheep would be left behind to find the straying one (Matthew 18:12). The key concern is the salvation of every one whom the Lord has brought to Himself: *"Thus it is not the will of your Father who is in heaven that one of these little ones perish"* (Matthew 18:14; note that "little ones" in context are believers – Matthew 18:6).

So in the Bible, discipline is about those who willfully sin against God, but who are believers. The goal is to restore them to fellowship. When it says, "Let him be to you as a Gentile and a tax-gatherer," that indicates that the conclusion has been reached, that such a person is not truly a Christian and needs to be the object of gospel preaching, hoping for conversion.

In churches that adopt the new model of corporate efficiency through a mission statement and a system that produces synergy of energy to reach the desired outcome, this process is much different. The synergy of energy is only possible when every member is pulling together to achieve the stated mission of the corporation. People are confronted and removed who insist on doing things in ways not consistent with the corporate mission state-ment. Inasmuch as the mission statement is not the gospel or the whole counsel of God, it is a truncated version of Christianity. Those who feel strongly that certain biblical commands (like cor-recting false teachers or preaching about the wrath of God against sin) should be followed are sand in the gears of the smoothly oiled corporate machine. They have to go. I have e-mails from people who were removed from Purpose Driven churches because they insisted on the need for gospel preaching and Bible teaching.

The disciplining of sincere Christians for failing to support a man-made mission statement is not what Matthew 18 is all about. In the context, the disciples were arguing about who was the great-est, and Jesus took a little child to make an object lesson. The "lit-tle ones" were believers who had no great status in the minds of others. They are to be treated with the utmost love and concern, even though as one straggling lamb they seem insignificant. What we have instead, in the new paradigm churches, are faithful "little ones" being booted for not supporting the corporate dreams of those who deem themselves important. This is a total reversal of what Jesus taught. We will look more deeply into how this works in the Purpose Driven movement in the next chapter.

Unity of What?

Unity is a biblical concept, but there is a huge difference between the concept of unity in a biblically defined church and that in the new Purpose Driven church. In the Bible, the goal is the unity of the faith: *"Until we all attain to the unity of the faith, and of the knowledge of the Son of God, to a mature man, to the measure of the stature which belongs to the fulness of Christ"* (Ephesians 4:13). The faith is the content of the gospel, including the entirety of the teaching as given by Christ and His Apostles: *"Beloved, while I was making every effort to write you about our common salvation, I felt the necessity to write to you appealing that you contend earnestly for the faith which was once for all delivered to the saints"* (Jude 1:3). One cannot decide anything about what unity is to be preserved without first deciding what "the faith" is.

For example, at the time of the Reformation, Luther was considered a heretic, a schismatic whose efforts were directed against the unity of the church. From the perspective of Rome, he was. However, that assumes that the Roman church and her practices were truly in accord with the gospel and the teachings of Christ and His Apostles. Luther believed that they were not and that to find the unity of the faith, churches needed to be established based on the true means of grace. Both Luther and Calvin taught that true churches were those where the Word was purely taught and the sacraments were kept according to the Lord's commandment. It is impossible to decide what constitutes a schismatic (one who causes divisions) without first deciding what constitutes a valid church!

Let us again consider Jude, where we were told to contend for the faith:

> But you, beloved, ought to remember the words that were spoken beforehand by the apostles of our Lord Jesus Christ, that they were saying to you, "In the last time there shall be mockers, following after their own ungodly lusts." These are the ones who cause divisions, worldly-minded, devoid of the Spirit (Jude 1:17-19).

According to this, the divisions are caused by worldly minded people whose lusts indicate that they are not truly regenerate. They are departing from the faith that was delivered by Christ and His Apostles.

Elsewhere we see the same thing: "*Now I urge you, brethren, keep your eye on those who cause dissensions and hindrances contrary to the teaching which you learned, and turn away from them*" (Romans 16:17). Notice that division is that which is contrary to the apostolic teaching. Here is another example:

> If anyone advocates a different doctrine, and does not agree with sound words, those of our Lord Jesus Christ, and with the doctrine

conforming to godliness, he is conceited and understands nothing;
but he has a morbid interest in controversial questions and disputes
about words, out of which arise envy, strife, abusive language, evil
suspicions, and constant friction between men of depraved mind
and deprived of the truth, who suppose that godliness is a means of
gain (1 Timothy 6:3-5).

Unity cannot be preserved when a clear biblical understanding of sound doctrine is absent. The unity of the faith is not the same as the unity of a religious corporation. Luther brought us closer to the unity of the faith (because he brought the church closer to sound doctrine), even though he appeared at the time to be a schismatic. Religious corporations that exist to meet the needs of the maximum numbers of religious consumers move us away from the unity of the faith because preserving sound doctrine is not in their stated mission.

A secular corporation can determine its marketing goals, mission, and protocol, and legitimately remove those who refuse to cooperate with the corporate mission statement. But is this valid with the church? The Bible defines the church. The doctrines of Christ and His apostles determine its unity. Church leaders who decide to change the church from its biblical definition for the sake of expediency and corporate success have no right to remove godly Christians for the "sin" of not being in unity with their man-made mission statement. They have no biblical authority to do this.

Growing the Invisible Church

Peter said, "*Obtaining as the outcome of your faith the salvation of your souls*" (1 Peter 1:9). The outcome based corporate management churches judge their success vis-à-vis their mission statement based on measurable outcome. They cannot measure the invisible church because it cannot be seen. The only outcome they can measure very accurately is the number of people joining the visible church. The biblically defined church seeks to nurture and grow the invisible church through the means of grace. Though we cannot know for sure who the elect are, we know for sure what means God uses to call people to Himself and sanctify them. If we faithfully provide those means, God will use them to nurture His flock which was purchased by the blood of Christ. The size of the visible church is not an important issue, but the existence and well being of the invisible one surely is. To grow the invisible church, we preach the gospel without compromise and provide the means of grace for the redeemed. God uses these to build Christ's church.

The redefined church of the Church Growth movement has mostly ignored the matter of the invisible church. They use the best means available based on pragmatic tests to make the visible church as big as possible, even if the light of the truth is so dim that only with difficulty will anyone be saved or sanctified. If happy religious consumers living better lives than they had outside of the church is the test of validity, then these huge and rapidly growing churches must be right. I do not believe, however, there is anything in the New Testament that validates seeking to maximize the visible church by means that tend to strangle the invisible one.

Consider the inspired words of Paul: *"Pay close attention to yourself and to your teaching; persevere in these things; for as you do this you will insure salvation both for yourself and for those who hear you"* (1 Timothy 4:16). That is how you insure that there is a growing invisible church enrolled in Heaven. Consider what Jesus told Peter: *"Feed My sheep"* (see John 21:15-17). Doing a Purpose Driven campaign hoping to gain twenty percent more people and money is not feeding Christ's sheep.

Redefining Vision

"Where there is no vision, the people are unrestrained, But happy is he who keeps the law" (Proverbs 29:18).

Biblical Vision

The process of redefining the church includes redefining terms that are found in the Bible. A key term that Rick Warren and his followers redefine is "vision." The passage cited above is often misunderstood because of this phrase in the KJV, *"Where there is no vision, the people perish"* (Proverbs 29:18a). This is taken to mean, "a corporate idea of an optimal future for the church." But as the full citation from the NASB shows, we have an example of Hebrew parallelism. The Psalms and Proverbs are full of synonymous and antithetical parallelisms. This simply means stating an idea, then restating it in synonymous terms, or stating an idea and then stating the opposite. Proverbs 29:18 is an antithetical parallelism. The contrast is between different outcomes when there is or is not vision. In making the contrast, the terms "vision" and "law" are used synonymously. So the vision was God's vision which is His revealed law.

Many years ago a preacher came to our church and preached on vision, citing this passage. His point was that our congregation needed to know what our vision was for our corporate future—how we were going to have an impact on those around us and what we would look like when that happens. His claim was that if we did not have a focused vision for our local church, we would perish. At the time, I did not understand Hebrew parallelism like I do now, so I could not see the error of his biblical interpretation. However, I felt that the teaching was somehow off base, thinking that all churches had the same vision because it had been given once for all by Christ. When I heard that message I lacked a mental image of an optimal future for this organization. All I had was the gospel to preach and the Bible to teach. Now I realize that gospel preaching and Bible teaching ARE the vision for the church, just like the law was God's vision for Old Covenant Israel.

Rick Warren wrote the foreword to Dan Southerland's book entitled *Transitioning; Leading Your Church Through Change*.[1] The book is designed to show pastors how to transition their traditional church into a Purpose Driven one. Rick Warren sells the book on the Purpose Driven Web site. Some of the chapter headings reveal how heavily it depends on the concept of vision: "Preparing for Vision; Defining Vision; Planting the Vision; Sharing the Vision; Implementing the Vision, etc." The future Purpose Driven church is what the vision is all about. The vision includes the process of removing people who oppose becoming Purpose Driven. This book is very revealing.

"What Happened to My Church?"

Reading Southerland's book will help people whose churches have changed from gospel preaching and Bible teaching churches to seeker churches understand what has happened to them. Southerland characterizes those who resist this transition as "leaders from hell" who are of the ilk of Sanballat who resisted Nehemiah.[2] It is clear that Pastor Southerland is convinced that he is like Nehemiah on a mission from God (i.e., to convert the church to being a Purpose Driven seeker church) and that all who resist are misguided, have evil motives, or are just unwilling to change because of their being caught in traditions.

There is, however, another side of the story. I have heard from many of these "evil Sanballat types", and they are heart-broken over what has happened to their churches. They love the gospel and hunger for solid Bible teaching. Besides being starved spiritually, they are now chastised as being evildoers. This e-mail from Canada is an example:

> We were labeled critical and divisive and negative in our Southern Baptist church for pointing out the watered-down gospel and twisting of Scripture in the book *Purpose-Driven Life*. Despite the concerns we raised, our church pressed ahead with their 40 day journey earlier this year and we found it too difficult to attend church over that period, where all the ministries of the church were geared to that study over that time. We have found the lack of discernment very alarming. We are shocked at the weak teaching of Scripture we are seeing, the lack of discernment, the ignorance of truth versus error, and the willingness to jump unquestioningly on every popular "Christian" bandwagon that comes along. We are very discouraged as we know of no solid, Bible-honoring, discerning church in our area and wonder what those of us who see these problems are to do.

Here is another lament from people whose church made the transition:

> We attend a large Baptist, though in reality nondenominational church. It seems our church, and many, many, others have embraced what I've come to call "Warrenism". . . What's disturbed us is the secularization of our church. It's become more and more worldly, while growing large in number (about 6,000 members). We have felt alone in our uneasiness with the "Warrenistic" culture of our church as it's grown stronger there, but we felt confused about it after some Sunday sermons in support of it. What we see now at our church is not enough evangelism without, and God's

House is very worldly within. This is what breaks our hearts. We hear sermons with only vague references to Scripture and have a secularized worship service many times. My wife asks me, "Shouldn't we be getting nourishment to prepare us for our battles as Christians?"

My question is this: "Are the resisters really leaders from hell or are they solid Christians who know the difference between the gospel as preached by Christ and His apostles and the Purpose Driven message that is tailored to appeal to the unregenerate and carnal minded?"

What most of these resistant people do not know is that their pastors have been trained in how to deal with them. Their pastors have been taught that "traditionalists" who do not get on board with the new vision will have to go if they cannot be placated or converted to the new paradigm. The reason for this is that the Purpose Driven franchise cannot succeed without conformity to its protocol. That is why Rick Warren makes all members of his church sign a unity covenant.[3] In his case, his church never was anything but Purpose Driven. The people who have come there mostly do not know the difference between a gospel church and a Purpose Driven church. They are happy to sign unity pledges because they are already convinced that Rick Warren and his processes are from God. But Warren's campaign to convert existing churches to become Purpose Driven creates a far different situation. It displaces thousands of people who know what real gospel preaching and Bible teaching are. They know that the synthetic alternative that pleases the unregenerate masses is not the same message. They, who were previously the stalwarts of the congregation, are now the "problem people" who have to be dealt with.

This transition is similar to what happens when one franchise company buys another. The employees of the purchased company have been trained in the vision and protocol of that company. The new one has an entirely different corporate agenda. What often happens is that long-time, loyal employees of the old company are fired because it is easier to bring in a new team that is sold on the new company's ways. This is painful enough in corporate America, but when it happens to a long-standing church that existed to preach the gospel, teach the Bible, and care for the flock, people who are mature, loving Christians find themselves removed from fellowship. They who love their Lord and His Word have, through no choice of their own, become characterized as wicked resisters who are standing in the way of what God wants to do.

The New "Reformation"

Dan Southerland's book reveals in a step-by-step process describing how to convert one's congregation from a Bible church to a Purpose Driven church.[4] Rick Warren's endorsement in the foreword of the book characterizes what is happening: "An incredible wave of renewal and revival is taking place in these churches that are willing to change."[5] This process is entirely based on the concept of vision, which includes eight steps that will convert one's church to a Purpose Driven church.

Before the vision process begins, pastors need to be convinced that what they are now doing is failing. Statistics are used to prove that most churches are failing and desperately need to transition to the new paradigm. Southerland writes, "According to recent studies, 80 percent of churches in North America are plateaued or in decline."[6] Church Growth advocates commonly cite this statistic. Southerland further asserts, "In the twenty centuries since Jesus handed us the keys to the kingdom, we have lost our way."[7] His answer is to regain the vision, a process which entails a second reformation: "The second reformation is about methods. It concerns how we should relate to the world around us; how we make the gospel culturally relevant so that men and women everywhere can come to know, love and serve Jesus Christ."[8]

In these few pages, Southerland tells pastors that they need a reformation and an entirely new model of how to "do church". He thinks (probably sincerely) that this is the biblical model. Yet he does no exegetical or theological work to prove from the Bible that the Purpose Driven model is that of Christ and His apostles. Still he asks, "How do we transition the church back to a Purpose Driven model?"[9] This is amazingly anachronistic. The Purpose Driven model is based on marketing principles that were not articulated before the 20th century. Do not be deceived, the Purpose Driven movement is not bringing us back to something that existed in biblical times, that was somehow lost in church history. This is a new movement that was founded by Robert Schuller in the 1960s. Schuller called for a similar reformation in 1982.[10] As discussed earlier, Schuller's reformation was somewhat limited because of the difficulty of replicating the Crystal Cathedral. Rick Warren has overcome that shortcoming by creating a model that can be adopted anywhere. Thus the reformation that Schuller envisioned in 1982 has been resurrected and restructured by Rick Warren in a way that might actually succeed.[11] What we need to decide is whether the Schuller/Warren reformation is biblical or whether it is actually a deformation.

To confuse this matter even more, C. Peter Wagner is calling for a "new apostolic reformation." Not to be left on the sidelines, in 1993 a group of feminists gathered at a re-imagining conference and proposed a feminist second reformation that would push their agenda.[12] That makes four reformations going on simultaneously. Schuller's reformation is based on self-esteem; Warren's on making the church exist so as to be relevant to unbelievers (which self-esteem teaching does); Wagner's on the emergence of latter day apostles and prophets in the church; and the feminists on the need for a more sensual spirituality.[13] One thing they all have in common is the desired end which is church growth through making the church more attractive to the world. Church growth was not an issue during the real Reformation; the Catholic church was growing just fine before Luther.

During a radio debate with a pastor who supports Rick Warren, I suggested that if Warren really believes we need a reformation, he should show in detail what exactly was wrong with the teaching and practice of evangelicalism that warranted a reformation.[14] His response cited surveys suggesting that most churches are not growing. Apparently growth is the one issue that fuels this movement. In a later chapter I will show that when Jesus Christ brought messages to seven churches in Revelation He never considered size or growth as an important matter. We have some major problems here. First we have to make the logical jump that lack of numerical growth warrants a reformation. Second, if we make that logical jump, then we have to decide which of the four reformations is right to join. Third, having joined one of them, we have to overturn everything we have been doing, even at the expense of alienating solid Christians who love their church and the gospel, in order to make our message and practice acceptable to the world (and thus facilitate growth).

Not a single epistle in the New Testament rebukes a church for not growing! Furthermore, when it comes to the church's relationship to the lost, there are warnings to not give needless offense, but there are no instructions to change the nature of Christian teaching and gatherings so that a target audience would find it appealing in their unregenerate state.[15] It seems to me that too many pastors are signing up for some version of this new reformation without critically examining the claims of its proponents by comparing them with Scripture.

The new reformation isn't designed to make anything more biblical; it is designed to do two things: 1) create a felt need in pastors by suggesting that they are failing God based on demographic studies and statistics, and 2) feed the appetite for success in the eyes of their peers (Who wants to fail?) by designing a system that will work to make their churches grow. Why be one of the miserable statistics of failure when you can sign up to become Purpose Driven? If you follow the protocol the way it is designed to be followed, your church is very likely to be deemed healthy. Southerland achieved this status by using these proven techniques to grow his church from 300 to 2,100.[16] This creates a dilemma for pastors: Either continue to preach the gospel clearly as preached in the New Testament in its native offensiveness to the unregenerate mind and be deemed a failure by the church growth experts, or join the new reformation and learn how to turn your sick church into a healthy one as defined by the church growth technocrats. If the numbers that Rick Warren cites are accurate, many pastors in America are choosing the second option.

How Vision Is Used to Change Churches

The concept *"vision"* is the key to converting one's church to becoming Purpose Driven. Southerland's book used the term "vision" continually, claiming that it is supported by the book of Nehemiah. He presents an eight-step program for pastors to follow that will transition their church to becoming Purpose Driven. The steps are all dependent on his concept of *"vision"*. I will show that the way he and other Church Growth advocates use the term *"vision"* is entirely different from how it is used in the Bible.

In order to understand this transitioning process, we need to understand what Warren and Southerland mean by the term *"vision."* The term *"vision"* is never found in the book of Nehemiah, though Southerland uses Nehemiah as a key example of someone who used the principle of vision to achieve something great for God. Nehemiah was on a mission that God endorsed to rebuild the walls of Jerusalem. But the vision for doing so was given many years previous by authoritative prophets from God; it was not dreamed up by Nehemiah.

The term *"vision"* in the Bible relates to special revelation, either true or false. True vision was God's authoritative word to the people (which is contained in our Scriptures), not someone having a plan for the future that they hoped to implement. In modern business jargon, the term *"vision"* does not have the same meaning that it did in the Bible. Southerland makes a major category error when he confuses the business meaning of vision with the biblical meaning.

False vision in the Bible was that which originated from man's imagination: *"Then the Lord said to me, 'The prophets are prophesying falsehood in My name. I have neither sent them nor commanded them nor spoken to them; they are prophesying to you a false vision, divination, futility and the deception of their own minds*'" (Jeremiah 14:14). Later in Jeremiah we find the same idea: *"Thus says the Lord of hosts, "Do not listen to the words of the prophets who are prophesying to you. They are leading you into futility; They speak a vision **of their own imagination**, Not from the mouth of the Lord"* (Jeremiah 23:16). The use of the term *"vision"* in modern business lingo concerns a visionary person seeing the marketing of a product all the way from research and development to marketing and support. This vision begins in the mind of a capable businessperson. Executing the vision follows the plan that Southerland lays out in his book: conducting market surveys of potential religious consumers; defining the business; selling the power brokers on it; selling the business team; selling the key workers and the common people on the concept; and dealing with opposition. This is a business marketing plan pure and simple. It starts with man's imagination, not God's authoritative vision contained in Scripture.

To show how Southerland and others who have bought into Warren's Purpose Driven paradigm are using the term *"vision"*, I will cite several examples. In the following sentences, Southerland tells what vision is and is not: "Vision is not just a destination, it is a journey. Vision is not just a product, it is a process. Vision is not just the finish line; it is the whole race."[17] These ideas have nothing to do with the biblical concept of vision as authoritative revelation from God given to His authoritative spokespersons. Southerland goes on, "Any business guru can tell you that research and development is a major part of producing a winning product."[18] Again, this has nothing to do with the biblical term *vision*. This is a modern, secular use of the term. I am convinced that the Church Growth movement uses the term because it sounds like something from the Bible and suits their purposes of selling a version of Christianity to the masses. To use the term in the business sense and simultaneously tell people that it came from the Bible is a blatant example of equivocation.[19]

Here is an example from Southerland's book where he confuses people by using the term *"vision"* in an unbiblical way: "Paul captured the essence of vision when he wrote these words: '*No eye has seen, no ear has heard, no mind has conceived what God has prepared for those who love him*'" (1 Corinthians 2:9). This passage is not the essence of what the Bible means by vision, it is the opposite. There is no vision in the sense of authoritative revelation from God for what is not revealed and no one knows! What Paul is describing will not be known until the end of the age when Christ returns. We only know that part of it that is revealed in Scripture. Southerland, however, makes this application: "For our eyes to see God's vision, for our ears to hear God's voice, and for our minds to conceive of God's plan, we must spend time in major preparation."[20] Exactly what preparation is going to give us what God has not chosen to reveal to anyone? The following shows that Southerland is using "*vision*" in the modern business marketing sense and not the biblical sense: "Before we can receive God's vision for His church, we must prepare for vision. God's vision for your church is big stuff, so the preparation for that vision must be big stuff as well."[21] He obviously is not speaking of what has been revealed once for all by God's authoritative prophets. Instead, he is speaking of what we get in our mind now from extra-biblical sources in order to conceive of a different future for our local church.

To make this equivocation process even more confusing, Southerland tells his readers that Nehemiah used this type of vision process in his ministry: "Nehemiah understood this vital principle: vision is best birthed out of thorough knowledge."[22] No, Nehemiah was not from the Peter Drucker school of the prophets. The term "*vision*" does not even appear in the Book of Nehemiah. The "*vision*" of rebuilding Jerusalem was given to the authoritative prophet Jeremiah years before: "'*Behold, days are coming,*' declares the Lord, '*when the city shall be rebuilt for the Lord from the Tower of Hananel to the Corner Gate*'" (Jeremiah 31:38). It was also spoken to Daniel: "*So you are to know and discern that from the issuing of a decree to restore and rebuild Jerusalem until Messiah the Prince there will be seven weeks and sixty-two weeks; it will be built again, with plaza and moat, even in times of distress*" (Daniel 9:25). Nehemiah was carrying out the plan of God that had been declared God's plan by God's biblical prophets. He was not using his imagination to dream big things for God; nor was he birthing a vision by some man-made process.

Southerland tells pastors how to birth their vision, supposedly based on Nehemiah: "First, go to school on *the unchurched people in your community*."[23] Nehemiah knew from Jeremiah and Daniel that God intended to restore Jerusalem. In our day, we do not have authoritative Scripture telling us that our churches should exist to meet the needs and expectations of the unregenerate. Nehemiah surveying the situation in Jerusalem to see what would be needed to rebuild is not analogous to pastors doing marketing surveys of potential religious consumers so as to design a church that suits their fancy. This is a huge category disconnect.

Yet Pastor Southerland is so absolutely convinced that the Purpose Driven paradigm is God's vision for the church that he is willing to take criticism for not preaching the gospel in order to fulfill this vision. When criticized for not preaching the gospel, he gathered his leaders, stood his ground, and said this: "This is where I have to go. I must do church for the unchurched; I can't go back to doing church for the already convinced. If you want to go with me, please do."[24] His vision of creating a Purpose Driven church is more important than anything else and he willingly suffered the loss of 300 members to create a church that appeals to the "unchurched" (which is code for the "unregenerate"). Why feed Jesus' little flock when you could have a huge group of happy religious consumers instead? He made a poor choice.

Biblical vision is from God. It is spoken authoritatively once for all Christians for all ages and it always applies in all situations. Vision that helps a pastor transition his church from a gospel preaching church to a Purpose Driven church comes from the imagination of men, is fueled by the wisdom of marketing gurus, and changes as often as the target group takes on different cultural characteristics. The modern business term has nothing to do with the Biblical one. Do not be fooled. The possibility thinker Robert Schuller and the exponential thinker Rick Warren have visions alright, but they did not come from the authoritative prophets of the Bible.

Why Christians are Only Important if They Join the Vision Team

The goal of the transition from a Bible church to a Purpose Driven church is to get everyone to buy the vision and agree to work to implement it. If this is happening in your church your pastor has probably already bought into the Purpose Driven franchise and is convinced that he is on a serious mission from God. He thinks that everyone who resists being Purpose Driven either has bad motives, is a slave of religious traditions, or is a tool of Satan. Such people will only hinder the implementation of the vision. In a chapter on dealing with opposition, Southerland admits that he was accused of not preaching the gospel.[25] So his "evil" opponents want the gospel preached, much like the many people who have e-mailed me after their churches were hijacked by Rick Warren's movement.

If you believe that the church should preach the law and gospel and feed the flock solid food through expository Bible preaching, you likely have enemy status in the eyes of the pastor and leaders of your church—especially if the decision to transition has already been made. Your church, once the transition is implemented, will no longer exist to feed God's flock and preach the gospel to the lost, but will exist to meet the felt needs of religious consumers (the target market niche).

Southerland makes it clear that the vision is about reaching a target group. He says, "The question in business jargon would be 'Who is our primary customer?'"[26] Determining this requires market research that will reveal who the church is targeting. Southerland writes, "We must determine who is in the center of the bull's-eye on the target."[27] For Rick Warren, the target was "Saddleback Sam," a composite, typical person that Warren designed his church services to please.[28] We must be clear about something: The market research that determines the target audience that these pastors want to reach is used to design a church service, not gospel preaching outside the church. The church is no longer to be a gathering of Christians around the means of grace; it is to be a place to attract the target audience by feeding their religious appetites, whatever they may be. Marketing is ultimately about satisfied customers.

Once this vision is established and refined to reach the market niche that seems most likely to respond favorably, all team members must get on board with the vision. This means that the long-standing church members' needs—being fed God's Word, prayer, fellowship, and opportunities to minister to one another—are no longer important. The felt needs of the target audience are what define the vision of the Purpose Driven church. Those who long to be fed God's Word are made to look selfish and unwilling to reach the lost.

Perhaps expanding on an earlier analogy will help clarify this. The Purpose Driven church is a church that has adopted a business marketing strategy. As we stated, the previous members are like employees of a company that was bought out by another. The new company has a different target audience with different appetites. Imagine you were an employee of a fried chicken restaurant and it was bought out by a pizza franchise. The new corporate vision will target people with an appetite for pizza. You will either have to work to follow company protocol so that the target group becomes satisfied customers, or you will have to give up your job. Pizza customers are never going to expect chicken at that location again.

If you were a member of a Bible church that consisted of people with a hunger for the whole counsel of God, the gospel preached without compromise, and worship designed to bring glory to God, and that church becomes Purpose Driven, that church now has a different purpose. That church will no longer exist to satisfy the appetites of those who love God's Word and hunger for the truth. It now exists to feed the appetites of religious consumers of the target market group. These religious consumers have no appetite for what that church used to provide, AND THEY NEVER WILL! People do not go to a pizza place if their appetite is for chicken, and they do not go to a Purpose Driven church if their appetite is for solid, unsullied Bible teaching. Whatever that church offers that satisfies their targeted religious consumers will have to continue to be offered. If this targeted market group had an appetite for the gospel and expository Bible preaching, that church would never have changed; they could have reached this group the way they were. Having changed, that church will now be a different entity, permanently.

If you were a member before the change, your only choices are to join the new vision and work to meet the felt needs of the targeted market group (religious consumers)—or leave. If you stay, you will have to spend your time helping the pastor achieve his vision (marketing plan). You will have to do this knowing that never again will God's Word be preached with authority and power from the pulpit (which religious consumers have no appetite for), because to do so would be to give up the vision which your pastor is trained to never do at any cost. If you loved chicken and chose to work in a chicken place because of that, once the pizza company buys your store, your chicken days are over. So it is when a Bible church becomes Purpose Driven. This is true because of one simple fact: "Saddleback Sam" has no hunger for the things of God. The old way was preaching the gospel to the lost. If they were converted they got a hunger for the things of God and then they joined a Bible church where they were fed. The new way is to make the church appealing to those who are not converted. This means it can never become a Bible church. As soon as it does, it would quit attracting the target market group.

Can you imagine what would happen if John MacArthur preached the gospel, week after week in the Crystal Cathedral? I can. Some people would be converted and their lives permanently changed by the power of God. The majority would be outraged, offended and leave the church. They come to get a self-esteem boost, not be told they are wretched sinners facing God's wrath. Of course this will never happen as long as Robert Schuller has anything to say about it. It cannot happen because the Crystal

Cathedral exists for other reasons than preaching the blood atonement. So does any Purpose Driven church. The differences between Schuller and Warren are merely superficial. Warren includes evangelical terminology and has a more orthodox statement of faith. But what is preached to the general public is very similar. That is the target audience. Warren says that "Saddleback Sam" is "skeptical of 'organized religion.'"[29] So are those who are attracted to the Crystal Cathedral.

Once this key change is in place, and the church leadership has bought the vision package, the members either become team players helping to make the new marketing plan work, or they are disloyal traitors who have to go. If you long for solid Bible teaching, you are in the wrong place if yours is a Purpose Driven church. That you will leave is a cost your pastor has already calculated and decided he is willing to pay. Reading *Transitioning*, which Rick Warren promotes, makes that crystal clear. Southerland tells pastors, "You will be criticized. It might as well be for doing the right thing."[30] From what he writes, one must conclude that he really believes that making the church a community gathering place for religious consumers rather than a gathering of the "called out ones" is the right thing. Southerland really believes he is like Nehemiah sent by God to rebuild Jerusalem. He really believes that people who hunger for gospel preaching and Bible teaching are the enemies of God's vision. If your church has bought the Purpose Driven franchise, your pastor probably does too. It is a sad, harsh reality, but you have lost your church. It's highly unlikely that it will ever again be a gospel-centric church.

In the next chapter we will examine the process whereby Rick Warren gets people to take oaths to support his program. In so doing he is redefining the nature of true Christian commitment. We will show that in launching his P.E.A.C.E. plan, touting it as a new reformation, he is refuting key principles of the real Reformation.

Redefining Christian Commitment

"But above all, my brethren, do not swear, either by heaven or by earth or with any other oath; but let your yes be yes, and your no, no; so that you may not fall under judgment" (James 5:12).

In the Bible, Christian commitment is based on faith in Christ and dependence on Him for grace to walk obediently in His ways. In church history hyper-pious people, believing it possible to become higher-order Christians, created religious orders. People who joined these orders took oaths they believed made them more pious and spiritual than the ordinary people who were only obliged to follow Christ's teachings.[1] The resulting abusive system was part of the reason for the Reformation.

Now we have Rick Warren bringing back the hyper piety of pre-Reformation Rome through nothing less than religious oaths, touting this as a "reformation." I will show that this process is unbiblical and takes the church away from the principles of the real Reformation. It is not surprising that Warren would fall into this error since he teaches that there are two classes of Christian, the preferred one being "world-class."[2]

On April 17, 2005, Rick Warren had 30,000 people stand at Saddleback Church's 25th anniversary celebration and make a covenant to express a "radical commitment to this global spiritual revolution."[3] The revolution is a planned "new spiritual reformation."[4] Warren further used the occasion to rally the troops to engage in his P.E.A.C.E. plan to wipe out world problems like poverty and disease.[5]

For Warren's congregation, entering a covenant was nothing new, since they have agreed to several covenants to become members of his church. The following is the entire text of the covenant document to which they agreed:

THE ANGEL STADIUM DECLARATION
April 17, 2005

Today I am stepping across the line. I'm tired of waffling, and I'm finished with wavering. I've made my choice; the verdict is in; and my decision is irrevocable. I'm going God's way. There's no turning back now!

I will live the rest of my life serving God's purposes with God's people on God's planet for God's glory. I will use my life to celebrate his presence, cultivate his character, participate in his family, demonstrate his love, and communicate his Word.

Since my past has been forgiven, and I have a purpose for living and a home awaiting in heaven, I refuse to waste any more time or energy on shallow living, petty thinking, trivial talking, thoughtless doing, useless regretting, hurtful resenting, or faithless worrying. Instead I will magnify God, grow to maturity, serve in ministry, and fulfill my mission in the membership of his family.

Because this life is preparation for the next, I will value worship over wealth, "we" over "me," character over comfort, service over status, and people over possessions, position, and pleasures. I know what matters most, and I'll give it all I've got. I'll do the best I can with what I have for Jesus Christ today.

I won't be captivated by culture, manipulated by critics, motivated by praise, frustrated by problems, debilitated by temptation, or intimidated by the devil. I'll keep running my race with my eyes on the goal, not the sidelines or those running by me. When times get tough, and I get tired, I won't back up, back off, back down, back out, or backslide. I'll just keep moving forward by God's grace. I'm Spirit-led, purpose-driven and mission-focused, so I cannot be bought, I will not be compromised, and I shall not quit until I finish the race.

I'm a trophy of God's amazing grace, so I will be gracious to everyone, grateful for everyday, and generous with everything that God entrusts to me.

To my Lord and Savior Jesus Christ, I say: However, whenever, wherever, and whatever you ask me to do, my answer in advance is yes! Wherever you lead and whatever the cost, I'm ready. Anytime. Anywhere. Anyway. Whatever it takes Lord; whatever it takes! I want to be used by you in such a way, that on that final day I'll hear you say, "Well done, thou good and faithful one. Come on in, and let the eternal party begin!"[6]

Much of this pious language sounds very noble minded. However, there are some serious problems. **First** and most important, this "covenant" involves taking oaths in a way that the New Testament forbids. **Second**, asking 30,000 people to stand and read this covenant in a spontaneous group event is very manipulative; the crowd dynamics insure nearly total compliance. **Third**, this statement presumes heavily on human abilities that we do not have. Who are we to make "irrevocable" decisions? What makes us think we have the power to live up to this statement? **Fourth**, this statement presumes on the future which is unknown to us. How are we going to find out what the future will of God (beyond Scripture) is that we have agreed in advance to do? **Fifth**, this covenant was made in the context of committing to a P.E.A.C.E. plan that was just unveiled. These people committed to serve a cause that may or may not be from God. Why make a radical commitment to what you have not had an opportunity to study and compare with Scripture? In this chapter I am going to explain the biblical warning against oaths and show that Rick Warren's use of covenants in his church membership plan is unbiblical. I will also show from Martin Luther's writings against oaths that Warren's reformation is a repudiation of the Reformation.

Covenants and Oaths

Most people know about the biblical passages in the New Testament that forbid oaths. They are found in Matthew 5:33-37 and James 5:12. Since Rick Warren uses the term "covenant" when he asks people to make a pledge, it appears on the surface that he is not in violation of the teachings found in these verses. However, a careful study of Scripture shows that the Old Testament uses the term for covenant when it involves an agreement between humans (as opposed to those between God and man) interchangeably with the term "oath" or "vow." Making a covenant between human parties is tantamount to taking an oath. We will examine several passages to show this.

In Genesis 26, Abimelech, king of the Philistines, made a covenant with Isaac: *"We see plainly that the Lord has been with you; so we said, 'Let there now be an oath between us, even between you and us, and let us make a covenant with you'"* (Genesis 26:28). This was one agreement, the oath and covenant being the substance of it. The following passage is even more clear: *"Now not with you alone am I making this covenant and this oath"* (Deuteronomy 29:14). Moses was speaking of one agreement, not two. The terms "covenant" and "oath" are synonymously parallel. Here is another example: *"So Jonathan made a covenant with the house of David, saying, 'May the Lord require it at the hands of David's enemies.' And Jonathan made David vow again because of his love for him, because he loved him as he loved his own life"* (1 Samuel 20:16, 17). Here, "made a covenant" and "vow" are synonymously parallel; there is no distinction between them.

Likewise, in the Book of Ezra, the terms "covenant" and "oath" are used of the same act: *"'So now let us **make a covenant** with our God to put away all the wives and their children, according to the counsel of my lord and of those who tremble at the commandment of our God; and let it be done according to the law. Arise! For this matter is your responsibility, but we*

will be with you; be courageous and act.' Then Ezra rose and made the lead-*
ing priests, the Levites, and all Israel, take oath that they would do according
to this proposal; **so they took the oath**" (Ezra 10:3-5). According to biblical usage, a covenant agreement is an oath. When God made a
covenant with Abraham, the Book of Hebrews tells us He did so
with an oath (Hebrews 6:13-18). Therefore, entering a covenant
agreement is taking a solemn oath.[7]

It is also interesting to note that the Greek term translated
"covenant" in the New Testament is never used there to describe an
agreement between two human parties. It only describes God's
covenants, either the Old Covenant or New Covenant. There is no
New Testament precedent for a religious leader creating a covenant
and enticing his followers to sign it or verbally swear to it. Whether
the term "covenant" or "oath" is used, there is still a problem with
this practice.

Oaths are Forbidden in the New Testament

Jesus referenced the Old Testament command about keeping
one's oaths and then forbade them altogether: "*Again, you have*
heard that the ancients were told, 'You shall not make false vows, but shall
fulfill your vows to the Lord.' But I say to you, make no oath at all, either by
heaven, for it is the throne of God, or by the earth, for it is the footstool of His
feet, or by Jerusalem, for it is the city of the great King. Nor shall you make
an oath by your head, for you cannot make one hair white or black"
(Matthew 5:34-36). The Jews wanted to avoid invoking God's name
when taking an oath in order to avoid the possibility of taking His
name in vain. So they swore by something else as a substitute. To
make a vow to the Lord and fail to keep it would be profaning
God's name. Jesus says that in some way, whatever one might swear
by is associated with God. Therefore swearing by something less in
order to lessen the guilt of failing to keep one's vow is hypocritical.

Oaths are often invoked by liars who would want to convince
their hearers that they are now telling the truth. Sometimes we
hear, "May God strike me dead if I am lying." True disciples are to
be characterized by truth telling so that oaths are not necessary to

convince others of their integrity. If one swears by anything, and that person breaks his or her vow it amounts to profaning God's name. Jesus went on to say, *"But let your statement be, 'Yes, yes' or 'No, no'; and anything beyond these is of evil"* (Matthew 5:37). Literally it says in the Greek, "from the evil one," i.e., Satan. Oaths also could be used to make a person seem pious to others. In Matthew 23 Jesus rebukes the hypocrisy of religious leaders who used unwarranted casuistry[8] at one and the same time make oaths and then escape from being obligated by them (Matthew 23:16-22). Jesus argues that all swearing is ultimately swearing by God Himself and therefore all breaking of oaths is profaning God's name.

When James teaches against taking oaths, he does so in the context of various abuses of speech. James writes, *"But above all, my brethren, do not swear, either by heaven or by earth or with any other oath; but let your yes be yes, and your no, no; so that you may not fall under judgment"* (James 5:12). These abuses include boasting (James 3:5), cursing (James 3:10), wrongly speaking against a brother (James 4:11), presumptuous speech about the future (James 4:13), arrogant speech (James 4:16), complaining impatiently (James 5:9, 10), and then "above all" taking oaths (James 5:12). Of all the abuses of human speech that James warns against, taking oaths is the worst. Those who do are likely to fall under judgment.

There are reasons for this. In light of Jesus' teaching, people who take religious oaths are invoking God's name whether they think they are or not. When they do, they profane God's name if they do not live up to their oath. Since humans are fallen sinners, not living up to an oath is a likely outcome. In James, there was the warning against the presumptuous businessmen who boasted of future profits as if they knew the future. They are rebuked (see James 4:13-16). Taking oaths that have to do with the future involves even more presumption. Those businessmen were told, *"Yet you do not know what your life will be like tomorrow. You are just a vapor that appears for a little while and then vanishes away"* (James 4:14). Boasting of the future is a failure to take into account human frailty and our lack of knowledge about the future.

Let us consider parts of the "covenant" (i.e., oath) that Rick Warren had 30,000 people take upon the launch of his P.E.A.C.E. plan:

> I've made my choice; the verdict is in; and my decision is irrevocable. I'm going God's way. There's no turning back now! I will live the rest of my life serving God's purposes with God's people on God's planet for God's glory.

This is a blatant example of boasting about the future. What sinner is able to make such a boast and be sure to not fall short of it and thereby break his oath, profane God's name, and fall under judgment? Are we so absolutely sure that we are incapable of even momentary backsliding that we will not break our oath? If we are, then we are sadly deluded: *"Therefore let him who thinks he stands take heed lest he fall"* (1 Corinthians 10:12). But Rick Warren has people swear, "I won't be captivated by culture, manipulated by critics, motivated by praise, frustrated by problems, debilitated by temptation, or intimidated by the devil." What person could swear to this and then live the rest of his or her life in perfect harmony with it? I am quite sure that if I were to foolishly swear an oath that I will never be "frustrated by problems" that I would become a covenant breaker within a week.

Oath taking does not have the power to make a liar tell the truth, a sinner righteous, or a weak person strong. It only has the power to put those who make foolish covenants under greater condemnation. Jesus said that it is from the evil one. I think He said this because Satan is the accuser of the brethren, and when Christians take oaths they set themselves up to fall under accusation. Satan tempts them to take oaths knowing that in so doing they play into his hands, giving Satan a stick to beat them with later. If leadership later uses these oaths to accuse people and place them under condemnation they are unwittingly doing the devil's work. Given this fact, Rick Warren is abusing his flock by requiring them to sign covenants. He is failing to look out for their spiritual well-being. He has them convinced that they are becoming disciples and committed Christians by doing what Jesus forbids.

Requiring an Act of Sin to Join a Church

Rick Warren has created a series of classes (101, 201, 301, and 401) that involve signing a series of covenants (oaths) at completion to go on to the next class and eventually become a fully committed member of Saddleback church.[9] All members must agree to unity: "At Saddleback Church, every member signs a covenant that includes a promise to protect the unity of our fellowship."[10] This is not an agreement to preserve either the "unity of the Spirit" (Ephesians 4:3) or strive for "the unity of the faith" (Ephesians 4:13), but a signed covenant that includes "following the leaders."[11] Since, as we have shown, the terms "covenant" and "oath" are used synonymously, Warren is requiring people to take an oath to follow leaders (among other things).

This brings into play all the problems with oaths that we discussed earlier. It is presuming on the future in at least two ways: 1) it presumes that the oath-taker will always have the future power and motivation to keep the oath, and 2) it presumes that the leaders who are being followed are not leading the people away from the truth. If these people later find the leaders going astray, they will either have to break their oath or follow these leaders into error. They have tempted God by purposely putting themselves in a potential ethical dilemma. This would be like Satan tempting Jesus to jump off the temple. Either the angels catch Him and lend endorsement to a foolish act or let Him fall and die. Jesus called this tempting God and refused to yield to the temptation. Forcing people to sign a covenant that may lead to sin is tempting God. Jesus said, "Let your yes be yes." More than that is from the evil one. Since Jesus forbade taking oaths, the act of signing the covenant itself is sin.

There are some who would argue that taking oaths is not a sin, but that Jesus was just rebuking the manner in which the Pharisees took oaths. I do not believe that this claim holds up under careful scrutiny. For example, as proof of this they point out that Jesus took an oath: "It was under oath that Jesus declared himself to be the Christ, the Son of God (Matthew 26:63, 64)."[12] As a matter of fact Jesus did not take this oath, but responded, *"You said it."* Peter, who was being unfaithful, did take an oath: *"And again he denied it with an oath, 'I do not know the man'"* (Matthew 26:72). The Book of Matthew is consistent that oaths are not to be taken.

The key to understanding the prohibition against oaths in Matthew is the context (as it was in James). In Matthew 5:21, 22 Jesus heightens the prohibition against murder to a prohibition against anger. In Matthew 5:27, 28 He heightens the prohibition against adultery to a prohibition against lust. And in Matthew 5:31, 32 He heightens the loose restrictions on divorce to a prohibition of divorce. Seen in this light, Jesus takes the requirement of keeping one's oaths and strengthens it into a prohibition of oaths all together. One's word is enough. Looking at the other issues addressed in this context, one could say, "Everyone gets angry at some times and who could totally avoid lust?" These are true observations, showing that we are sinners who need a Savior and forgiveness. Do you suppose that if someone swore an oath to never be angry again, he would be able to keep that oath? Of course he would not. But that does not mean that anger and lust are thereby justified.

Considered in the light of the context, Jesus is prohibiting oaths just as much as He prohibits divorce. This will help us understand the issue. Some say that people take marriage vows and are required to take oaths in courts of law, so how could Jesus be prohibiting oaths? Likewise Jesus prohibited divorce but anticipated reasons it might happen (like unchastity – Matthew 5:32). Paul allowed for the situation that a person might become a Christian and his unbelieving wife would leave (1 Corinthians 7:12). Nevertheless, this does not mean that Jesus' prohibition against divorce is not binding. Likewise, if one is asked by civil authorities to take an oath in a court of law, he may decide that it would be the greater good to take the oath even though Jesus forbade it than to disobey civil authorities which the New Testament tells us not to do (Romans 13). If there is any valid covenant between two people in the New Testament it is marriage. We know this from the analogy of marriage being a type of Christ and the church (Ephesians 5:22-32). In my opinion, this implies that marriage has covenant status which would make marriage vows valid. Ultimately, we find that Jesus upholds marriage and forbids divorce because God Himself joins the man and woman; and therefore in the marriage covenant He states, "what God has joined together let no man separate." Therefore God has made a covenant between two people.

Let us apply what we have learned from the context in Matthew to Warren's covenants that he requires of church members. If we consider any of the other prohibitions in this section of Matthew, we can see what the problem is. Would it be appropriate to require church members to lust, be angry, or divorce to join the church? No, that would be absurd. So why then, is it valid to require them to take an oath which is forbidden in the same context and with the same seriousness? Even if it could be argued that sometimes oaths are necessary (like in court) it does not follow that we should purposely require them and furthermore imply that disobeying Jesus' teaching on this is an act of piety. So that rather than the lesser of two evils, Warren is promoting oaths as a positive good that is pleasing to God and required for unity.

What is interesting in the Purpose Driven covenants is that Warren uses marriage as an analogy for joining the local church. Here is what Warren says:

> The most important part of a marriage ceremony is when the man and woman exchange vows, making certain promises to each other before witnesses and God. This covenant between them is the essence of the marriage. In the same way, the essence of church membership is contained in the willingness to commit to a membership covenant. This is the most important element of our membership class.[13]

By making membership in a local church like marriage, Warren raises the stakes. By requiring oath-taking as in a marriage ceremony, he ties people to his local organization in a way that cannot be severed without the type of pain and guilt associated with divorce. He gives church membership the covenant status like marriage. That gives him power over people since they have no valid way of separating without displeasing God.

Let us make this clear. A local church organization is not sacrosanct in the way marriage is. These local organizations cannot be confused with the true body of Christ that was purchased by the blood of the Lamb as was in the chapter on redefining the church. One joins the true body of Christ at conversion. Local expressions are important but their constitution and bylaws exist in order to function legally within the civil government, not to serve as covenant documents before God. Membership requirements should be biblical and should reflect Jesus' teaching about "letting your yes be yes." People should feel free to disagree with leaders if need be, or leave if they must without feeling like they have broken covenant with God. To create a human organization and claim that joining it is tantamount to one's covenant relationship with God—that is abusive. Leaving it would be like divorce or apostasy? Preposterous! Such abuse is reminiscent of what Luther fought during the Reformation.

Luther's Teaching Against Oaths

It is ironic that upon the announcement of a new reformation, Rick Warren had 30,000 people stand and recite a vow (called "covenant" which we have shown is synonymous with an oath or vow in Scripture). The irony is that Warren's reformation begins with a repudiation of one of Luther's important reforms—the removal of special, religious vows. Warren claims that while Luther reformed the church's beliefs, Warren will reform her practice. The truth is that Luther reformed both teaching and practice, and that one of the practices that Luther reformed was the taking of special religious vows. Luther wrote a lengthy essay demonstrating that

Scripture rejects the validity of monastic vows.[14] The particular vows he rejects are those of celibacy, poverty, and obedience that characterized monastic orders. But in his writings on this, Luther dealt with essential issues that very much apply to the vows of the Purpose Driven church and Warren's new reformation.

One key issue for Luther was that the monastics went beyond the gospel and made commandments out of matters that God has not commanded, and in so doing sought to achieve a superior standing before God. One such example was celibacy. Luther argued that vowing something that God had not commanded is sinful: "The very foundation of the monastic vows is godlessness, blasphemy, sacrilege, which has befallen them because they spurn Christ, their leader and light, and presume to follow other things they think better."[15] They thought they could improve on the teachings of Christ and live a superior spirituality by swearing oaths to live pious lives beyond anything Christ required of His people. Luther condemned this as sinful. Luther wrote, "If you obey the gospel, you ought to regard celibacy as a matter of free choice: if you do not hold it as a matter of free choice, you are not obeying the gospel. . . . A vow of chastity, therefore, is diametrically opposed to the gospel."[16] So in Luther's Reformation, he taught that Christians were in error and sin if they bound themselves by oath to a practice not required by Christ. Though they may think themselves more pious than ordinary Christians because of their special vows, Luther called them gross sinners.

Taking such oaths was not only contrary to God's Word; Luther said they were against faith. Luther wrote, "Here let us lay our rock and foundation, our first principle of faith, namely, the words of Paul in Romans 14:23, 'Everything that is not of faith is sin.' From this we infer that monastic vows, if not of faith, are sins. Moreover, if these vows are lifelong, compulsory, and not optional, they are not of faith."[17] Religious vows that go beyond the teachings and requirements of Scripture ultimately rest on human volition, human fortitude, and trust in human ability to not fail one's solemn oath. The same spirit of works and human ability that

Luther saw in monastic vows can be seen in the covenant Warren had his followers swear to:

> To my Lord and Savior Jesus Christ, I say: However, whenever, wherever, and whatever you ask me to do, my answer in advance is yes! Wherever you lead and whatever the cost, I'm ready. Anytime. Anywhere. Anyway. Whatever it takes Lord; whatever it takes! I want to be used by you in such a way, that on that final day I'll hear you say, "Well done, thou good and faithful one. Come on in, and let the eternal party begin!"[18]

A circumspect sinner, coming to God by faith, doubts his own ability and trusts only in God's mercy and grace. How do I know that I will even correctly know what Jesus will ask me to do in the future, much less perfectly obey it? Like the monks vowing obedience to their superiors for the rest of their lives, Warren has Christians vowing obedience to some future unrevealed will of God. I suspect that how these people will find out what Jesus wants them to unquestioningly do and obey will be from Rick Warren's future directives (perhaps when he makes more details of his P.E.A.C.E. plan known). The person of faith approaches God only based on the finished work of Christ, not by offering oaths of his or her own presumed future obedience. Luther condemns such oaths as against faith, and I agree with Luther.

Luther made this very clear: "But are not all such vows, and works performed in fulfillment of vows, works done apart from faith? Show me one single person who would presume to assert that his vow was pleasing and acceptable to God."[19] Only the knowledge that I am in Christ (having His imputed righteousness and not my own) can give me assurance that my works are of faith and pleasing to God. Consider further what Luther taught: "How shall I, and all the works I do, not please God if Christ is mine and I am Christ's? Can Christ ever be displeasing to God?"[20] Taking religious vows in order to convince ourselves or someone else of our sincerity, piety, and future obedience is a failure of faith. Such vows, for Luther, are works of the law: "Thus Paul cries out to the Galatians, 'You who are justified by the law are fallen from grace' (Galatians 5:4). Vows and the works of vows are but law and works. They are not faith, nor do they issue from faith, for what else is a vow but some kind of law?"[21]

Luther charged with heresy those who take high and holy sounding oaths presuming to achieve piety superior to that of ordinary Christians: "They not only think that their obedience, poverty, and chastity are certain roads to salvation, but that their ways are more perfect and better than those of the rest of the faithful. This is an open, obvious lie, and an error and sin against faith. All they have is hypocrisy and a branded conscience."[22] The Roman Catholic doctrine on this is called "supererogation" and teaches that some can and should do deeds beyond that which is required by Christ for all Christians.[23] This doctrine was rejected by Luther and the other Reformers on the grounds that even the Christian duties required of all could never be perfectly performed even by the greatest of saints.[24] Luther further argued that what he called the vow of baptism, legitimately covered all Christian duties. But even with baptism, he saw through the understanding of faith and not works:

> But perhaps you will object (and say), "If this opinion were accepted, then it would not be permissible to make a vow to God in baptism, since both faith and the fulfillment of the commandments of God are not in our hands but God's alone." I reply: That is beautifully and well said if the case were at all the same in the matter of baptismal vows as it is with your vows. In baptism it is God who makes the promise and the offer; we vow nothing else but to accept Christ who is offered us. It is a happy vow indeed which does not promise to give anything, but which only accepts good things and holds on to what has been accepted.[25]

To summarize his logic here, if one swears an oath to some

Christian duty, is it to a legitimate duty that is enjoined of all Christians or is it to some work of supererogation (above and beyond duty)? If it is a general Christian duty, we have no need for such oaths. We have agreed to them in becoming Christian and being baptized. If they are duties that are beyond Christ's requirements, we are sinful hypocrites who think by our pious oaths we can add to faith and Christ's finished work.

In baptism and marriage there is a public affirmation of what God has done (i.e., took a person's sins away through Christ and joined a man and woman together). Other religious vows are about what we claim we are going to do—they are presumptuous.

Luther argues that pious oaths are not only against faith, they are against Christian liberty. He shows that no oath that is deemed necessary for righteousness and salvation is acceptable to God because such an oath would be of works and not faith. Therefore, only unnecessary oaths are permissible, and therefore can be freely rejected:

> "Since therefore it is absolutely certain from these arguments that no vow is acceptable to God unless it is a kind not deemed necessary for righteousness and salvation, and since God has not commanded the taking of any vow, it clearly follows that this kind of vow is a matter of free choice and can be laid aside."[26]

Luther wanted to free himself and others from oaths they had foolishly taken previously, thinking at the time they were pleasing God. He taught that evangelical (gospel) freedom forbids vows: "In fact, we are proving that evangelical freedom forbids vows. Paul is asserting evangelical freedom when he says in Galatians 1:8, 'But if an angel or someone else from heaven were to teach anything other than what you have heard, let him be anathema.' And later, 'You, brethren, are called to freedom'[27] (Galatians 5:13)."

Luther claimed that any godly vow should include the freedom to retract it:

Let us go back then to what was said earlier. The vow to chastity and the whole of monasticism, if godly, ought necessarily to include the freedom to retract the vow. The vow should be interpreted something like this: "I vow to thee obedience, chastity, and poverty, together with the whole rule of St. Augustine until death. I do it of my own free will, which means that I would be free to change my mind if it seemed good." If you interpret the vow otherwise, or take a different view of it, you sin against the divine freedom God ordained for us, as you can see from the earlier arguments. Under no circumstances can God accept anything else without revoking his own freedom, that is, without denying himself.[28]

That is an important insight. When we vow something that supposedly becomes God's requirement for us for the rest of our lives, if that vow turns out to not be within God's providential intentions for us, we have, with our vow, taken away God's freedom to work as He pleases in our lives. The vow becomes a man-made law that rules us, rather than God's moral law revealed in Scripture, and God's providential will revealed as history unfolds. For example, the monk who vows celibacy has ruled out God's freedom to have him marry in the future.

Let us again consider Rick Warren's vow: "Today I am stepping across the line. I'm tired of waffling, and I'm finished with wavering. I've made my choice; the verdict is in; and my decision is irrevocable." The irrevocable oath is precisely what Luther condemned as impinging on God's freedom, and therefore unacceptable to God. This proves that in using an oath to launch his new reformation, Rick Warren has repudiated the key teachings of the Protestant Reformation. He is not building on the Reformation, he is rejecting it. Warren is promoting a repudiation, not a reformation. He is bringing us back to the concepts of the pre-reformation Rome that Luther fought against, including "supererogation."

Vowing to Pay Tithes

The second covenant Warren's church members sign (from class 201) includes tithing.[29] He has them sign a card they will carry: "The signed covenant cards are collected, I sign them as a witness, we laminate them, and then they are returned so people can carry them in their wallets."[30] There is a picture of one of these in his book.[31] One side of the card includes: "My 1992 Growth Covenant," "A weekly tithe to God," and "Giving the first 10 percent of my income."

Warren cites Nehemiah 9:38 as justification for his practice of having his members sign a covenant document that is also signed by leaders.[32] The spiritual covenant in Nehemiah that Warren uses for biblical justification was about keeping the Law of Moses: *"Are joining with their kinsmen, their nobles, and are taking on themselves a curse and an oath to walk in God's law, which was given through Moses, God's servant, and to keep and to observe all the commandments of God our Lord, and His ordinances and His statutes"* (Nehemiah 10:29). The signers were agreeing to the blessings and curses that already attended the Mosaic covenant. However, as Paul points out, this amounts to being under a curse: *"For as many as are of the works of the Law are under a curse; for it is written, 'Cursed is everyone who does not abide by all things written in the book of the law, to perform them"* (Galatians 3:10). It was not long before the people who had returned to the land and took the oath with Nehemiah were cursed: *"'You are cursed with a curse, for you are robbing Me, the whole nation of you! Bring the whole tithe into the storehouse, so that there may be food in My house, and test Me now in this,' says the Lord of hosts, 'if I will not open for you the windows of heaven, and pour out for you a blessing until it overflows'"* (Malachi 3:9, 10).

Paul's warning to the Galatians was that if they went back to keeping the requirements of the Mosaic Covenant, they would be cursed and not blessed, because blessing comes by faith, not works. Tithing was a requirement of the Mosaic Covenant just as were circumcision, food laws, and Sabbath keeping. Paul in harsh words condemns those who require keeping Old Covenant law:

You foolish Galatians, who has bewitched you, before whose eyes

Jesus Christ was publicly portrayed as crucified? This is the only thing I want to find out from you: did you receive the Spirit by the works of the Law, or by hearing with faith? Are you so foolish? Having begun by the Spirit, are you now being perfected by the flesh? (Galatians 3:1-3).

Tithing is not required under the new covenant any more than circumcision or Sabbath keeping: *"Therefore let no one act as your judge in regard to food or drink or in respect to a festival or a new moon or a Sabbath day— things which are a mere shadow of what is to come; but the substance belongs to Christ"* (Colossians 2:16, 17).

Giving that is commended under the New Covenant is done freely, not under compulsion: *"For I testify that according to their ability, and beyond their ability they gave of their own accord"* (2 Corinthians 8:3). Paul instructed: *"On the first day of every week let each one of you put aside and save, as he may prosper, that no collections be made when I come"* (1 Corinthians 16:2). The first incident of tithing in the Bible was before the Mosaic covenant when Abraham paid tithes to Melchizedek (Genesis 14:20). Though it says "He gave him a tenth of all," the context shows that it was a tenth of the booty from the war of the kings. Gordon Wenham comments on this passage, "'Everything' in context must refer to all the booty captured from the fleeing kings, since it was on his way home that Abram met Melchizedek."[33] Abraham freely chose to tithe without being required to do so by a covenant.

Since there is no command to tithe in the New Covenant, it is voluntary. Giving for Christians is important, but how much and to whom is a matter of Christian liberty. A Christian is free to have his children circumcised, but if he commands others to do so by making it a religious requirement he is sinning (see Galatians 2:3, 4; Galatians 5:1-12). The same principle holds for food and days of worship. People are free to follow Old Covenant practices as long as they do not suppose these practices make them more pleasing to God or preach that others must follow these practices to be pleasing to God. If they do, they put themselves and their followers under the curse of the Law. Requiring a tithe of "the first ten percent of my income" as Rick Warren's covenant does, forces people under pains of breaking their oath (with the laminated written witness card in their pocket to testify against them), to follow as law what the New Testament makes a liberty. Paul says, *"But it was because of the false brethren who had sneaked in to spy out our liberty which we have in Christ Jesus, in order to bring us into bondage"* (Galatians 2:4).

Many Christians tithe because it is their joy to do so and their way of honoring God. As they do so in faith like Abraham and not through works prescribed and demanded by Christian leaders, they are blessed in their giving. We are told to give generously, regularly, and freely in the New Testament. There is no prescribed law code that says exactly how much, to whom, and under what circumstances. Nobody has the right to become God's law-giver to church members.

Conclusion

Requiring oaths about things we know Christ has commanded is wrong for several reasons:

1. We have seen from Scripture that making a covenant is the same as taking an oath.

2. Doing so presumes on our own abilities to obey which is tantamount to trusting man (Jeremiah 17:5).

3. Jesus told us to not take oaths; therefore doing so is purposeful disobedience to the Lord.

4. The act of taking an oath has no power to deliver from future sin. If it did, every Christian could vow to never sin again and thereby be perfected.

5. Taking an oath brings us under condemnation as James said.

Since these are good reasons for not taking oaths about things we know to be God's will, how much worse it is to take oaths about things that may not be God's will! Doing so tempts God and presumes on His future providential will, which is for now unknown to us. Swearing to uphold Rick Warren's P.E.A.C.E. plan does just that. Those who have done so should follow Martin Luther's advice to monks and renounce their vows, realizing that it was sinful to take them in the first place.

One might ask why Warren would require vows and what would motivate people to take them. The answer is that he is holding out to them the hope of being a higher class Christian. That is what motivated people to join monasteries in Luther's day. Warren teaches that there are two classes of Christians, the preferred one being "world-class."[34] He has found that asking people for a big commitment actually helps get people to join his church. He writes, "People *want* to be committed to something that gives significance to their lives."[35] What could promise more significance than swearing allegiance to a movement that promises to solve the world's biggest problems and becoming "world-class" in the process? Asking for a big commitment turns out to be part of creating a product with market appeal.

In the next chapter, we will examine how the gospel itself has been changed and redefined in the Purpose Driven Life. We will begin to see that Rick Warren's process of redefining key aspects of Christianity and the Christian life is making a new product that differs from the biblical message. This new product has more market appeal than the gospel of the Bible.

The "Gospel" According to
The Purpose Driven Life

The key religious product that Rick Warren has produced to reach unchurched people and target them with his message is *The Purpose Driven Life*.[1] If, as I claim in this book, Warren's plan is to create a version of Christianity that the world will be attracted to, *The Purpose Driven Life* is his masterpiece. Sales figures prove that his plan has worked, since the world is clearly attracted to his message.

In business terms *The Purpose Driven Life* is the product, religious consumers are the target market, and *The Purpose Driven Church* is the marketing agency. To maximize the market share, the product has to appeal to the broadest possible audience. The broadest possible audience consists of those who Warren calls "unchurched" and the Bible calls "sinners."

It is clear that Warren is targeting the general public with his book. The book is dedicated to "you," whoever you might be.[2] It addresses readers who have no relationship with Jesus Christ,[3] and it describes to the general public how to find out God's purpose for their lives. So it is a gospel presentation using the technique of making the gospel a special journey to find out one's purpose. The problem is that in so doing, Warren changes or obscures the key issues of the biblical gospel. The result is a presentation of the gospel quite different from any found in the Bible.

His use of the term "purpose" is confusing and frequently unbiblical. I will explain why this is a significant problem, what the true nature of the biblical gospel is, and then show how Warren has redefined the gospel through deletion, obscuration, and mixture.

Is God's Purpose Declared or Discovered?

Warren begins, "This is more than a book; it is a guide to a *40-day spiritual* journey that will enable you to discover the answer to life's most important question: What on earth am I here for?"[4] Right up front we have a major problem. His claim that people will discover their purpose through reading his book assumes that God's purpose for all people ultimately is the same, and that the two classes of people are those who have discovered their purpose and those who have not. The truth is that God's purposes must be divided into His **revealed** purposes and those that are **not revealed**. What God has not revealed will not be discovered on a spiritual journey. That which God has revealed can be declared up front so that people know what God has said. Therefore a journey of discovery is unnecessary. The only reason to propose such a venture is that the idea of a spiritual journey of discovery appeals to people's religious appetites.

Let me explain why understanding what is and is not revealed is important. The fact is that God's revealed purpose includes both salvation for those whose names are in the book of life, and damnation for those who are not: *"And if anyone's name was not found written in the book of life, he was thrown into the lake of fire"* (Revelation 20:15). It is just as much God's purpose that those who reject the gospel be damned as it is that those who believe it be saved. Since it is impossible for people to know which group they are in unless the terms are clearly proclaimed to them, we must preach the law and the gospel. The law declares that all who sin must die and suffer God's wrath against their sin for all eternity. God's righteousness requires that rebellious lawbreakers receive perfect justice, because God is always a just God. God's purpose is to save some out of this mass of rebellious humanity to become

His people. What is **not revealed** now is whose names ultimately are in the book of life (reading of the names happens at the final judgment). What **is revealed** are terms by which one can receive eternal life.

Since God's revealed will is that all should repent and believe the gospel, this must be clearly preached to all. Also, every sinner needs to know what will happen if he doesn't repent. Knowing the terms, and knowing that God's revealed purpose is to grant eternal life to all who believe and eternally damn all who reject the gospel, sinners then know all they need to know about God's purposes. A 40 day program is worthless when the simple facts can be explained forthrightly right up front!

God's providential purposes for the future includes BOTH life and damnation. His purpose for those who believe His gospel is salvation, and damnation for those who reject it. At best, Rick Warren has obscured the only starting point and essential issue relative to God's purposes for us: repenting and believing to obtain salvation in the gospel through the forgiveness of our sins.

This means that in a most important sense, God's ultimate purpose for an individual is unknown and will remain that way until their response to the gospel is known. A spiritual journey of self-discovery is worthless for determining one's purpose if the gospel has not been preached. There is no reason to propose, much less begin such a journey, when the terms for finding peace with God are already clearly revealed in the Bible and the preacher has the ability to declare those terms. Any failure of a preacher to clearly declare those terms is inexcusable.

What the sinner can know is that if he refuses to repent and believe, God's purpose is and shall remain to be execution of the judgment of His wrath against sin upon that sinner. Clear preaching makes this known. We may not know, for now, whether a given sinner will ever repent, but the sinner himself can know what will happen if he does not. Conversely, those who do repent and believe can know that they have eternal life (1 John 5:13). Only those with a saving knowledge of Jesus Christ can understand the rest of God's revealed purposes for the Christian. Warren treats the saint and sinner alike in regards to God's purposes and thus creates confusion.

Therefore, telling a sinner to go on a spiritual journey to find out his purpose is utterly foolish. Until he or she decides whether or not to believe the gospel, there is nothing more to find out! Until the gospel is preached in a clear and forthright manner, God's purposes will be totally obscure in the sinner's mind. So a spiritual journey of self-discovery is worthless for a sinner. Likewise, since God's purposes for the Christian are revealed in the New Testament, the Christian doesn't need a spiritual journey either—just solid Bible teaching. Warren offers neither clear, unsullied preaching of the law and the gospel to the sinner, nor clear, unadulterated Bible teaching for the Christian, but rather a journey of self-discovery to one and all. God's revealed purposes are thereby obscured and confused. What God has not revealed cannot be discovered by any means. The sad truth is that *The Purpose Driven Life* cannot do what it claims it will do.

True Gospel Preaching or *The Purpose Driven Life*

So that we are not confused on this matter, I will describe what gospel preaching is all about and compare that to how *The Purpose Driven Life* presents Christianity. Gospel preaching describes a problem and a solution. The problem is that sinners have spurned God's law and face His wrath against their sin. The solution is that God sent Jesus Christ, who lived a sinless life, bore God's wrath for us through His death on the cross, and overcame sin and death through His resurrection. We must repent and believe the gospel for our sins to be forgiven and for us to receive the gift of eternal life. Any preaching that fails to define the problem of sin and God's wrath against it is not the gospel preaching the Bible teaches. Only the blood atonement that Christ has provided can provide hope for law-breakers, i.e., all of Adam's descendants.

At this key issue most modern preaching is deficient. The definition of the human need that is addressed by the gospel too often is changed in order to present the gospel in terms that will not offend people. This is precisely what the *Purpose Driven Life* does so very well.

How does *The Purpose Driven Life* define the problem for which its "gospel" provides the cure? The problem, according to Warren, is the lack of identity and purpose that is caused by the lack of a relationship with Jesus Christ. He says, "You discover your identity and purpose through a relationship with Jesus Christ."[5] He promises his readers, "You may have felt in the dark about *your* purpose in life. Congratulations, you're about to walk into the light."[6] This fits his motif of a journey of discovery, but it has changed the issue from escaping God's wrath to learning one's purpose.

Warren's understanding of the nature of the Bible also shows his view of the problem from which the gospel is going to deliver us. As mentioned elsewhere, he considers the Bible an "Owner's Manual."[7] He says, "To discover your purpose in life you must turn to God's Word, not the world's wisdom."[8] However, what does the Bible say about itself? It says this: *"And that from childhood you have known the sacred writings which are able to give you the wisdom that leads to salvation through faith which is in Christ Jesus"* (2 Timothy 3:15). Paul is not speaking of being saved from having a lack of purpose, he is speaking of being saved from sin and damnation.

In chapter 3 Warren discusses what drives people: guilt, anger, fear, materialism or the need for approval.[9] He suggests, "Without a purpose, life is trivial, petty, and pointless."[10] Of course people often feel guilty, angry, afraid, and feel like life is not what they would like it to be. A gospel that offers to meet those needs is not offensive, but desirable. Warren is merely telling people they have normal, human concerns and needs. Thus, Rick Warren's gospel starts by addressing felt needs. These are summarized as the need for purpose.

He then describes the following benefits of knowing one's purpose: meaning, a simplified life, focus, motivation, and preparation for eternity.[11] Having described a set of problems that most people could identify with and a set of desirable conditions that most people would want, Warren brings people to a crucial question that he says God will ask: *"What did you do with my Son, Jesus Christ?"*[12] This question, according to Warren, determines where one will spend eternity.[13] He also tells us what God will not ask:

> God won't ask about your religious background or doctrinal views. The only thing that matters is, did you accept what Jesus did for you and did you learn to love and trust him?[14]

The Purpose Driven Life version of the gospel offers to bring many benefits to its adherents, including eternal life, if they, without regard to doctrine, accept what Jesus did for them (which has not been clearly explained) and learn to love Him.[15] So (to summarize the gospel according to *The Purpose Driven Life*) the problem is not that sinners are facing God's wrath, but that people have common human needs. The solution is not the blood atonement, that averts God's wrath for those who repent and believe, but accepting what Jesus did and finding purpose.

These are interesting claims. If God will not ask us about doctrinal views, then that means He will not ask us about our doctrine of Christ. Let us suppose a Mormon reads this. Any Mormon would be willing to accept what Jesus did, as long as what he did is defined in Mormon terms (i.e., according to Mormon doctrine). Since doctrinal views will not matter in eternity, then Mormons should be fine. They believe in Jesus Christ. They believe that Jesus is the son of God. They believe Jesus died for sin. They accept Jesus and do not reject him. They claim that they love Jesus. The problem is that Mormon doctrine changes nearly everything the Bible says about the person and work of Christ.[16] Since *The Purpose Driven Life* does not clearly articulate the doctrine of Christ and states that doctrine and religious background are not of eternal consequence, many people could easily decide that they are fine and headed for heaven when they are, in fact, lost.

If people are going to truly accept what Jesus did for them, they must be told much more than Warren has told them. First of all they need a description of who Jesus is and exactly what He did. Not enough is told us about the Person and work of Jesus to tell an uninformed reader what and who it is they are accepting. If God is indeed going to ask us, "What did you do with my Son, Jesus Christ?" then we need to know not only who Jesus Christ is, we need to know what God expects us to do.

What *The Purpose Driven Life* presents is what Ray Comfort aptly rejects as "life enhancement preaching."[17] The idea is that there are many wonderful benefits to becoming a Christian. Warren has promised satisfaction, focus, simplification, purpose, and motivation. And beside all these great benefits, one gains eternal life as well. All they have to do is accept what Jesus did for them.

One searches in vain throughout Warren's book to find clear articulation of the gospel, but rather bits and pieces of certain gospel truths scattered throughout. These facts are so scattered that the uninformed could never put them together into a cogent description of the gospel. People who are already Christian can scour through the book and find some gospel truths, but the people with the greatest need to hear the truth could never put it all together.

Warren returns to the theme of eternity in the next day of purpose. There he says, "If you learn to love and trust God's Son, Jesus, you will be invited to spend the rest of eternity with him."[18] Exactly what does it mean to "learn to love and trust God's Son?" We surely need to love the Lord. We need to trust Him as well. The problem is that many nominal Christians think they do, though they have never been converted. People from other backgrounds have no idea of what it means that Jesus is God's Son, how they could love Him, or what it would mean to trust Him. Why should we trust Him, and what should we trust Him about? What were we trusting before that we should now give up? Why do we have to learn to love Him? Is it because He is innately less than lovable? These unanswered questions leave many ambiguities about the gospel as presented in *The Purpose Driven Life*.

When I was a young man in Bible college, I went door to door witnessing in the neighborhood around a small church I attended. I asked people questions like, "Have you accepted Jesus?" The answers were interesting. Many said, "I never rejected him." Others said, "I have been in church all my life, are you telling me that I am not a Christian?" People have pictures of Jesus on their wall and love Him very much, but have no clue about what saving faith is. They have never come to Him on His terms. They never will if those terms are not clearly described. What I did not know then was that I was failing to preach the gospel. I was using common evangelical lingo that meant something to me, but not my hearers. They were mostly church people who had different terminology. Identifying with evangelical terminology is not the same as believing the gospel.

The Gospel and Human "Needs"

If people are told that they should "Come to Jesus and find purpose, motivation, focus and satisfaction," they are being offered results that are not exclusive to Christianity. I recently received an e-mail from a former pastor who is now an atheist. In it he states that now that he has freed himself from Christianity, his life is much better. This is a quotation from his email:

> Since concluding that atheism is a far more honorable world view than Christianity, my wife and I have enjoyed excellent health, prospered financially, our sons happily married, we have a grandchild and another on the way, and we have had numerous trips abroad. My observation is that there is no correlation between God's promises or God's threats and actual observable experience, e.g. there is a huge reality gap. . . [As atheists] our minds are free to question, think, and reason without fear of retribution or taking our every thought captive to a mythical Christ. That, to me, is the essence of what it means to be human.

There are others who claim to have purpose, motivation, and satisfaction, etc., after joining other religions. They think they have the way to eternal life as well.

Rather than telling people of the wonderful benefits of accepting Christ, we need to proclaim the law and the gospel. We cannot know for sure that someone's life will get objectively better now if they become a Christian. Down through the centuries the opposite has been the case for many who have believed. I replied to that atheist that the Bible never claims that a person's relative well-being vis-à-vis others is a sign of true faith. What we do know is that God's absolute law shows that all are sinners facing the just penalty for sin, which is death and eternity in hell. We also know that the Bible claims that Jesus satisfied God's wrath against sin through the blood atonement for all who believe. We can preach with certainty that those who truly repent and believe will be forgiven.

How Jesus Dealt With "Felt Needs"

In John, chapter 6, we have a biblical example of people more than willing to come to Jesus and be His followers because He met their needs. They even wanted to make Him king! The story begins with Jesus multiplying bread and fish to feed five thousand people (John 6:1-13). The result was initially good: The people rightly recognized that Jesus was the "Prophet" about whom Moses prophesied in Deuteronomy 18:15-18 (John 6:14; notice Jesus said in John 5:46 that Moses wrote about Him). However, Jesus withdrew from them when they intended to *take Him by force to make Him king* (John 6:15). After that, Jesus walked on water and ended up with His disciples on the other side of the sea. The multitudes followed in small boats.

There, at Capernaum, Jesus exposed their motives: *"Jesus answered them and said, "Truly, truly, I say to you, you seek Me, not because you saw signs, but because you ate of the loaves, and were filled"* (John 6:26). "Signs," in the New Testament, point to the Person and work of Christ. They are not ends in themselves to meet human needs. They evidently wanted Jesus to be king because of

His power to multiply bread. Imagine how much work that would save! Jesus, knowing their hearts, pointed them elsewhere: *"Do not work for the food which perishes, but for the food which endures to eternal life, which the Son of Man shall give to you, for on Him the Father, even God, has set His seal"* (John 6:27). This prompted them to ask about the "work of God." Jesus told them, *"This is the work of God, that you believe in Him whom He has sent"* (John 6:29). They were to put their faith in Christ—on His terms. Their mind was still on bread! They alluded again to Moses, this time referencing manna (John 6:31). Their idea was that Jesus would fulfill the role of Moses and give them food to eat that they would not have to work for. That was their felt need.

This dialogue led to Jesus proclaiming Himself as the "Bread of life" and His flesh and blood as food and drink (John 6:35; 53). They "grumbled," (John 6:41) which is a reminder of the wilderness wanderers who grumbled over Moses and manna. It seems that no matter what God provides, the recipients find cause to grumble. People whose minds are on their own perceived needs quickly become grumblers. Jesus repeatedly called upon them to believe (John 6:35, 40, 47). However, between these calls to faith, Jesus said this: *"No one can come to Me, unless the Father who sent Me draws him; and I will raise him up on the last day"* (John 6:44). The word for "can" is *"dunatai"* which denotes the power of ability. They are not even able. The word for "draws" means "drag" (the same Greek word used in John 21:6 for dragging in a catch of fish; see Acts 16:19; Acts 21:30; and James 2:6 for uses of the same Greek word). Since it is true that no one has the ability to come to Jesus unless the Father graciously brings them, one might as well preach the truth, whether it is popular or not. That is what Jesus did.

Not only did Jesus refuse to tell them what they wanted to hear or give them what they wanted to receive, He told them what offended them. The real need was for Jesus' flesh and blood to become their food and drink. Those who believed Christ and came to Him on His terms will be raised up on the last day. Most were unwilling: *"As a result of this many of His disciples withdrew, and were not walking with Him anymore*" (John 6:66). A few, with Peter as their spokesperson, believed in spite of the "offense" (see John 6:61): "*Simon Peter answered Him, 'Lord, to whom shall we go? You have words of eternal life. And we have believed and have come to know that You are the Holy One of God*'" (John 6:68, 69). The majority were offended, and a minority came because God graciously opened their eyes to see the truth of the gospel, even in its native offense.

This scenario is a microcosm of the effects of the gospel throughout the ages. Sinners have many needs and desires. They are willing to embrace religion if they see that it meets those needs and desires. Those who offer to meet their self-perceived needs will be popular. Those who do not will be rejected. Rick Warren is one who has studied the self-perceived needs of sinners and promised to meet them. Jesus refused to do this.

In His case, when they approached Him with their needs, He pointed them instead to the true need for a blood atonement. The rationale for this was that they could not come anyhow, unless the Father gave them to the Son (John 6:37). All the Father has given will come and be raised up (John 6:39). When the gospel of salvation (through the rejected and crucified Jewish Messiah) is accurately preached, God uses it to bring in all He has given the Son. This has been the case throughout church history. The flip side is that the same message offends seekers and drives them away.

Why *The Purpose Driven Life* Does not Offend Sinners

Rick Warren manages not to offend either by taking out the offensive parts of the gospel or burying them in chapters that do not address the terms of coming to God. He then accentuates the perceived benefits of finding one's purpose. The results speak for themselves—his movement is massively popular. The few who are unhappy with it are long-time Christians who recognize that Warren's message is not the same gospel as preached by Christ and His apostles. What happens is the reverse of John 6. The masses of seekers embrace it and the handful of committed disciples find it offensive.

Let us examine Day 7, the part of *Purpose Driven Life* where Warren tells his readers how to become Christians. He says, "God will give you what you need [the strength to live for God] if you will just make the choice to live for Him."[19] This is not how the gospel is presented in the Bible. The Bible says, "Repent and believe the gospel" (see Mark 1:14, 15; Luke 24:47; Acts 20:21).

Warren uses a passage from *The Message* to reinforce his theology: "*Everything that goes into a life of pleasing God has been miraculously given to us by getting to know, personally and intimately, the One who invited us to God*" (2 Peter 1:3). Here is a more literal translation: "*Seeing that His divine power has granted to us everything pertaining to life and godliness, through the true knowledge of Him who called us by His own glory and excellence*" (2 Peter 1:3 NASB). What is clear in the NASB is that "us" are those who are already Christians. Peter made that clear: "*Simon Peter, a bond-servant and apostle of Jesus Christ, to those who have received a faith of the same kind as ours, by the righteousness of our God and Savior, Jesus Christ*" (2 Peter 1:1, NASB). Therefore verse 3 is not an invitation to become a Christian, but a description of what is true for those who already are Christian. But Warren says, after citing it, "Right now, God is inviting you to live for His glory by fulfilling the purposes He made you for."[20] This is a misuse of Scripture. Furthermore, *The Message* soft-pedals the true meaning of the passage by replacing "called" with "invited." The term "called" in this passage means the effectual call (or internal call as some describe it) whereby God calls His elect out of the mass of perdition (see Romans 8:28-30). Everyone who hears the gospel hears the external call (the command to repent and believe). Those who hear the internal call are effectually redeemed by God's grace. Peter shows his meaning of "called" in verse 3 by returning to the idea in verse 10: "*Therefore, brethren, be all the more diligent to make certain about His calling and choosing you; for as long as you practice these things, you will never stumble*" (2 Peter 1:10 NASB). One needs to be diligent in one's practice of the faith so as to have more certainty about having been called. Therefore, "invited" as used by Warren and *The Message* changes Peter's meaning and claims that he is speaking of the external call, when the context (that he is speaking particularly to Christians) shows that he is speaking of the internal call. Plus, "invited," even when used of the universal, outer call of the gospel, is weak compared to the biblical terminology which "commands" all people to repent (Acts 17:30 KJV).

Why does this matter? It matters because this illustrates why Warren's gospel does not offend, while the gospel preached by Jesus and His apostles was always offensive. In Acts 17, when Paul preached the gospel to the Athenian philosophers, commanding all to repent, they scoffed at him (Acts 17:32). Most of them rejected this message. This is exactly what happened in John 6, as we have seen. But Rick Warren issues a nice, soft, invitation as we just saw. People invited to fulfill God's purposes and thereby find their own purpose, are not likely to be offended. They just have to accept God's offer and "receive and believe."[21]

Even "believing," for Warren, is couched in terms different from how the Bible presents the gospel. He writes, "Believe God loves you and made you for his purposes. Believe you are not an accident."[22] The problem is that this does not describe any uniquely Christian ideas. Moslems, Mormons, or any theist, other than pantheists, already believe these things. It is easier to get people to accept a "gospel" that does not require changing their beliefs.

The next sentences do add some Christian ideas: "Believe God has chosen you to have a relationship with Jesus, who died on the cross for you. Believe that no matter what you've done, God wants to forgive you."[23] But let us unpack these ideas. First, "Believe God has chosen you." Since, as we have pointed out, this is addressed to readers in general, and here people who do not yet have a relationship with Christ—this call, to believe God has chosen you, is curious and confusing. On what basis would a non-Christian believe that he or she had been "chosen by God" any more so than anyone else? The very concept of God choosing a person implies not choosing others. When the Bible (for example in Ephesians 1) teaches the doctrine of election, it is applied to Christians. If we were to preach to all people everywhere, "God has chosen you," then the concept of choosing would become meaningless. God would then have chosen no one in particular. Many Christians believe this, but why tell people to believe that God chose them when in fact you do not believe God has chosen anyone in particular. That is as meaningful as a piece of junk mail that says, "You have been chosen to buy our product." What Warren suggests here is confusing.

Then he adds, "To have a relationship with Jesus, who died on the cross for you." Why would I believe that I have been chosen for such a relationship and what does this relationship entail? Why would a historical person die on the cross for me and for what purpose? Warren's readers do not know. It is unclear, partly because he has not told us what relationship we had with Christ before, so that we do not know what needs to change. The Bible makes it clear: We were enemies who, in our sin cursed condition, abided under the wrath of God. Consider how the Bible describes this matter:

> But God demonstrates His own love toward us, in that while we were yet sinners, Christ died for us. Much more then, having now been justified by His blood, we shall be saved from the wrath of God through Him. For if while we were enemies, we were reconciled to God through the death of His Son, much more, having been reconciled, we shall be saved by His life (Romans 5:8-10).

Conversion is the reconciliation of enemies and requires the blood atonement. This is far different from believing Christ died on the cross when it is not clear why He died or what it has to do with the sinner and his sin.

There is another matter to unpack, "Believe that no matter what you've done, God wants to forgive you." Believing that "God wants to forgive" skirts the issue that God is offended by my sin and that I, a sinner, abide under God's wrath unless something is done to avert that wrath. Warren's version sounds innocuous. It does not offend sinners to hear that God wants to forgive them no matter how bad they are. Many of them already believe that. In fact, many believe that they are going to Heaven because God is kind and understands. But if you tell them that God is a just judge, who is angry at sin, and that unless payment is made, they will face eternity in hell—that offends them! They rail against a "God" who would be that way. So once again, Warren has deleted those aspects of the gospel that offend, and kept those that do not. The question is: "Is it still the same gospel?" The blood atonement, which was central to both the Old and New Covenants, is gone.

This presentation found on pages 58 and 59 is missing another key aspect of the gospel. The resurrection of Christ is not taught as an essential belief for salvation. The resurrection is mentioned a couple of times in passing elsewhere in *The Purpose Driven Life*, but not in the context of saving faith. This is a departure from the consistent preaching of the gospel in the New Testament. Here is what the Bible says:

> But what does it say? "The word is near you, in your mouth and in your heart"— that is, the word of faith which we are preaching, that if you confess with your mouth Jesus as Lord, and believe in your heart that God raised Him from the dead, you shall be saved; for with the heart man believes, resulting in righteousness, and with the mouth he confesses, resulting in salvation. (Romans 10:8-10).

The belief in Christ's literal, bodily resurrection is central to the gospel message in the New Testament. Every account of gospel preaching in the book of Acts included the resurrection. Paul made it definitely essential to the gospel (1 Corinthians 15:1-4). When Warren does not even mention it in the context of believing unto salvation, He fails to follow the biblical pattern.

Having urged his reader to believe and receive (as shown above), he has them pray this prayer: "*Jesus, I believe in you and I receive you.*"[24] He then assures them, "If you sincerely meant that prayer, congratulations! Welcome to the family of God!"[25] Supposedly, it is that simple. Say this little prayer and believe that God wants to forgive you and have a relationship with you, and you are a Christian. There is nothing offensive here. We have not heard enough about the uniqueness of Christ to offend people who have a different doctrine of Christ. We have not heard enough about the reason for Christ's death to be offended that God considers us His enemies. We have not heard enough about the bodily resurrection of Christ to distinguish between Him from other founders of world religions who died. Warren's non-offensive version is very different from the scandal of a crucified Jewish Messiah as taught in the Bible.

An Inoffensive Cross

It would be unfair to suggest that *The Purpose Driven Life* does not mention the cross. Rick Warren does teach that Christ died on the cross. He explains his understanding of the cross as follows:

> If you want to know how much you matter to God, look at Christ with his arms outstretched on the cross, saying, "I love you this much! I'd rather die than live without you." God is not a cruel slave driver or a bully who uses brute force to coerce us into submission. He doesn't try to break our will, but woos us to himself so that we might offer ourselves freely to him.[26]

Warren is again repeating commonly used evangelical lingo. The problem is that many popular ideas of modern evangelicalism are not biblical. The Bible does not teach that the cross shows how much we matter to God. It teaches how utterly loving God is! God could live without us; but chose to redeem for Himself a people to demonstrate His mercy. Yes, God demonstrates His love through the cross. But Warren's description of this gives us the impression that God was lacking without us, not the other way around.

Warren then goes to the unbiblical notion of "wooing." God does not "woo" people; He commands them to repent, and through effectual grace He regenerates them. Warren portrays the sinner in the decisive role. According to this theology, God wishes He could have a people, but has to woo them, hoping some will decide He is worthy to be served. Though this approach is very popular, it is not biblical. The theology of "wooing" is why people try to "dress up" God to make Him look more attractive to sinners, hoping they will "make a decision." The fact is that sinners hate God and will never respond to wooing unless God first graciously changes their hearts.

Warren uses the following passage to show his understanding of the cross (i.e., how important we are): *"But God demonstrates His own love toward us, in that while we were yet sinners, Christ died for us"* (Romans 5:8 NASB).[27] Yes, Christ dying for us does show God's love toward us. But is the emphasis on "us" being important to God, or on how amazing God's love is that he would show it to undeserving sinners? The verses before and after the one cited by Warren show the real emphasis:

> *For while we were still helpless, at the right time Christ died for the ungodly. For one will hardly die for a righteous man; though perhaps for the good man someone would dare even to die. . . . Much more then, having now been justified by His blood, we shall be saved from the wrath of God through Him* (Romans 5:6, 7, 9).

Paul's emphasis is on how ungodly, unworthy, and helpless we were, facing God's wrath. The cross saves us from this wrath. In Warren's version, God is trying to woo us by making Himself look appealing. God, then, would be like a young man trying to attract a young lady who was the object of his attention, but apparently uninterested. Plus, Romans is written to believers, and Warren is applying the passage to the general public.

The huge problem is that the Bible teaches (1 Corinthians 1:23) that the cross is not attractive to sinners—it is offensive! In this section where Warren teaches about the cross and God's love, he never tells us why it would be necessary for God to have His own Son brutally killed and why that should attract us to Him. Since, in Warren's gospel, we do not know we are under God's wrath, we do not know that there is a need for the shedding of blood for the remission of sins. We do not know that Christ died as a substitute, and so therefore we would have no way to understand how Christ's death on the cross demonstrated His love. The essential information is missing! If we do not understand the importance of being saved from wrath, then we will not be attracted to God by Christ's death on the cross.

Many people can be wooed when they think of Christ as a great teacher of religious ethics, but these same people will often mock the message of the cross. The reason is that the cross shows how wicked we must be that such a horrible sacrifice would have to be paid. When Jesus was dying on the cross, eyewitnesses mocked Him and expressed willingness to believe on their terms: *"He saved others; He cannot save Himself. He is the King of Israel; let Him now come down from the cross, and we shall believe in Him"* (Matthew 27:42). They wanted nothing to do with "saving" if it meant the cross.

So Warren's cross shows us how much we matter to God. Perhaps it could possibly do so had he told his readers why the cross was necessary. But lacking that information, we get the impression that we have something God wants and He has to woo us to get it. This is not how the New Testament writers describe the cross or salvation.

Why Rick Warren Downplays Doctrine

The gospel of *The Purpose Driven Life* is not the same as the gospel of the Bible. *The Purpose Driven Life* gospel is inoffensive, attractive, winsome, popular, and easy to believe. The gospel of the Bible is offensive and hard to believe.[28] It is a narrow gate and narrow path with few adherents (Matthew 7:13, 14). The danger, of course, is that many who are entering the wide gate offered by *The Purpose Driven Life* will falsely assume they have become Christians when they have not.

Does this mean that Rick Warren does not know about the issues I am addressing? I do not think so. His apparent reason for devising a spiritual journey to discover one's purpose is to create a religious product that would appeal to his target audience. Biblical doctrine does not help Warren's purpose. It is telling that every time he mentions the term "doctrine" in *The Purpose Driven Life,* it is given a negative connotation. For example, "Jesus said our love *for each other*—not our doctrinal beliefs—is our greatest witness to the world."[29] This statement is completely false. When Jesus prayed for Christian unity in John 17, He never contrasted it negatively with the importance of true doctrine or teaching (the Greek word often translated "teaching" can also be translated "doctrine"). Warren expresses distaste for doctrine, but Jesus considered it important: *"But in vain do they worship Me, teaching as doctrines the precepts of men"* (Mark 7:7). Do not be fooled, teaching is doctrine. Since Warren's book is filled with the precepts of men propped up by many misuses of the Bible and bad translations, this confusing amalgamation is his "doctrine." Jesus called this sort of thing "vain worship." The gospel is too important to be stripped of its key doctrines, accessorized with human wisdom, turned into a spiritual journey of self-discovery, and sold to the unsuspecting world as "Christianity." Its very nature requires that it be proclaimed with bold clarity.

Sadly, Rick Warren has not done that. He says that his book is biblical because of the numerous Bible citations. In the next chapter we will examine how he uses the Bible and show that the Bible is being misused in the same way the gospel is misused—to make it appealing to the unregenerate mind. Warren's product is *The Purpose Driven Life,* and his buyers are the world and deceived Christians. The issues of truth or error, life or death, pleasing God or pleasing man are too important to allow *The Purpose Driven Life* to be the new "Christianity" that evangelicalism is presenting to the world.

6

How Misused Bible Translations
Support a Journey of Self-discovery

Rick Warren appears to wants his Purpose Driven movement and ministry philosophy to be true to his Baptist roots. So it needs to be biblical. This movement, however, also desires to be seen as appealing to the felt needs of the target audience—potential religious consumers. The problem is that the target audience does not feel the need for a religion that is biblical; in fact they have a built-in hostility to the truths of the Bible. James says, *"You adulteresses, do you not know that friendship with the world is hostility toward God? Therefore whoever wishes to be a friend of the world makes himself an enemy of God"* (James 4:4). Paul wrote, *"The man without the Spirit does not accept the things that come from the Spirit of God, for they are foolishness to him, and he cannot understand them, because they are spiritually discerned"* (1 Corinthians 2:14 NIV). Because the Bible is inspired by the Holy Spirit, the unregenerate do not accept it (unless God does a work of grace).

We keep coming back to the same problem. Warren wants to make the church attractive to the world. The problem is that if the church and its message are truly from God, then the world will not listen and will actually be hostile to it (1 John 4:6; Romans 8:7).

Warren's solution to the problem is to use his marketing acumen to circumvent the resistance of the target audience. His plan is to draw from dozens of translations (including loose paraphrases), to choose the ones that will support the motif of a journey of self-discovery (already proven to be popular with the world), mix these various Bible citations with citations of popular worldly writers that seem to be saying the same thing, and make a seamless, religious product that speaks the world's language but appears to come right out of the Bible. Genius! The result is *The Purpose Driven Life*. This is the product for the Purpose Driven church to market to religious consumers.

Selling the Product

Warren uses clever ways to convince people they need his product. First he describes its benefits. He promises this to those who discover God's purpose for their lives through this journey: "Having this perspective [purpose] will reduce your stress, simplify your decisions, increase your satisfaction, and, most important, prepare you for eternity."[1] To gain these important benefits, his readers are asked to sign a covenant with Rick Warren to set aside 40 days, "To figure out what God wants you to do with the rest of them [your days]."[2] The covenant document is included on page 13 along with places for the reader and a partner to sign, Warren's signature is already provided. Evidently believing in closing a sale quickly, he does so before day one of the journey.

In Warren's approach, people are asked to sign a binding covenant before witnesses without knowing whether what they are committing to is a valid or biblical. He entices them into a program without their knowing any details about what they are buying into.

This technique is similar to TV infomercials where someone presents a teaser about a process that will help ordinary people become wealthy. The scheme involves convincing the people to commit to a process, the details of which are unknown. Having signed up with high hopes of living a life of luxury, the buyers get some information that contains the secrets to unlocking wealth. When hopes are high and a group of others claims that the process has worked for them, buyers tend to believe in the process and ignore signs that something is wrong. Another factor is that people who have made a purchase (or commitment) want to believe that it was a good one. They do not want to lose face in a group setting where everyone else seems to think it is a good product.

In Warren's case, one also makes a commitment first, usually in a group setting (during a Forty Days of Purpose campaign), and finds out later what was bought. The individual who has bought the product (signed the covenant) is carried along by the process and is not likely later to want to publicly admit that he or she has doubts about the process. The thinking is like this: "Everyone else in this group is excited and successful, what is wrong with me?" Pyramid sales schemes often capitalize on this proven technique. The method works.

As we showed in the last chapter, preachers of the gospel in the Bible declared God's purposes up front. Biblical gospel preachers were willing to see the majority of their hearers reject their message. The hearers knew what the issues were, what the claims of the gospel are, and what was expected of them. In Warren's book the details are muddy and people sign a covenant while knowing none of the details. If Warren declared God's purposes as clearly as they were preached by Christ and His apostles, most of Warren's readers would respond in the same way—they would reject them.

How, then, does a journey to discover one's purpose receive a massive positive response when the Bible's declarations of God's purposes were mostly rejected? Rick Warren accomplishes this by leading his readers down a path of self-discovery that is paved with mistranslations of the Bible that turn a message that is offensive to sinners into a winsome tale of gaining purpose, a more satisfied life, and eternal life thrown in as an extra benefit. With quality writing and the skill of a master motivator, Warren seamlessly intertwines his aphorisms with Bible verses from whatever translation or paraphrase that supports the point he wants to make. In doing so,

Warren usually does not concern himself with the meaning of the biblical author who wrote the original passage, but instead selects translations that suit his own purpose. This approach works to sell his product, *The Purpose Driven Life*.[3]

The misuse of Scripture is so widespread in *The Purpose Driven Life* that a whole book could be written just to correct them all. But that is not my purpose here. Instead, I will illustrate the manner in which Scripture is misused to show how this misuse works to make the religious product attractive to the world.

Ephesians 1:11

Let us begin our examination of Rick Warren's use of the Bible with the very first verse cited in the *The Purpose Driven Life*. It is found right after the copyright information, before the table of contents. Warren says, "This book is dedicated to you."[4] He tells us that God planned this moment. He writes, "Before you were born, God planned *this moment* in your life. It is no accident that we are holding this book."[5] If this is accurate, then it is also no accident that I am holding the book right now in order to refute it. The idea that God is working all things according to the "counsel of His will" (Ephesians 1:11) is true. Therefore it follows that a person reading Warren's book is part of the "all things" that God works. It does not follow that God therefore approves of Warren's book and its contents. He is confusing his readers by making a category switch. If they had been reading some other book, that would just as well fall into the category of "all things" through which God is working. Warren is misusing the passage by confusing God's providential will (works all things) with His revealed will (what God says is true or false, right or wrong).

Let me explain further about the "no accident" idea from Ephesians 1:11 before I proceed to critique the particular translation that Warren uses for the passage. Since, according to Ephesians 1:11, God "*works all things according to the counsel of His will*," then anything in particular is no accident. This is a description of the doctrine of providence. God is sovereignly overseeing His own creation.

Nevertheless, within this providential oversight are good and evil events. We could say that it was no accident that Hitler rose to power. The Bible teaches that God establishes the authorities (Romans 13:1). Since Hitler was an authority in Germany, he fit into that category. However, that does not mean God approved of Hitler or his policies. Morally, according to God's revealed will, Hitler was sinful.

Now let us apply this understanding to Warren's use of Ephesians 1:11. He says, "It is no accident that you are holding this book." However, that does not prove that it is God's revealed moral will for a person to believe what is in the book. It is just as possible that God is allowing people to be led astray because they refuse to listen to the gospel as preached by Christ and His apostles. Whether *The Purpose Driven Life* is good or bad cannot be determined by the fact that someone is providentially ordained to read it. So, even if Warren had used a valid translation of Ephesians 1:11 (which he did not), he would still be misusing it.

However, the problem is much deeper than the category error of confusing God's providential will with His moral will. Warren uses a translation that introduces concepts not found in Ephesians 1:11. Here is the passage as cited by Rick Warren, *"It's in Christ that we find out who we are and what we are living for. Long before we first heard of Christ and got our hopes up, he had his eye on us, had designs on us for glorious living, part of the overall purpose he is working out in everything and everyone.* (Ephesians 1:11 *The Message*).[6] Here is the passage in the New American Standard Bible: "...*also we have obtained an inheritance, having been predestined according to His purpose who works all things after the counsel of His will.*"

The Message translation introduces several key changes from Paul's meaning. *The Message* says, *"It's in Christ that we find out who we are."* How nicely this mistranslation fits with the journey of self-discovery motif of *The Purpose Driven Life* about finding one's identity. But, the phrase in a literal translation is, *"We have obtained an inheritance,"* an "inheritance" that only applies to Christians. Warren addresses his book to a general audience, not just to people who are already Christians. Ephesians 1:11 is not about people in general finding their purpose, it is about Christians in particular having obtained an inheritance. Warren, through using an inaccurate translation and applying it to a different set of people than Paul had in mind, misleads and confuses his readers. *The Message* translation suggests that Christ will help people find their identity. The inheritance Paul is speaking of is Messianic salvation and all of its benefits, not an enhanced sense of self-identity. These are two completely different concepts.

The next concept in *The Message* version of Ephesians 1:11 is even farther removed from the meaning of the text in a literal translation: "*Long before we first heard of Christ and got our hopes up, he had his eye on us, had designs on us for glorious living. . .*" The actual idea is much more concise: "*having been predestined according to His purpose. . .*" The category shifts are significant. The Bible is God-centered in that God, based on nothing in us, predestined us (Christians), assuring that we will obtain the inheritance. The version Warren uses says that God "*had His eye on us,*" which implies that there was something in us that caused God to act.[7] The idea "*had designs on us for glorious living,*" also obscures Paul's meaning. Paul said that God predestined us to obtain an inheritance so that we "*should be to the praise of His glory*" (Ephesians 1:12 which is incorporated into Ephesians 1:11 as Warren uses it). The God-centered writing of Paul (His glory) becomes the man-centered idea Warren wants to promote (designs on us for glorious living). Rather than Christians glorifying God as the passage teaches, people in general find out who they are and enjoy glorious living, according to Warren's version.

We have seen that the version Warren cites fits perfectly with his motif of a journey to discover one's purpose (self-discovery). We have also seen that the biblical passage cited would not fit that motif if a correct translation were used. In the process, a message that sounds appealing to the world is substituted for the true message of the passage that does not apply to the world and would be scoffed at by the unregenerate.

When a Paraphrase is Not a Paraphrase

The Message introduces concepts that are not present in the passage it claims to be paraphrasing. Here is the dictionary definition of "paraphrase:" "a restatement of a text, passage, or work giving the meaning in another form."[8] Notice that it says, *"giving the meaning."* The meaning is the meaning of the original author, in this case Paul's. Once biblical interpretation departs from the historical, grammatical method which focuses on determining the meaning expressed by the biblical author (who was inspired by the Holy Spirit), the door is opened for much mischief. *The Living Bible* was the first paraphrased text. Its purpose was to unpack complex ideas, put them in other words, and make those ideas easier to understand.

The preface of *The Living Bible* shows a good understanding of what it means to paraphrase. It says this,

> To paraphrase is to say something in different words than the author used. It is a restatement of an author's thoughts, using different words than he did. . . . Its [The Living Bible] purpose is to say as exactly as possible what the writers of the Scriptures meant, and to say it simply, expanding where necessary for a clear understanding by the modern reader.[9]

If a different meaning were to be introduced, one would not have a paraphrase. In the case of *The Living Bible*, the preface states that they are committed to an evangelical position and that the intention was to avoid introducing ideas different from the meaning of the original text. How well they managed to do this can be disputed, but the principle behind it is valid.

The Living Bible came out when I was in Bible College in the early 1970s. At the time we were told that a paraphrase like that was not useful for doing serious theology. Its purpose was to introduce the Bible to people one might meet at a coffee house outreach. It certainly would not be appropriate for an evangelical author to use to describe something as important as God's eternal purposes. Ephesians 1 contains complex but important theology. *The Message* as cited by Warren, does not even come close to the standards set out in the preface to *The Living Bible*. That Warren cites this very poor paraphrase at a key point in his book, with no supporting exegetical work, is very substandard theology.

What happens when a paraphrase departs not merely from the original author's words, but also from his meaning? The result, as in the case of *The Message* version of Ephesians 1:11 and many other verses, is a book called "The Bible" which is not the Bible, but the uninspired ideas of a man. In fact, the very passage that Warren uses on his cover page to justify the thesis of his book is an example of such an abuse. This is troubling. Let's consider other examples.

Matthew 16:25

To show that the misused poor translation issue on the cover page is not an isolated problem, let us consider how the 40-day journey begins. Warren writes, "It's not about you."[10] He correctly teaches that we need to find out what God says from the Bible about our purpose, and not look to ourselves to find purpose. He says, "You could reach all your personal goals, and *still* miss the purposes for which God created you."[11] This is true. How great it would be if Warren actually did what he promised to do (show us what the Bible says about God's purposes), rather than turn to passages from invalid paraphrases that change the meaning of the Bible.

Warren wishes to distinguish *The Purpose Driven Life* from the typical self-help genre' of books.[12] To prove that we do not need self-help, Warren turns again to *The Message*: "The Bible says, '*Self-help is no help at all. Self-sacrifice is the way, my way, to finding yourself, your true self.*'"[13] This citation of Matthew 16:25 introduces ideas that are not from Matthew 16:25 and consequently obscures the gospel. Here is the passage from the NASB: "*For whoever wishes to save his life shall lose it; but whoever loses his life for My sake shall find it.*" The biblical alternative to self-help is not finding yourself, but losing one's life through the cross.

Let us analyze what is going on here. *The Message* offers "self-help" as a paraphrase of "wishes to save his life," which is a defensible paraphrase. The context, however, shows that the key issue is taking up one's cross (Matthew 16:24) versus gaining what the world has to offer (Matthew 16:26). It is about being willing to die to one's life of seeking self-fulfillment in this life because of the more important matter of finding eternal life. "Self-help," however, is not the main problem with *The Message* paraphrase.

The next phrase in *The Message* version departs from the meaning of the text: *"Self-sacrifice is the way, my way, to finding yourself."* There are two problems here. First, self-sacrifice is not the same as losing one's life (i.e., dying to our old life through the cross). Second, the concept of finding yourself is not found in Matthew 16:24-26. The passage says, *"Whoever loses his life for My sake shall find it."* What is found is life, eternal life, new life in Christ for the one who has lost his old life through embracing the cross. Finding yourself fits with Warren's theme of a journey of self-discovery, but dying to self through the cross does not. So he has chosen a paraphrase that does not paraphrase but changes the meaning of the passage. It gets worse.

The idea of losing one's life "for Christ's sake" is missing from *The Message*; the concept of the phrase was not just paraphrased, it was removed entirely. This is a huge problem because "for My sake" links this back to the previous discussion about the cross (also missing from *The Message*). So the cross is out, for Christ's sake is out, and finding yourself through self-sacrifice is in. Does the Bible teach that we can find ourselves through self-sacrifice? It does not. We do not find ourselves, we find our life, i.e., eternal life. We do not find this eternal life through self-sacrifice, we find it through the cross (Matthew 16:24). The old self does not need to sacrifice more; it needs to die! This section of Scripture is central to the gospel that Jesus preached. Warren has chosen to obscure the true gospel of death to self through the cross and replace it with a new message of finding one's self through self-sacrifice. This is much more appealing than the gospel, but it will save no one.

The "self-sacrifice" idea is common to most other religions that teach salvation by works. It is appealing to religious consumers. By replacing death to self through the cross with finding one's self through self-sacrifice, the biblical passage is distorted so that it sounds like other religious ideas that the world accepts. This is very alarming because Matthew 16:24-26 is a key part of the gospel as preached by Jesus Christ.

The Message paraphrase as cited by Warren introduces another concept that is foreign to the passage as written in Matthew: "*Finding yourself, your true self.*" In Matthew 16:25, Jesus is contrasting forfeiting one's soul for eternity with finding eternal life through the cross. The concept of finding one's "true self," absent from the passage, is popular in some psychological theories and in New Age thinking. The idea is this: A pristine person comes into the world and becomes messed up by bad parenting and the things that happen in life. Shaming messages force this pristine person inward so that a false "self" is presented to the world to satisfy others. Finding one's "true self" (also called "higher self") is the process of recovering that "inner child" in his or her pristine state, and making it safe for this true self to be presented to the outer world without fear. This unbiblical theory is popular, but why introduce the idea of a "true self" using a Bible paraphrase when the Bible says nothing about this concept? Perhaps because "finding your self, your true self" fits with Warren's theme of a journey to discover one's purpose. Besides that, finding the true self is popular with the world and therefore marketable.

What has happened in this case is that the message of the cross, which is central to the gospel, is set aside in favor of finding a "true self" through self-sacrifice. The offense of the gospel is removed and replaced by something that interests people. Consider how *The Message* translates the previous verse in Matthew: "*Then Jesus went to work on His disciples. 'Anyone who intends to come with Me has to let Me lead. You're not in the driver's seat; I am. Don't run from suffering; embrace it. Follow Me and I'll show you how.*" (Matthew 16:24). Now compare that to the NASB: "*Then Jesus said*

*to His disciples, 'If anyone wishes to come after Me, let him deny himself,
and take up his cross, and follow Me.'"* A person carrying a cross in the
first century had already been sentenced to death. Such a person
was a "walking dead man." He had no hope in this world. He was
not making a self-sacrifice to find his purpose. The graphic terminology that Jesus used is replaced by a discussion of who is in the
driver's seat. Jesus was not teaching us to embrace suffering and
practice self-sacrifice. He was saying that we must die to all our
hopes in this world if we are going to be His disciples. The reward
is the free gift of eternal life.

By citing *The Message* translation of Matthew 16:25, Warren has
obscured the gospel, and changed it. *The Message* teaches that
through embracing suffering and practicing self-sacrifice, a person
can find their true self. All world religions teach self-sacrifice. Only
Christianity has the cross. The cross is offensive because it is an
executioner's device. Taken literally, the passage teaches that one
must deny self and embrace the cross. The life that is thereby
found is new and it is eternal. In this case, again, *The Message* is not
a paraphrase because it does not carry the same meaning. It is
man's wisdom being presented as God's words. However, this mistranslation does fit Warren's purpose of bringing his readers on a
journey of self-discovery. What they would have discovered had
Warren cited the passage as it was written, was that the self they are
going to discover is so wicked that it needs to die! But that idea is
offensive.

Warren's Explanation of the Many Translations

Before analyzing another example of using a translation that
changes the meaning of a text (again from God-centered to man-
centered), I want to quote Rick Warren's stated reason for using so
many different translations:

I have intentionally varied the Bible translations used for
two important reasons. First, no matter how wonderful a
translation is, it has limitations. [He references the fact of

the Hebrew, Aramaic, and Greek words] Obviously, nuances and shades of meaning can be missed, so it is always helpful to compare translations. Second, and even more important, is the fact that we often miss the full impact of familiar Bible verses, *not* because of poor trans- lating, but simply because they have become so familiar. . . I have deliberately used paraphrases in order to help you see God's truth in new, *fresh* ways.[14]

I will respond to both of his stated reasons. If the first reason is what is important to him, then his practice would be to find the translation that best brings out the meaning of the Hebrew or Greek. That is a valid thing to do if you know that a different version brings out the author's intent more faithfully than the one you usu- ally use. I do this myself at times. In writing the book, however, Warren does not show that he is concerned with the translation that best demonstrates the biblical author's meaning. As we have seen, he often uses versions that are not even valid paraphrases, much less translations. That casts suspicion on his first stated reason.

Secondly, he claims that using unfamiliar versions helps us think more carefully about passages that have grown dull through familiarity. This can happen. Studying a passage in other English versions might help bring clarity. (It is even better to use Hebrew and Greek language tools if one has them available and scholarly commentary on a given text.) But again the actual practice in *The Purpose Driven Life* makes one wonder. *The Message*, which many times departs far from the original meaning, is cited over 100 times in Warren's book. This does not help us understand overly famil- iar passages better—it often obscures the meaning of the passages. We have shown two examples of this, and there are dozens of oth- ers. Unless the actual citations in *The Purpose Driven Life* can be shown to bring better clarity to the biblical author's meaning as determined by solid grammatical, historical study, Warren's stated reason for using them becomes suspect.

1 Corinthians 2:7

Let us consider the very next biblical citation in *The Purpose Driven Life* after Matthew 16:25. It is also from *The Message*: "*God's wisdom . . . goes deep into the interior of His purposes. . . . It's not the latest message, but more like the oldest—what God determined as the way to bring out His best in us*" (1 Corinthians 2:7, *The Message*).[15] Here it is from the NASB: "*...but we speak God's wisdom in a mystery, the hidden wisdom, which God predestined before the ages to our glory.*"

The passage is about Paul's message which is the gospel. The purposes of God are revealed through the gospel, though it is considered foolishness to the world. Paul told us the content of this "wisdom" that he spoke: "*For I determined to know nothing among you except Jesus Christ, and Him crucified.*" (1 Corinthians 2:2). God's wisdom is revealed through a crucified Jewish Messiah. It is offensive to the Jews, and foolishness to the Gentiles (see 1 Corinthians 1:23). This wisdom is a mystery because it could not be found out until God revealed it.[16] God predestined that this plan of salvation, through a crucified Messiah, would bring His people, believers, to glory.

The passage, as cited by Warren from *The Message*, again changes the meaning of the biblical author (Paul). Paul was defending his message, the gospel, in light of the fact that it was considered "foolish." *The Message* removes the key verb in the passage "we speak." This takes the focus off of the gospel, where Paul had it. Next, the passage as cited by Warren says, "*What God determined as the way to bring out His best in us.*" What God predestined was to save a people through the crucified Messiah. "To bring out His best in us" fits with Warren's motif of finding one's purpose. This, however, obscures the key point of the passage which is the gospel that Paul preaches. The verse is about the content of Paul's preaching and also the content of God's wisdom.

Here is the context of Warren's use of the passage in *The Purpose Driven Life*:

It [the Bible] is our Owner's Manual, explaining why we are alive, how life works, what to avoid, and what to expect in the future. It explains what no self-help or philosophy book could know. The Bible says, *"God's wisdom . . . goes deep into the interior of his purposes. . . It's not the latest message, but more like the oldest—what God determined as the way to bring out His best in us"* . . . To discover your purpose in life you must turn to God's Word, not the world's wisdom.[17]

While it is true that we should study the Bible, it is not true that the Bible is an "Owner's Manual." That would make it a "how to fix things" book. Paul was not talking about that. He was speaking of the "mystery" of God's plan to save Jews and Gentiles through a crucified Messiah. The "Owner's Manual" analogy obscures the fact that we are lost sinners abiding under God's wrath as sinners who need a means of escape. It suggests that we need information, not redemption. The Word of God is a means of grace, not information about "our purpose."

Some have suggested that Warren is only addressing Christians who already know the gospel, giving them information about having purpose in their lives. Not so; the book is addressed to the general public. On the same page on which the 1 Corinthians 2:7 citation is found, he says this: "If you don't have such a relationship [with Jesus Christ], I will later explain how to begin one."[18] He has failed to tell his readers that 1 Corinthians 2:7 is about the gospel, saying instead it is about God bringing out the best in us, as if there were some "best" worth bringing out. That is not offensive to sinners. But the idea that our sins are so grievous that Christ's blood was shed to avert God's wrath against them is offensive. That was Paul's point in 1Corinthians chapters 1 and 2. The world does not accept this message. Warren avoids this rejection at this point in his book by using a paraphrase that obscures the fact that his proof text is about the gospel. Thus again, he takes what would not be popular with the world, changes it, and presents a different idea that is popular with the world.

Ephesians 1:4a

Let us study one more passage from the very beginning of *The Purpose Driven Life* to establish that from the cover page to Day 1 to Day 2, the book consistently uses faulty Bible translations to introduce ideas that the biblical passages do not contain. Then, in the next section, we will examine more examples to show that this pattern continues to the end.

In the Day 2 study, Rick Warren says this: "God's motive for creating you was His love. The Bible says, *"Long before He laid down earth's foundations, He had us in mind, had settled on us as the focus of His love"*[19] (Ephesians 1:4a *The Message*). As we saw a few pages earlier, Warren told those who are not Christians and are reading his book that he would tell them later how to have a relationship with Jesus. He has not done so yet. Therefore, on Day 2 he is addressing people in general, not Christians. Therefore "us" in Ephesians 1:4a, as used by Warren, is not the church but people in general. Here is the same passage from the NASB: *"Just as He chose us in Him before the foundation of the world."* Even *The Message* paraphrase, if taken in context, makes it clear that "us" is the church, true Christians, not people in general. Warren's use of it as a generalization about all people is not a valid use of Ephesians 1:4a in any translation. The verse does not apply to anyone but Christians.

But Warren ignores this fact and goes on to make more generalizations: "God designed this planet's environment just so we could live in it."[20] He is not saying God designed the planet so that Christians could live here, but people in general. This proves that Warren is not applying the passage to Christians only, although that his how Paul meant it to be understood.

Using Ephesians 1:4a the way Warren does confuses and misleads the reader. The passage teaches that God chose His people before the foundation of the world. He did so "in Christ." *The Message* makes the passage man-centered: *"He had us in mind, had settled on us as the focus of his love."* But even though it removes the important concept, "in Christ," it nevertheless still teaches the doctrine of election that Warren obscures. "Settled on us" means that believers are in some sense uniquely the focus of God's love. Warren even misuses the paraphrase in his application. He uses it to teach that God's motive for creation was a general love for all people. The paraphrase does not teach that, nor does a literal translation of the verse. Consider the whole passage in context:

> *"Just as He chose us in Him before the foundation of the world, that we should be holy and blameless before Him. In love He predestined us to adoption as sons through Jesus Christ to Himself, according to the kind intention of His will"* (Ephesians 1:4, 5).

It obviously only applies to Christians. It says that God predestined us to adoption, and it tells us this is God's sovereign doing. There is nothing in this passage that says that the reason God created the world was His general love for all mankind. Even if that concept were true, this passage does not teach it.

In Warren's *The Purpose Driven Life*, passages that are God-centered and declarative of gospel truths are changed and misapplied so that they become man-centered and amenable to the motif of a journey to discover one's purpose. This pattern continues throughout the book. Warren does not explain, clarify, or expound the Bible. Rather he selects texts that can be massaged to support a journey of self-discovery. The gospel, as preached by Christ and His apostles, was never presented as such a journey.

1 Thessalonians 1:8

We could work through the entire book this way, chapter by chapter, showing how the Bible is misused. But to keep this process reasonably short, I will select a few more representative examples to show that this pattern does not change.

On page 289, Warren cites part of 1 Thessalonians 1:8 from *The Message*: *"Your lives are echoing the Master's Word . . . The news of your faith in God is out. We don't even have to say anything anymore—you're the message!"* Let us again compare the NASB: *"For the Word of the Lord has sounded forth from you, not only in Macedonia and Achaia, but also in every place your faith toward God has gone forth, so that we have no need to say anything"* (1 Thessalonians 1:8). In *The Message*, their lives are the message, not God's Word. In the more literal translation, the "Word of the Lord" goes out from the Thessalonian Christians. There is a big difference.

People in other religions sometimes live pious lives. People in other religions have some sort of faith. People in other religions are sometimes so exemplary that they and whatever faith they hold are held in high esteem by their contemporaries. By removing the preaching of God's Word and replacing it with the idea, "You're the message," the paraphrase changes an important concept and removes what is distinctively Christian. The next verse in 1 Thessalonians shows what it is that was truly exemplary about them: *"For they themselves report about us what kind of a reception we had with you, and how you turned to God from idols to serve a living and true God."* (1 Thessalonians 1:9 NASB). They had believed Paul's gospel preaching, repented, and left behind idol worship to serve God on His terms.

Again, Warren takes a God-centered passage about the gospel and its power and turns it into something man-centered. Rather than the gospel being the message, people are. Again we have an invalid paraphrase being used to introduce a concept not found in the Bible. Though unbiblical, this mistranslation helps support Warren's motif of a journey to find one's purpose; and as in all of these cases, this process creates a message that the world finds attractive.

Genesis 6:8

A few weeks before I read *The Purpose Driven Life*, I preached on the Noah narrative in Genesis 6. A key point in this passage is that God showed grace to Noah and ultimately to the whole world. He did so through preserving Noah's family and thereby preserving the promise given to Eve in Genesis 3:15, that the seed of the woman would crush the serpent's head. This is the first Messianic prophecy in the Bible. Concerning Genesis 6:8, one scholar says, "Here, Noah received sovereign grace and escaped the catastrophe. No one escapes divine judgment apart from grace."[21] Another scholar writes about the passage, "'To find favor' is a formal expression often used when someone is making a request of a superior or when someone in authority helps someone without status."[22] If one is to understand the flood narrative and understand how God keeps His promises, one must understand Genesis 6:8. From this verse we learn that God shows grace even in the midst of judgment.

Now, let us see how Warren used the same passage: "But there was one man who made God smile. The Bible says, 'Noah was a pleasure to the Lord'"[23] (Genesis 6:8 The Living Bible). I read that, and I was shocked. Warren's interpretation is opposite from what I had learned through careful study of Genesis 6. Rather than God showing grace and mercy in the midst of judging a horribly perverse situation, Warren's version has man imparting something to God. This is a reversal of the meaning of the text. The NASB says, "But Noah found favor in the eyes of the Lord." The New King James uses the term "grace," "But Noah found grace in the eyes of the LORD." The only other version I found that makes the passage man-centered was The Message which says: "But Noah was different. GOD liked what He saw in Noah." The paraphrased versions (both The Living Bible and The Message) remove the idea of God giving grace or favor and replace it with a man-centered concept. Warren cites this passage in his chapter about making God smile (Day 9).

The result is that a passage that could be used to preach the gospel (how God's grace preserves a man and his family in the midst of judgment so that the promise of future Messianic salvation is preserved and prefigured) is turned into a passage that suggests we have something to offer God that makes Him smile. Here is how Warren paraphrases the paraphrase: "God said, 'This guy brings me pleasure. He makes me smile. I'll start over with this family.'"[24] So rather than God graciously keeping and preserving Noah, Noah provided God with an opportunity that evidently He would have lacked had Noah not been there. This is a man-centered idea that is not God-honoring. By misusing a passage that should have led people to see their need for the gospel, Warren leads people away from seeing that need.

In the flood narrative we see many important aspects of the

gospel: the Lord kept His promise to Eve (Genesis 3:15); the Lord preserves a remnant when He brings judgment (Romans 9:27); salvation is by faith (Hebrews 11:7); the salvation of Noah and his family prefigures salvation through Christ, who was raised (1 Peter 3:20, 21); the judgment of the wicked world at the time of Noah prefigures the judgment coming at the end of the age (Luke 17:26, 27), and therefore we need to repent and believe the gospel or we will perish just as surely as the wicked in Noah's day perished when they refused to listen to his preaching (2 Peter 2:5). Alas, Warren's readers learn none of these things from the story of Noah. Instead, they learn five ways to make God smile.[25]

Even when Warren touches on the issue of Noah's faith, citing Hebrews 11:7, he misses the point:

> Imagine this scene: One day God comes to Noah and says, "I'm disappointed in human beings. In the entire world, no one but you thinks about Me. But Noah, when I look at you, I start smiling. I'm pleased with your life, so I'm going to flood the world and start over with your family. . ."[26]

On the contrary, the point of having faith is not that God is pleased with us, but that He is displeased with our sin, and that by faith we can escape judgment, if we come to Him on His terms. That idea is missing from Warren's use of the passage. No wonder he uses a passage that makes God the recipient of a benefit from Noah, rather than Noah the recipient of a benefit from God.

In Genesis 6:8, as cited in *The Purpose Driven Life*, yet another verse from the Bible is used in a poorly worded paraphrase that changes a God-centered idea into a man-centered one. This process goes on throughout the *The Purpose Driven Life*. The cumulative result is that Warren's readers are led astray from the gospel.

Our Responsibility to Handle the Word of God Carefully

One could conclude that Rick Warren is unable to do solid biblical exegesis, and that the cases highlighted above, and many others, are caused by a simple preacher trying his best, but lacking scholarly tools. This, however, is not the case. On pages 195 and 196 he offers solid, well reasoned, and accurate exegesis of Romans 8:28-29.[27] I was surprised when I found this quality of biblical interpretation in a book filled with just the opposite. This proves that Warren is capable of sound biblical interpretation and teaching when he sees fit. My question is, "If he is capable of expounding the truth of a passage accurately, what excuse does he have for not doing so with hundreds of other passages?"

The fact that Warren has accurate translations available, a quality education, scholarly analysis, and the demonstrated ability to understand and apply these to proper biblical exegesis but often fails to interpret the Bible properly, only reinforces my opinion that he is willing to put out material that is substandard theologically in order to make his message sound like what the world wants to hear. I do not believe that God gives us the option to do this. Preachers are responsible, every time they proclaim a text, to make sure they understand what the Holy Spirit has inspired the biblical writer to say, and to carefully convey and apply that meaning to the contemporary audience. As a whole, *The Purpose Driven Life* too often fails to do so. The underlying basic issue is whether we have the right to modify or soften the message to make it appealing to the unconverted.

The Bible does not offer a journey of self-discovery to find one's purpose; Warren does. In order to provide such a journey and make it seem biblical, he chooses poor translations of Bible verses that fit with the motif of a journey to discover one's purpose. Warren rarely provides any exegetical work to help his readers understand how to properly interpret Scripture (with the exception noted above). Rather, "proof texts" are inserted to create a seamless tale of a journey to discover one's purpose. The seamlessness of the process blurs the distinction between Warren's philosophy and the teachings of Scripture. That will be the subject of the next chapter.

7

Redefining God's Wisdom

"For the word of the cross is to those who are perishing foolishness, but to us who are being saved it is the power of God" (1 Corinthians 1:18).

"For since in the wisdom of God the world through its wisdom did not come to know God, God was well-pleased through the foolishness of the message preached to save those who believe. For indeed Jews ask for signs, and Greeks search for wisdom; but we preach Christ crucified, to Jews a stumbling block, and to Gentiles foolishness" (1 Corinthians 1:21-23).

Human wisdom appeals to the unregenerate mind. When Paul preached the gospel to the philosophers on Mars Hill, they mocked the idea of the resurrection of Jesus Christ. When Paul left Athens, he went to Corinth. He preached the same gospel there. Paul did not take up human wisdom because it appeals to the Greek mind. Paul said, *"Greeks search for wisdom, but we preach Christ crucified."* Here he had an opportunity to appeal to seekers but laid aside what they wanted, and preached instead what they needed—a crucified Jewish Messiah.

Rick Warren has mastered the wisdom of man and cleverly integrated it with bad paraphrases of the Bible or passages taken out of context to make a seamless religious product, *The Purpose*

Driven Life, that appeals to the unregenerate. His process is the opposite of the one Paul describes in 1 Corinthians. Paul did not invite people on a journey to discover their purpose; he preached the gospel. We can read about his ministry in Corinth in the Book of Acts:

And he was reasoning in the synagogue every Sabbath and trying to persuade Jews and Greeks. But when Silas and Timothy came down from Macedonia, Paul began devoting himself completely to the word, solemnly testifying to the Jews that Jesus was the Christ. And when they resisted and blasphemed, he shook out his garments and said to them, "Your blood be upon your own heads! I am clean. From now on I shall go to the Gentiles" (Acts 18:4-6).

Paul's message was not carefully crafted to appeal to their religious sensitivities; it was designed to show them from Scripture that Jesus was the Messiah. Acts tell us what he did after leaving the synagogue: *"And he settled there a year and six months, teaching the Word of God among them"* (Acts 18:11). This is what God used to establish the church in Corinth. This teaching (Christ crucified) was summarized in 1 Corinthians.

According to his own public statements, Rick Warren's message has broad appeal, even to members of other religions. Part of the secret of his success is his ability to integrate his own aphorisms with statements from people the world admires, combining these with partial biblical passages taken out of context, to create a hybrid message that is simultaneously marketed to the world and the evangelical church. Everyone gets something they like. The problem is, Paul claimed that the message of the crucified Messiah and the wisdom of the world are totally incompatible. Has Rick Warren found a valid way to bridge these two messages, or has he compromised the Christian message to make it seem to be compatible with the world's wisdom? The facts will show that the latter is the case.

Human Wisdom Contradicts God's Word

Rick Warren's human wisdom makes grand claims that he presents in a manner that makes them seem as if they are God's words. For example, "Nothing matters more than knowing God's purposes for your life, and nothing can compensate for not knowing them—not success, wealth, fame, or pleasure."[1] He follows this with a list of benefits including meaning, simplification, focus, and preparation for eternity.[2] "Nothing matters more" is a very strong truth claim and is a presentation of Rick Warren's philosophy, but it is not the truth of the gospel. If we are going to say, "nothing matters more" we have to first determine if we are speaking to Christians or non-Christians (as we have seen, Warren is writing to people in general). For non-Christians nothing matters more than escaping God's wrath against sin through the gospel: *"He who believes in the Son has eternal life; but he who does not obey the Son shall not see life, but the wrath of God abides on him"* (John 3:36). "To "believe in the Son" is not the equivalent of "knowing God's purposes." If it were, Rick Warren could have told his readers right up front who Christ is, what He did, and why they need Him, and he could have called them to believe the gospel. Those who responded in faith would have embraced God's purposes. But instead he makes knowing God's purposes the key to everything and leaves the issue of believing in the Son until later. Then, as we have shown, he leaves out many of the key gospel issues or obscures them so they have little impact. Thus, his human philosophy replaces God's Word.

Besides this, many people know God's purposes but go to Hell. So how can that be so primary that nothing else is more important? For example: *"But the Pharisees and the lawyers rejected God's purpose for themselves, not having been baptized by John"* (Luke 7:30). We are not saved by knowledge, but by grace through faith. So a person could know God's purposes, reject them, and yet be lost. So therefore the statement, "nothing matters more than knowing God's purposes for your life. . ." is false if applied to non-Christians. What really matters is knowing what is revealed about

God's purposes and embracing those purposes by coming to God on His terms.

For Christians, his "nothing is more important" statement is equally invalid. There are many things more important than knowing God's purposes. For example, consider Paul's statement: *"More than that, I count all things to be loss in view of the surpassing value of knowing Christ Jesus my Lord, for whom I have suffered the loss of all things, and count them but rubbish in order that I may gain Christ"* (Philippians 3:8). Paul further elaborates what is most important to him: *"That I may know Him, and the power of His resurrection and the fellowship of His sufferings, being conformed to His death; in order that I may attain to the resurrection from the dead"* (Philippians 3:10, 11). The wisdom presented in *The Purpose Driven Life* gives the impression that some hidden, special knowledge exists that will come to light as a person follows the 40-day journey, and acquiring this knowledge will provide everything the journeyer has been missing. The truth is that knowing Christ and embracing the cross as Paul did is what is most important. The result is not finding meaning and focus; it is attaining to the resurrection of the dead and thus knowing Christ in perfect, eternal fellowship. Such knowledge is not the result of a 40-day spiritual journey—it is the result of believing the gospel.

Rick Warren likely believes the truths that I cite from Philippians. The problem is that he obscures these truths from his readers, and instead entices them to join the spiritual journey to find purpose. Apparently, he hopes to lure them in first and later bring Christian truths in through the back door. In the next chapter I will show from Scripture why this practice is invalid. Anything less than being straightforward about the truth of the gospel is unacceptable.

Is Reality a State of Mind?

On page 41, Day 5 of the *Purpose Driven Life*, Warren cites both a partial Bible verse and a writer of female erotica to substantiate his idea that life and one's destiny is the product of how he or she sees it and defines it (i.e., one's state of mind). The partial Bible passage is this, "What is your life?"[3] The wisdom from Anaïs Nin is this: "We don't see things as they are, we see them as we are."[4] It is disturbing that he cites Nin's "wisdom." It is literally like citing Hugh Heffner approvingly. But setting aside the source, the "wisdom" itself is false. It is a version of subjectivism that undermines the gospel.

Warren gleans the following from these citations: "The way you *see* your life *shapes* your life. How you define life determines your destiny."[5] These are not biblical concepts, but Warren's human wisdom elevated to appear to be something derived from the Bible. His assumption is that we have some mental image that determines how we live and defines our destiny. Supposedly we must discover this mental picture in order to find out how it influences our destiny. He says, "If I asked you how you picture life, what image would come to your mind? That image is your *life metaphor*."[6] This life metaphor may be held unconsciously.[7] What he is saying is that there may be a secret mental image that determines your destiny. This idea is unbiblical. Yet he raises it to the level of Scripture by suggesting that the Bible offers "life metaphors" that are "the foundation of purpose-driven living."[8]

Before we rush on (as Warren's readers likely do) to discover our life metaphor and then to discover the exciting biblical life metaphors that can make us purpose-driven, let us back up and examine the partial Bible verse and statement from the worldly author. These supposedly lay the groundwork for Warren's philosophy that a mental image determines our destiny.

The passage supposedly says, "What is your life?" This is from James 4:14. The verse says this: *"Yet you do not know what your life will be like tomorrow. You are just a vapor that appears for a little while and then vanishes away"* (James 4:14, NASB). Warren cites just part of the NIV version: *"Why, you do not even know what will happen tomorrow. **What is your life?** You are a mist that appears for a little while and then vanishes,"* calling it "James 4:14b." Actually he takes one small phrase from the middle of the NIV version and cites it totally out of context. He ignores the fact that the Bible is not raising a question to entice us to the self-discovery of a life metaphor (Warren's application), but is a warning against presumption. James teaches that we do not know what tomorrow will bring so we should not boast or brag about future would-be accomplishments (see the entire context, James 4:13-16). Warren raises his human wisdom (that we need to discover a life metaphor) to the level of Scripture by using very poor exegesis and application. This misuse of Scripture is inexcusable for a person like Warren, who has the means and ability to interpret the passage correctly—if he saw fit to.

This citation from Nin is very problematic: "We don't see things as they are, we see them as we are." This statement is entirely relativistic. If taken as true, it would undermine everything we believe. Let me explain. If something that is true about the subjective "knower" determines how the world is seen, then verification of truth is impossible. Every individual seeing would only see what his or her mental processes determined could be seen. There would be no way to be sure that any two witnesses to a supposed event saw the same thing. If this type of relativism were true, we could know neither science nor history.

Furthermore, this thinking would give credence to the theory that Jesus was not really raised from the dead, because the disciples just thought He was. They so badly wanted it to be true they saw a resurrected Jesus in their minds. They did not see Jesus as He is, they saw Him as they were, if indeed Nin's philosophy is true. So the worldly wisdom of Anaïs Nin undermines the possibility of knowing the truth. The Bible says that we must know the truth. Not only is her "wisdom" irrational and unbiblical, it comes from someone whose fame was in writing erotic literature. I am amazed that Warren would try to integrate this into a version of Christianity.

From the faulty foundation of misquoted, misinterpreted and misapplied Scripture, coupled with a relativistic philosophy from a perverse source, Warren builds his own structure replete with strong claims. For example, he claims, "Your unspoken life metaphor influences your life more than you realize. It determines your expectation, your values, your relationships, your goals, and your priorities."[9] He told us that this metaphor may be unconscious. This means that for people in general (Warren's audience) everything important about life is determined and that by something they likely did not even know existed—their life metaphor. This is an earthshaking discovery in the realm of anthropology, sociology and psychology if it is true. But is it?

This version of determinism falls victim to the same problems that attend all versions of determinism. If determinism is true, how does the person teaching it get free from its grips himself, and how can anyone else get free? Think about the problems with these claims. Warren cited Nin approvingly (right up there with a biblical passage) saying that we do not see things as they are. Rather, they claim that what we see is determined by processes internal to us. If this is true for all, then it is true for Rick Warren. If it is true for Rick Warren, then Rick Warren does not see "things" (including such matters as people being determined by life metaphors) as they are, but as he is. If this is true, then maybe Warren has an unconscious life metaphor that causes him to see life metaphors to be deterministic. If that is so, it may be that for the rest of us, our life metaphors are not determined in our subjective worlds; that is true only in Rick Warren's world. So how did Rick Warren extract himself from his own subjectively determined life metaphor to examine all of humanity and know for certain that everyone else is determined by a life metaphor?

If this is confusing to you, it should be. Welcome to the world of man-made philosophy and relativism. The Bible knows nothing of these determinative life metaphors, and as I have shown, the concept is self-defeating rationally. If you accept this worldly philosophy, you cannot be sure you will ever be free. Warren, on one hand, says a subjective metaphor determines everything important but then suggests that all we have to do is choose the new ones he offers and thereby change everything in our lives. If a simple choice of a life metaphor can change our destinies, then we were never determined in the first place.

Life metaphors do not determine our destinies. Our future depends on whether we stay under the wrath of God against sin or flee from it through faith in Christ's finished work. The truth is that values, relationships, goals, etc. are not determined by life metaphors, but by whether we live according to the flesh or according to the Spirit (Romans 8:5-13). Warren cites Romans 12:2 from the TEV as his proof text for needing new "biblical" metaphors. Here is the passage from the NASB: *"And do not be conformed to this world, but be transformed by the renewing of your mind, that you may prove what the will of God is, that which is good and acceptable and perfect."* The term "prove" from the Greek means, "put to the test."[10] The person whose mind is renewed is able to objectively distinguish between what is of the world and what is God's will by putting whatever is before him or her to the test. I fail to see how this passage serves as proof that we can change life metaphors and thereby change the process and destiny of our lives.

Let me explain why this does not work. The first alternative life metaphor Warren offers is, "Life on earth is a test."[11] He cites stories from the Bible where God tested people. Those stories do nothing to prove that we need a life metaphor, but simply show that for people of faith, God does put them through tests. However, one does not need to be a Christian to adopt a life metaphor that, "life is a test." Every Hindu who believes in reincarnation would gladly accept that life metaphor. Life on earth for them is a test, and they have to keep coming back until they pass it. One problem with Warren's worldly philosophy is that it is perfectly acceptable to non-Christians. Another is that it is unbiblical. Warren's "life metaphor" wisdom is totally unacceptable and obscures the gospel.

The "Power of a Focused Life"

One of the frustrating things about reading *The Purpose Driven Life* is that it has so many self-contradictions that it is nearly impossible to decide what Warren really believes. On the one hand he starts by saying, "It is not about you," and on the other hand the entire book is about "you" in the sense that it is a journey of self-discovery. The book reads like a self-help book and seems like a self-help book, but Warren tells us it is not a self-help book. The general public loves the book because it seems to be speaking their language. However, if orthodox Christians challenge his many unbiblical claims, they can find a place in the book that says what they believe. Everyone gets something they like. The problem is that self-contradiction is ultimately irrational and meaningless.

Sometimes the confusion and contradiction comes from his taking a biblical passage and making implications from it that fit common human wisdom when the real, biblical implication is something entirely different. For example, Warren says, "There is nothing quite as potent as a focused life, one lived on purpose."[12] This is Warren's human wisdom. But then he implies that this is a biblical principle by using Paul as an example:

> "For instance, the apostle Paul almost single-handedly spread Christianity throughout the Roman Empire. His secret was a focused life. He said, *I am focusing all my energies on this one thing: Forgetting the past and looking forward to what lies ahead.*"[13]

This is an abuse of Paul's teaching. Paul never claimed that the key to his ministry was the principle of a focused life. That is Rick Warren's human wisdom, not Paul's biblical teaching. What was important to Paul was not the abstract principle of being focused, but his faith in Christ. Warren cites the New Living Translation of Philippians 3:13 because it contains the word "focus," thus making it a useful proof text for his human wisdom. However, the passage in Philippians is about Paul's willingness to lay aside all that this world has so as to attain to the full knowledge of Christ. Paul's secret was not a "focused life," but his relationship to Christ—and that was no secret. Here is what Paul really said, in context:

That I may know Him, and the power of His resurrection and the fellowship of His sufferings, being conformed to His death; in order that I may attain to the resurrection from the dead. Not that I have already obtained it, or have already become perfect, but I press on in order that I may lay hold of that for which also I was laid hold of by Christ Jesus. Brethren, I do not regard myself as having laid hold of it yet; but one thing I do: forgetting what lies behind and reaching forward to what lies ahead (Philippians 3:10-13).

Warren cited a poor translation of the verse, cited only part of the verse, and cited it out of context. By so doing, he finds his human wisdom in the Bible. The passage tells us that Paul's focus was knowing Christ and attaining to the resurrection of the dead, even though he had not yet attained the full knowledge of Christ that is possible only in eternity. Paul said that Christ had "laid hold of" (meaning to "seize" or "apprehend") him, which was God's prior action that gave Paul his basis to focus on the eternal hope of total conformity to the image of Christ and fully knowing Christ. Paul did not discover a secret to success through focus and purpose. Christ apprehended Paul, and what Paul discovered was the infinite value of knowing Christ.

Warren again cites a mistranslation of Philippians to reinforce his human wisdom of success through focus and purpose: "You can be busy without a purpose, but what's the point? Paul said, *"Let's keep focused on that goal, those of us who want everything God has for us."*[14] This is Philippians 3:15 from *The Message*. Again, he finds a translation to prove text that supports his human wisdom of the power of a focused life. Had he cited the same paraphrase he used for Philippians 3:13, he would have cited this: *"I hope all of you who are mature Christians will agree on these things. If you disagree on some point, I believe God will make it plain to you."* The NLT actually is quite accurate on this verse (though it misses the word play Paul is making with the term "attitude" which is used elsewhere in Philippians), so it would not suit his purposes. *The Message* version distorts the passage and makes it seem to teach Warren's principle of focus, especially since he cites only part of the passage. Because of the way Warren uses these paraphrases his readers never find out that the goal Paul stresses is to fully know Christ in eternity through the resurrection. All they hear about is the human wisdom of the power of a focused life.

Later in his book Warren does speak about Christians being changed to be like Christ.[15] He is not distorting Paul's teaching in Philippians 3 because of a failure to believe what Paul teaches there about conformity to the image of Christ; he simply selects what he wants, to teach his human wisdom of a focused life which is attractive to the unregenerate mind. A couple of paraphrases taken out of context suit that purpose. This is what I mean by being confusing and contradictory. Businesspeople can read pages 32 and 33 and find something that speaks to them (the power of a focused life) and get excited about it without being troubled by the fact that Paul is not even speaking of some generic principle like that. The average Christian reader will gloss over those pages and find what they believe later on page 119. Everyone hears what they want to hear. To be honest to his readers right up front, Warren would have told them that plenty of people with focused lives (like Hitler for example) end up in Hell.

To make matters worse Warren follows his use of Paul, citing socialist George Bernard Shaw to reinforce Warren's human wisdom: "This is the true joy of life: being used up for a purpose recognized by yourself as a mighty one; being a force of nature instead of a feverish, selfish little clot of ailments and grievances, complaining that the world will not devote itself to making you happy."[16] The implication is that Paul's focus and Shaw's purpose both prove the power of a focused life. Never mind that Paul was speaking of eternity with Christ and Shaw was speaking from his socialist ideals. This leaves the impression, at least in this part of the book, that any focused life will do—a Christian one or a socialist one. Later, he will make statements that only a Christian-focused life is acceptable. This creates confusion.

By weaving his human wisdom together with citations from

New Agers, a socialist and a writer of erotica and combining this mix with out-of-context citations of mistranslations of the Bible, Warren creates the impression that the world's wisdom and the Bible are all saying the same thing. This is false. Biblical truth is at odds with the world and its wisdom. When later in the book Warren also weaves some true biblical doctrine into this mix, it only serves to create more confusion. The true biblical doctrine is at odds with what he said elsewhere. The result is everyone gets something they like. But can this unholy mixture convert sinners and edify Christians? I think not.

Spiritual Disciplines

For those who are not content with the means of grace given in the Bible, men have created alternatives that spring from human wisdom. These are called "spiritual disciplines." Though many are fooled by the false piety of people who invented these practices, they have no power to conform people to the image of Christ, because they are based on human effort rather than God's grace. The idea is that some elite, spiritual masters have discovered practices that unlock the secret of a higher order piety. Rick Warren promotes such practices and those who invented them.

Warren promises to reveal "six secrets of friendship with God."[17] To start with, there are no such secrets. God has revealed the terms and means by which we must come to Him in the Bible; this is public, revealed truth. Warren offers secrets that were supposedly discovered by pious people in church history. The first secret concerns how to have a running conversation with God. This secret was discovered by Brother Lawrence, a 17th century monk, and is revealed in his book *Practicing the Presence of God*.[18] Another special technique that Warren offers to help his readers discover the secret of friendship with God is the "breath prayer."[19] This involves the continual repetition of a phrase, over and over, as one breathes. This unbiblical practice supposedly helps us obey Paul's command to "pray without ceasing." Do not be fooled, Paul did not teach breath prayers; they cannot be found in the Bible.

Jesus warned against such practices: *"And when you are praying, do not use meaningless repetition, as the Gentiles do, for they suppose that they will be heard for their many words"* (Matthew 6:7).

Warren's human wisdom says, "Practicing the presence of God is a skill."[20] On the contrary, God's presence with His own people is promised in the Bible: *"He Himself has said, 'I will never desert you, nor will I ever forsake you'"* (Hebrews 13:5b). We know we have God's presence because we have the promise of His presence that is for all who have believed the gospel. Practicing human techniques that are derived from human wisdom will not make God more present, and it will not lead to learning secrets, as Warren falsely promises.

Another secret Warren reveals is the practice of "venting" (using the modern psychological idea of being honest about one's feelings). Supposedly this is a practice we can learn that will help make us best friends with God. As is often the case, Warren uses bad exegesis and bad Bible translations to find his human wisdom in the Bible. He says:

> Job was allowed to vent his bitterness during his ordeal, and in the end, God defended Job for being honest, and rebuked Job's friends for being inauthentic. God told them, *"You haven't been honest either with me or about me—not the way my friend Job has . . . My friend Job will now pray for you and I will accept his prayer"*[21]

This mistranslation, coupled with Warren's misinterpretation, gives credence to concepts of "emotional honesty, venting, and authenticity" that are not biblical ideas, but human wisdom. The Bible does not teach that we gain authenticity by venting our emotions. Job surely did complain bitterly to God, but that was not what God commended Job for to his comforters. Warren has totally distorted the passage, and thereby changed the message of Job. Here is what Job 42:7 really says: *"And it came about after the Lord had spoken these words to Job, that the Lord said to Eliphaz the Temanite, 'My wrath is kindled against you and against your two friends, because you have not spoken of Me what is right as My servant Job has.'"* Job was not called God's "friend" but his "servant." Warren used a bad translation to give credibility to his idea that he is teaching "secrets to friendship with God." God did not commend Job for emotional honesty and authenticity, as Warren claims, but for speaking what was right about God. What Job said that was right is found in the immediate context, not in his supposed ventings: *"Then Job answered the Lord, and said, 'I know that Thou canst do all things, And that no purpose of Thine can be thwarted'"* (Job 42:1, 2). That truth is what God commended in verse 7.

Concerning Job's complaints, God spent three chapters rebuking and questioning Job (chapters 38-40). Here is the dialogue where God confronts Job for questioning Him:

> *Then the Lord said to Job, "Will the faultfinder contend with the Almighty? Let him who reproves God answer it." Then Job answered the Lord and said, "Behold, I am insignificant; what can I reply to Thee? I lay my hand on my mouth. "Once I have spoken, and I will not answer; Even twice, and I will add no more." Then the Lord answered Job out of the storm, and said, "Now gird up your loins like a man; I will ask you, and you instruct Me. Will you really annul My judgment? Will you condemn Me that you may be justified?"* (Job 40:2-8).

God did not commend Job for emotional honesty or venting; God rebuked him. God commended him for repenting: *"Therefore I retract, And I repent in dust and ashes"* (Job 42:6). Warren took a bad translation of Job 42:7 out of context, and used it to promote the very opposite idea that is being taught in Job. The lesson that Job learned was *"I know that Thou canst do all things, And that no purpose of Thine can be thwarted,"* not that God was pleased with his authenticity and emotional honesty. Thus, Warren finds watered down pop-psychology in the Bible, by doing a very sloppy job of biblical interpretation.

Spiritual disciplines are the accumulation of religious, human wisdom that promises practices that will make us closer to God. Warren cites mystics such as Henri Nouwen[22] and St. John of the Cross[23] to reinforce the idea that certain people have discovered secrets to friendship with God. The number of possible spiritual disciplines that could be invented is endless. They can be gleaned from many sources, but they are not taught in the Bible. The truth is that no one can get any closer to God than he or she gets through Christ Who sits at the right hand of God. The human wisdom of medieval and contemporary mystics cannot make anyone closer to God than they have come through the blood atonement. These disciplines create a sense of human piety that makes people feel more spiritual. Those who follow these unbiblical practices are usually drawn aside from what would nurture their faith—the pure teaching of God's Word.

Rick Warren further promotes spiritual disciplines on page 221:

> If you practice something over time, you get good at it. Repetition is the mother of character and skill. These character building habits are often called *"spiritual disciplines,"* and there are dozens of great books that can teach you how to do these. See appendix 2 for a recommended reading list of books for spiritual growth.[24]

Appendix 2 is entitled "Resources." Here are the resources for spiritual disciplines: *The Purpose Driven Life Journal, The Purpose Driven Life Scripture Keepers Plus, The Purpose Driven Life Album, The Purpose Driven Life Video Curriculum, The Purpose Driven Church, Foundations: 11 Core Truths to Build Your Life on* (for Purpose Driven living), *Doing Life Together,* and *Planned for God's Pleasure* (music CD for the message of *The Purpose Driven Life*).[25] Besides these sale items, there are free resources that are all Rick Warren's material. Evidently the spiritual disciplines are whatever Rick Warren is doing or selling. Nothing else is offered in Appendix 2.

People alive during the time of the Apostles grew in the grace

and knowledge of the Lord and they never heard of spiritual disciplines. Medieval monks with too much time on their hands and a
theology of personal piety that came from a lack of appreciation for
the finished work of Christ invented spiritual practices (or borrowed
them from the East as the case may be) that made them feel closer to
God. Now, Rick Warren has popularized some of these by including
them in his massively popular book. He has added other practices of
his own invention and attached the promise that these practices will
make one a close friend of God's to whom God will share secrets.[26]
These are man-made practices and are based on human wisdom, not
the revealed will of God. They should be rejected.

Hundreds of Rick Warren Aphorisms

I have dealt with several instances of Warren's practice of combining human wisdom with poor translations or out-of-context
Scripture that promotes his human wisdom as if it were God's wisdom, which it is not. *The Purpose Driven Life* contains many hundreds of others. Rather than tediously explaining and refuting
each one, I will list them with page numbers so that interested
readers can look them up for themselves.

"The greatest tragedy is not death, but life without purpose" –
page 30.

Paul's "secret" was a focused life. – page 32.

"How you define life determines your destiny" – page 41.

We need a life metaphor – page 42.

"St. Irenaeus said, 'The glory of God is a human being fully
alive'" – page 55.

There are "secrets" to friendship with God – pages 87-91.

The need for "emotional honesty" – pages 93-94

"The truth is—you are as close to God *as you choose to be*" – page 98.

"You are a spirit that resides in a body. . ." – page 101.

Warren promotes Gary Thomas' *Secret Pathways* — page 103.

Warren promotes mystics St. John of the Cross and Henri Nouwen – page 108.

Supposedly we need to have our feelings validated — page 141.

Warren urges a group "covenant" that includes sharing "true feelings" – page 151.

We need to "ventilate vertically" like David supposedly did – page 154.

"People don't care what we know until they know we care" – page 156.

"Unity is the soul of fellowship. Destroy it, and you rip the heart out of Christ's Body" – page 160.

"Longing for the ideal while criticizing the real is evidence of immaturity" – page 162.

Warren uses his human wisdom to intimidate people into not correcting error – pages 162-164.

People who are "disrespectful of leadership" are to be removed – page 166.

Warren requires a "covenant of unity" – page 167.

"Your character is essentially the sum of your habits ..." – page 175.

"Tell me what you are committed to, and I'll tell you what you will be in twenty years" – page 180.

"Every behavior is motivated by a belief, and every action is prompted by an attitude" – page 181.

"You are only as sick as your secrets" – page 213.

"The fear of what we might discover if we honestly faced our character defects keeps us living in denial" – page 220.

"The unconscious worry is that if I let go of my habit, my hurt, or my hang-up, who will I be?" – page 221.

"*Impression* without *expression* causes *depression*" – page 231.

"The *last* thing many believers need today is to go to another Bible study" – page 231.

Warren promotes his SHAPE program which involves a careful study of one's self as a means of discipleship – pages 234-248.

Warren promotes ideas of great human potential – page 242.

Warren promotes Jungian and Platonic temperament theories (without naming the source) – page 245.

"In determining your shape for serving God, you should examine at least six kinds of experiences from your past" – page 246.

Paul suffered from doubt and depression – page 248.

We must "discover" our shape, accept it, and develop it to best serve God – page 249.

We need to keep a "spiritual journal" – page 252.

"Service starts in your mind" – page 265.

"God uses money to test your faithfulness as a servant. That is why Jesus talked more about money than he did about either heaven or hell" – page 267.

Jesus is an example of having a "secure self-image" – page 269.

Gideon had "low self-esteem" – page 275.

"Ministry begins with vulnerability" – page 276.

"Vulnerability is emotionally liberating" – page 276.

"Our strengths create competition, but our weaknesses create community" – page 277.

"Blessed are the balanced; they shall outlast everyone" – page 305.

Warren promotes the need for spiritual checkups and a spiritual journal and sells products to facilitate these – page 307-308.

"Your life is a journey and a journey deserves a journal" – page 309.

Supposedly we need to develop a life "purpose statement." – pages 312-313.

"Your *mission statement* is a part of your life purpose statement" – page 315.

As we can see, many of these claims come from various versions of pop-psychology. The need for "vulnerability" is a good example. So is "diagnosing" Biblical characters using categories from modern pop psychology. Earlier in the book Warren says this, "To discover your purpose in life you must turn to God's Word, not the world's wisdom."[27] I totally agree with that statement. But if Warren really believes that, why is his book filled with the world's wisdom? He further states, "You must build your life on eternal truths, not pop-psychology, success-motivation, or inspirational stories."[28] Again, I totally agree. But having said this, his book is filled with many instances of what he earlier claimed we do not need. This is contradictory and confusing.

Who Speaks for God?

Warren's many statements and claims that are expressed as aphorisms (wise sayings) are presented in the tone of authoritative statements of truth. In literature this style is called, "the omniscient narrator." Some of these statements may have some truth to them. But they are not God's authoritative commands. By weakening biblical truth through use of bad translations, Scripture taken out of context and misapplied, and his own simultaneously issued decrees about what we must do, Warren has lowered Scripture to the level of human wisdom and elevated human wisdom to the level of God's authoritative word. His readers are given the impression that everything he says is what they should believe and do. The fact is that Rick Warren does not speak authoritatively for God. His human wisdom can safely be ignored or rejected. There is no reason to do or believe anything he says other than when he accurately explains and applies the meaning of God's inerrant Word. The same is true for me or any other writer. We must search the Scriptures to see if these things be true.

The key product of the *Purpose Driven Church* is this amalgamation of human wisdom, poor use of the Bible, and enough truth to give the entire product credibility with Christians. The reason Warren has been able to package this product and sell it to a vast array of churches is that they long for the promised results. Very few local pastors have the brilliance, motivation, and organizational abilities of Rick Warren. Very few could consistently create a religious product that seemed biblical and yet was popular with the unregenerate. Warren has done all the work for them, packaged it, and offered a means for them to share his success. Thousands are jumping on board. The result is that millions of people who could be hearing the authoritative Word of God from their churches are instead getting the non-authoritative, fallible, and often false words of a man. They should not be fooled by this process. Rick Warren does not speak for God UNLESS he is accurately interpreting, explaining, and applying the Bible. He has the ability to do so, but when he has the biggest audiences, he too often chooses not to.

In the next chapter we will examine the practice of holding true beliefs privately but proclaiming something else publicly. We will see that when one of Christ's own apostles tried to follow this practice, he was publicly rebuked by the apostle Paul.

The Problem with Private Confession

"Everyone therefore who shall confess Me before men, I will also confess him before My Father who is in Heaven" (Matthew 10:32).

Rick Warren believes the orthodox truths of the Christian faith. He has documents that say so. Insiders at Saddleback Church say that they know Warren is orthodox. However, when I read *The Purpose Driven Life* I saw many teachings that are very different from historical orthodoxy. How can this be?

My earliest experience in church life made clear to me that a church could have one set of beliefs on official documents, but proclaim another message from the pulpit. My experience sheds light on why one cannot judge orthodoxy by official documents. Here is the story.

Growing up in Iowa in the 1950s and early 1960s, I was taken to church every Sunday without fail. The church was of a mainline Protestant denomination that had embraced liberalism many decades before when the modernist movement of the early 20th century had swept through the denomination. As I sat in church, week after week, I tried to understand what it was I was supposed to believe and do. The pews faced a platform that had two pulpits, one on the left from our perspective and the other on the right. At the appointed place in the liturgy, the pastor would go over to the pulpit on the left and open a huge, gold-leafed Bible and read a passage from it. When it came time for the sermon, he would go to the pulpit on the right and preach on various issues of human affairs, rarely from the Bible but often from *Readers Digest* or from another magazine. As far as I could understand the teaching of the church, the point was that we were to go out and be good people, following the example of the Good Samaritan. To their credit, the adults I knew in that little country church did live good lives and were mostly exemplary citizens. Many were strongly committed Christians.

When I turned 12, I was required to go through membership training classes. This happened for me during Spring 1963. I hated those classes. They happened on Saturdays, during the school year! I cannot remember what we learned in them, but I vaguely recollect that it was more material about the need to be a good person. I do remember, however, one of the last classes before we were to go before the congregation on a Sunday morning to swear that we believed certain things to join the church. During our instruction we were grilled on what the questions would be and what our answers were to be. These questions had to do with historical, Christian orthodoxy. We had to say that we believed in the Person and work of Christ. I dutifully obeyed and was received into membership.

All was well for a couple of years until I started thinking more seriously about what I believed. I was studying science and learning the theory of evolution. I had serious doubts about God's existence. I would pray on occasion and ask God to forgive all my sins, just in case there was a God and something might happen to me. I kept my doubts to myself for those years. In Summer 1967 I went to a week of summer church camp that was sponsored by our denomination and signed up for a class that was to discuss the Bible. Being away from my home church I felt safe to ask questions. At the end of one of the sessions I asked to speak with the pastor who was teaching the class. I confided in him about my doubts. His answer shocked me. He asked, "You don't think you have to believe the stories in the Bible really happened do you?" I responded, "I thought I was supposed to, and I feel guilty about my doubts." He then reassured me that there was no Adam and Eve, no Noah, no Jonah, and that Jesus did not do miracles nor was He raised from the dead. I asked, "Then why are those stories in the Bible"? He answered, "They are there to inspire us to be better people."

I felt like I was a naïve fool. I felt like I was 16 years old and had just found out there was no Santa Claus. I had spent a couple of years feeling guilty for doubting things that never actually happened. I really did not buy the idea that I had to listen to mythological stories to be a better person. I resolved that as soon as I could get away from the church permanently, without disgracing my parents (for whom I had and always have the highest respect and admiration), I would. I ended up on the golf course on Sunday mornings playing "skins" with my Catholic friends who went to sinner's mass on Saturday night.

Later, after I was converted through the gospel in 1971, I thought back on my experience with theological liberalism. It seemed so very wrong to me that I had to swear to believe historical Christian doctrine to join the church, only to find out that some ordained ministers of the church did not believe these doctrines. I remember that we cited the Apostles' Creed in our liturgy, which stated our belief in the Person and work of Christ. Yet I was later told that this faith was based on myth and not fact. I learned that the best indicator of what is believed in a given church is what is preached from the pulpit week by week, not what is found in the statement of faith. Official documents are rarely changed, even when many no longer believe what is in those documents.

True Christian Confession Must Be Consistent and Public

Today we encounter a problem that in some ways is the mirror image of the problem I encountered in the liberal church. Then, the liberal church publicly confessed orthodoxy (through the recitation of creeds in the liturgy) but privately denied it. Today, popular preachers like Rick Warren privately hold orthodox doctrine, but when put into the public spotlight, they do not fully confess what they privately believe. I think that the cause in both cases is found in the culture. In rural Iowa in the 1950s, the culture supported Christian ideas. The pastor who privately did not believe was willing to publicly confess by reciting the creeds because the culture demanded it. Today, things are much different. The culture punishes public confession (witness the removal of the 10 Commandments and prayer) but allows private confession. So now we have much pressure to keep quiet in public and push our confession into the private sphere.

Let me illustrate how Rick Warren approaches this. The Web site for Saddleback Church contains this line in their statement of faith: "Through His Holy Spirit, God lives in and through us now."[1] The statement does not qualify who "us" is, so the casual enquirer would take that as meaning all people (which would be what they like to hear). The public statement sounds universalistic. However, if one digs deeper by clicking a link on the site, he finds out that this statement is only true for Christians.

Another example of this is what Warren has to say to his *Ladies Home Journal* readers. In the March 2005 issue Warren offers five truths that will supposedly boost a person's self-esteem. The first of these truths is that we should accept ourselves because "God accepts us unconditionally."[2] This again implies universalism. If there are no conditions for God's acceptance, then all people are accepted whether or not they believe the gospel. Why should anyone repent and believe the gospel if they are already accepted by God without doing so? The next point is that we need to love ourselves; but the story he tells to illustrate this truth is not about loving one's self at all, but about his wife learning more about God's love for her. That is not the same as loving self. The next point is, "Be true to yourself." This is not a biblical idea at all, but is popular worldly wisdom. We do not need to "get to know ourselves" as Warren teaches; we need to get to know God. Self is a sinful rebel who refuses to submit to God. Warren never tells his *Ladies Home Journal* readers about the sin nature.

The next point is "Forgive yourself." This is false teaching, pure and simple. It leads people away from facing their true need, which is God's forgiveness. It implies that self is a valid court of judgment, and that self can appeal to self for forgiveness. What we really need to know is the terms whereby God is willing to forgive us. He is the Judge—we are not. Warren is leading his readers astray. The last point in the article is the worst of all: "Believe in yourself." Here is how he concludes: "It's your choice. You can believe in what others say about you or you can believe in yourself as does God, who says that you are truly acceptable, lovable, valuable, and capable."[3]

Think of the horrible role reversal Warren proposes. The truth is that as sinners we already trust self, which is precisely why we need to repent and come to God on His terms. Warren has God believing in the sinner and the sinner forgiving self, as if the self were the ultimate judge. The truth is we need to believe in God and find His forgiveness through the blood of Christ.

What is confusing is that Rick Warren is not a universalist; he teaches that there is a literal Heaven and Hell. What he says in *Ladies Home Journal* is at odds with what he teaches elsewhere. Warren believes that we must have a relationship with God through turning to Christ to be saved. But his *Ladies Home Journal* readers, most of whom are not Christian, get the impression that everything is fine as it is. According to Warren, God believes in them, God accepts them, and they just need to bolster their self-esteem using Warren's methods. If they take what he writes seriously, they have no reason to think they need the gospel.

Rick Warren, in my opinion, presents a disjunction between what he confesses privately to evangelical Christians and what he confesses publicly to a worldly audience. Since I published an article critical of Warren a couple of years ago I have received correspondence from several people who are upset with me. Some have said that if I would go to Saddleback Church and see what Warren really believes, I would know that he is an orthodox Christian. Let us accept for the sake of discussion that this is true. We still have a problem. The problem is that the people who hear Rick Warren on secular news programs, who read him in *Ladies Home Journal*, and who read his most popular book get one message; those who are "insiders" at Saddleback get another message. This is unacceptable. Let me show you why.

Paul Publicly Rebukes Peter

In Galatians 2, Paul recounts an incident where he publicly corrected Peter:

> But when Cephas came to Antioch, I opposed him to his face, because he stood condemned. For prior to the coming of certain men from James, he used to eat with the Gentiles; but when they came, he began to withdraw and hold himself aloof, fearing the party of the circumcision. And the rest of the Jews joined him in hypocrisy, with the result that even Barnabas was carried away by their hypocrisy. But when I saw that they were not straightforward about the truth of the gospel, I said to Cephas in the presence of all, "If you, being a Jew, live like the Gentiles and not like the Jews, how is it that you compel the Gentiles to live like Jews"? (Galatians 2:11-14).

Paul publicly rebuked Peter for publicly denying in action what Paul knew Peter privately believed. Paul called Peter's actions, "[being] *not straightforward about the truth of the gospel.*" Peter's actions implied that Gentile Christians were still "unclean" unless they submitted to Jewish food laws. This is a denial of what was decided at the Jerusalem council in Acts 15. They had determined there not to require that the Gentiles follow the Law of Moses.

The irony is that Peter himself was the spokesman who convinced the church that this was right:

> And after there had been much debate, Peter stood up and said to them, 'Brethren, you know that in the early days God made a choice among you, that by my mouth the Gentiles should hear the word of the gospel and believe. And God, who knows the heart, bore witness to them, giving them the Holy Spirit, just as He also did to

us; and He made no distinction between us and them, cleansing their hearts by faith. Now therefore why do you put God to the test by placing upon the neck of the disciples a yoke which neither our fathers nor we have been able to bear? But we believe that we are saved through the grace of the Lord Jesus, in the same way as they also are' (Acts 15:7-11).

Paul knew that he and Peter believed the same thing; they had both agreed to the decision of the council. There was no reason to go to Peter privately to correct his belief. Paul immediately dealt with the issue publicly, *"in the presence of all."* Peter's public practice negated his private confession. Being "straightforward about the gospel" means that what we preach and practice in public must be the same as the beliefs we hold privately. The New Testament calls any disjuncture between the two "hypocrisy."

This is not the first time Peter faced the issue of public confession. When he was with Jesus and the band of disciples, he confessed, *"Thou art the Christ, the Son of the living God"* (Matthew 16:16b). But before a servant-girl he later said, *"I do not know the man"* (Matthew 26:72b). Privately, Peter still believed in Christ (he wept bitterly when he realized he had denied the Lord three times), but publicly he said something different. In both of these incidents Peter was restored and became a great man of God who preached Christ until he was martyred. But the lesson is that true Christian confession requires that our private beliefs and public confession match. The message of the gospel must be preached and lived in a straightforward manner, or we are denying what we claim to believe.

Paul was a model of consistency in that way. Whether he was before Jews in synagogues, philosophers in Athens, the Praetorian Guard in Rome, or before kings in a courtroom, Paul confessed Christ and the resurrection. There was only one gospel message and everyone heard it. Concerning his imprisonment in Rome for the gospel, Paul rejoiced because those who saw him confessing the gospel before hostile Rome were emboldened:

Now I want you to know, brethren, that my circumstances have turned out for the greater progress of the gospel, so that my imprisonment in the cause of Christ has become well known throughout the whole praetorian guard and to everyone else, and that most of the brethren, trusting in the Lord because of my imprisonment, have far more courage to speak the Word of God without fear (Philippians 1:12-14).

Not only did Paul consistently confess his faith in the gospel publicly, but he refused to tamper with the message to make it appealing to the unregenerate mind. He was adamant about the need for clear, consistent, public proclamation of the gospel:

But we have renounced the things hidden because of shame, not walking in craftiness or adulterating the word of God, but by the manifestation of truth commending ourselves to every man's conscience in the sight of God. And even if our gospel is veiled, it is veiled to those who are perishing, in whose case the god of this world has blinded the minds of the unbelieving, that they might not see the light of the gospel of the glory of Christ, who is the image of God. For we do not preach ourselves but Christ Jesus as Lord, and ourselves as your bond-servants for Jesus' sake (2 Corinthians 4:2-5).

The temptation for "craftiness" is to hide certain essential features of the message, so as to get people to accept us and our message. Paul renounced any such practice. For Paul, the veiling of the gospel was never because of failure to proclaim it, but because of spiritual blindness in the hearers. The answer to this is faithful proclamation and nothing more. God will supernaturally turn on the light in the hearts and minds of those who will be saved.

Rick Warren's entire program portrays the opposite of Paul's practice. The key aspects of the gospel that the world finds offensive are smoothed over and hidden until the audience is given a chance to warm up to Warren's message. He speaks their language as much as possible, then later mixes in some Christian truths. His close friends are adamant (because they know Warren intimately) that he has fully orthodox beliefs. They are probably right. But what they miss is that what is publicly proclaimed is the biblical test for discernment, not what is privately believed but not confessed.

Testing the Spirits

The Bible makes confessing, or the lack thereof, the objective test for the source of a teaching. Conversely, we might "feel" that something or someone is from God because they seem nice or we get a good impression, but this is not the biblical criteria. The following passage shows how we are to discern teachings that claim to be from God:

> Beloved, do not believe every spirit, but test the spirits to see whether they are from God; because many false prophets have gone out into the world. By this you know the Spirit of God: every spirit that confesses that Jesus Christ has come in the flesh is from God; and every spirit that does not confess Jesus is not from God; and this is the spirit of the antichrist, of which you have heard that it is coming, and now it is already in the world (1 John 4:1-3).

This test concerns the spiritual source behind the teaching of a person who claims to speak for God ("*false prophets have gone out into the world*"). Those who are from God confess the Person and work of Jesus Christ. The phrase "that Jesus Christ has come in the flesh" means that one proclaims all the implications of the incarnation. This does not mean merely to utter this phrase. It means to publicly proclaim that Jesus Christ pre-existed as God and with God (John 1:1). "Came in the flesh" implies pre-existence. Also included in this is the concept that Jesus lived a sinless life as a man in a real, human body. Jesus died in the flesh on the cross, shedding real blood for our sins, and that Jesus was raised in the flesh from the dead on the third day. All of this is included in the biblical doctrine of the incarnation. Those who speak from the Spirit of

God will confess this publicly whenever they get a chance.

Conversely, those who do not confess publicly show themselves to be not from God. Notice that the passage says "does not confess" rather than "deny." Keeping silent about the person and work of Christ, when the situation demands public confession is considered tantamount to denial in the New Testament. We are commanded to "discern" using this test and accept its conclusion. This is not optional. Those who fail to confess are to be considered by the church and its members as not speaking for God. If Christians applied this simple test, many of the popular preachers in America today would go out of business for lack of support.

Further evidence that failure to confess is considered denial is found in Matthew 26. Jesus predicted that Peter would deny Him three times: *"Jesus said to him, 'Truly I say to you that this very night, before a cock crows, you shall deny Me three times'"* (Matthew 26:34). However, the first incident was more of an evasion: *"Now Peter was sitting outside in the courtyard, and a certain servant-girl came to him and said, 'You too were with Jesus the Galilean.' But he denied it before them all, saying, 'I do not know what you are talking about'"* (Matthew 26:69, 70). The Bible calls evading a question that calls for confession of Christ, "denial."

Many do not want to make this confession because such statements make it impossible for them to be popular with the world. Those motivated by the Spirit of God will be like Christ and His apostles. They will confess the person and work of Christ publicly and forthrightly and be more than willing to suffer ridicule and scorn as the result. John discusses this in the next part of 1 John 4:

> *You are from God, little children, and have overcome them; because greater is He Who is in you than he who is in the world. They are from the world; therefore they speak as from the world, and the world listens to them. We are from God; he who knows God listens to us; he who is not from God does not listen to us. By this we know the spirit of truth and the spirit of error* (1 John 4:4-6).

The world, whether pagans or religious consumers, hates the message of the crucified Jewish Messiah. It offends their religious sensibilities. The world listens to those who fail to confess Christ but will not listen to those who do. Any preacher who lusts for popularity is going to be severely tempted to fail to confess. Why? Because of what Jesus said: *"Enter by the narrow gate; for the gate is wide, and the way is broad that leads to destruction, and many are those who enter by it. For the gate is small, and the way is narrow that leads to life, and few are those who find it"* (Matthew 7:13, 14). Preaching what the world hates, even knowing that God will use it to save those who will enter through the narrow gate, does not appeal to those who want to maximize the size of their audience. John says that the world does not listen to us, but the world has masses of people entering the wide gate—they have the largest audience. We could take the option to enhance church growth by widening the narrow gate through failure to confess—but that is an unacceptable option.

Partial Confession to Please Men

Because of the huge disparity of the size of the potential audience, the temptation to modify the Christian confession to make it more appealing is very great. The true confession of the person and work of Christ will never fit the agenda of a person who wants popularity with the masses. In much of church history the true confession has resulted in persecution, and even martyrdom. For this reason, it serves as a test of spirits. Those wrongly motivated will not confess consistently and publicly; those motivated by the Holy Spirit will confess.

Examples of what I mean can be seen in the differences between Rick Warren's responses and John MacArthur's when interviewed on "Larry King Live." When chatting with a panel of religious people of diverse backgrounds, (including Deepak Chopra) John MacArthur said this:

Back to the question about God—again, I hear all these responses, but we have to go back to some authority outside of ourselves. I mean, I can't define God for the universe from starting with me. God in the Scripture is the Creator and Sustainer of the universe, He's the sovereign over everything...who was incarnated in Jesus Christ, came down and died on a cross to provide atonement, so that the sins of those who repent were paid for in full, and therefore heaven was open to them.[4]

On another occasion Larry King interviewed Rick Warren about his best selling book. Warren said this:

KING: Does that mean that a Jew, a Muslim, an agnostic, an atheist could benefit from this book?

WARREN: If that's the question, sure. Anybody can benefit from it. In fact, the other day, I heard about a story of a lady who was at a little league, she was Jewish and the lady sitting next to her was Muslim. The Jewish lady was reading *The Purpose Driven Life*, and the other lady next to her said, what are you reading? She said, I'm reading *The Purpose Driven Life*. She said, I'd like to read it, too. She said, well, take mine, I'll get another copy. And I thought, OK, here's a Christian pastor writing a book that a Jewish lady is passing on to a Muslim lady. OK.[5]

This story tells us what we already know: Warren has crafted a version of Christianity that is not offensive to non-Christians. Warren later gets closer to explaining his beliefs:

WARREN: Nobody's going to make it on their own effort. It's kind of like — a lot of people think God grades on a curve. That if, you know, your good things on this side, and your bad things— well, you know, you kind of—but the truth is, God is perfect. And if you've got the *Titanic* and you got a criminal and you've got Mother Teresa, they're both going to sink with it, because the *Titanic's* sinking. And the human predicament is nobody's perfect. Not me, not you, not the Pope. So God sent a Savior to be perfect for us. I tell a story of a guy who took his son and three kids to a carnival for his birthday. And at every carnival ride, he'd give his son a ticket, and he'd give his three friends a ticket. And he'd go to the next ride, give his son a ticket, give his three friends a ticket. On about the fourth little ride, he looks down and he sees a fourth hand, a little kid out there he's never seen before. He said, "Who are you?" And the guy goes, "I'm your son's new friend." And he said, "This kid said that if I was his friend, his dad would give me a ticket."

This story hardly does justice to the gospel. But it is appealing to people. The Bible says: *"You are My friends, if you do what I command you"* (John 15:14). Warren is then asked a question about the religious right, from whom he distances himself. He goes back to what he sees as more important:

WARREN: You know, everybody's life is driven by something. That's why I called this book "The Purpose Driven Life." Some people are driven by fear. You know people like this. They are driven by the opinions of others. They live for the expectations of their parent, or husband, or boyfriend, or something like that. Some people are driven by worry. They're driven by guilt. They're driven by shame. Some people are driven by loneliness. And I don't think God wants any of our lives to be driven by these things. I think the bottom line is that we were put on Earth for a purpose. Part of that purpose is to know God, and then part of that purpose is to help other people.[6]

This is a deficient and obscured gospel. The person and work of Christ is not clearly explained. Later, in explaining a new book he is writing, Warren says this:

WARREN: I am going to write another book. I'm not going to write it this year. It's actually going to be—well, this book is on what on Earth are we here for? This next book is going to be on asking—dealing with the question, what are you doing with what you've been given? Because I believe that we all fundamentally—everything we have is a gift. I believe, because I believe in God, I believe that everything I have—my life is a gift.

KING: It's very Eastern philosophy.

WARREN: It's all a gift. And so we're stewards. We're stewards. And by the way, there's truth in every religion. Christians believe that there's truth in every religion. But we just believe that there's one Savior. We believe we can learn truth—I've learned a lot of truth from different religions. Because they all have a portion of the truth. I just believe there is one Savior, Jesus Christ.[7]

Notice how he wants to maintain both an openness to other religions so as not to be offensive, but still believe only in Christ. He has not yet given a clear confession of the Person and work of Christ. He doesn't reject King's assessment that his ideas are Eastern nor does he help King understand the many differences.

Later, under specific questioning he gets closer:

CALLER: Yes, I would like to ask the reverend if he believes that non-Christians can get into Heaven and be with God when they die.

WARREN: My question would be this, who gets to make the rules? Does God have a right to decide who gets into his place? And I would say, my opinion really doesn't matter. I would say this, and I would say this humbly. Jesus said this – He said, I am the way and the truth and the life. And nobody comes to the father except through me. Now, you know what, that's a pretty radical statement when you think about it.

KING: So, what you're saying the Jew is not going to heaven?

WARREN: I'm saying nobody's going to Heaven, except people who go to Heaven God's way. And I don't get to make the rules. I don't go to heaven, you don't go to Heaven.[8]

This is true, but in some ways evasive. However, Warren does talk about the cross:

WARREN: Why would anybody reject the love of Jesus? He's done everything possible. You saw the Mel Gibson movie. Jesus stretches out his hands out on the cross, I love you this much. It's like, I'm doing everything possible. I'm doing everything possible so that you don't have to go to hell. So that you don't have to depend on your own efforts.

Because it is my grace. The message of the evangelical, the message of the Bible is not judgment. The message is grace. Is that, I don't deserve it, but I get to go if I trust him.[9]

This is the same obscuring of the cross that is found in his book. The message of the Bible **is** about judgment—judgment that shows the need for grace and forgiveness. God has decreed the death penalty, an eternal one at that, for sinners. The cross showed God's wrath against sin being poured out on His own Son, whose blood averts God's wrath for those who repent and believe. The Holy Spirit was sent to convict the world about sin, righteousness and judgment (John 16:8). If we believe, as evangelicals, in the work of the Holy Spirit, we have to have a message about judgment.

Rick Warren is not "straightforward about the truth of the gospel" in certain settings, though he is an evangelical. He is doing what Peter did that Paul rebuked him for in Galatians 2. Peter wanted approval, so he was not straightforward about the truth of the gospel. That is what Warren is doing. He apparently wants broad-based approval for his message (even among followers of other religions) so he carefully crafts his message so that it is not as offensive as it would be in its native form. In Peter's case there was no doubt about his belief in the truth of the gospel, but Paul rebuked Peter for obscuring what he knew to be true. We know from this that it is not acceptable to obscure the truth in order to gain approval, even if we still firmly believe the truth.

Proponents of the seeker movement often cite Paul to justify their practice: *"To the weak I became weak, that I might win the weak; I have become all things to all men, that I may by all means save some"* (1 Corinthians 9:22). Comparing this passage to the incident described in Galatians 2, we see that Paul did not mean to condone compromise of a clear gospel confession. Rather, he wanted to have every opportunity to present a clear confession of the gospel and not let any non-essential cultural issue keep him from that opportunity.

The temptation to be less than bold and forthright about the gospel faces every one of us. John tells of people who failed to confess: *"Nevertheless many even of the rulers believed in Him, but because of the Pharisees they were not confessing Him, lest they should be put out of the synagogue; for they loved the approval of men rather than the approval of God"* (John 12:42, 43). Knowing how great the temptation is to mute or obscure the message, Paul asked for prayer: *"...and pray on my behalf, that utterance may be given to me in the opening of my mouth, to make known with boldness the mystery of the gospel, for which I am an ambassador in chains; that in proclaiming it I may speak boldly, as I ought to speak"* (Ephesians 6:19, 20). It is so hard to be bold when we know that the bolder we are, the more the world will hate us. Paul needed prayer, so do all who know Christ, including me.

File Cabinet Orthodoxy

Some friends of mine moved to a different city a few years ago. When they got there they began looking for a church within a reasonable distance. They sought out and obtained statements of faith from dozens of churches from many denominations. They told me that the surprising thing was that the statements were nearly identical. Based on those statements, they would have concluded that the churches in the area were all preaching the same message. But the reality was quite different. There were seeker churches that were mostly entertainment and had little or no message. There were liturgical churches. There were wild and raucous churches. There were churches with very strange doctrinal quirks. After visiting many of these churches, they determined that the statement of faith usually has little relationship to what is preached from the pulpit.

My point is that what is preached from the pulpit is the true confession of a church, not what the church has on file, in case someone might ask. In writing articles correcting serious doctrinal aberrations, I have received the response, "If you asked the person you are writing about, they would have sent you their doctrinal statement which is very orthodox." My response has often been, "The liberal church I grew up in had an orthodox statement of faith, but they failed to preach the gospel." When the modernists took over most of the mainline denominations 100 years ago, those denominations did not reject their historical creeds and confessions. They just quit preaching them from the pulpit.

For example, one person I know visited relatives on Easter and went to church with them. The sermon declared that Easter stands for renewed hope, just like the grass turns green every spring—the cycles of nature. This was a church of a major denomination. There is not a single Protestant denomination that has an official statement of faith that says, "Resurrection means the cycles of nature." This shows the common disconnect between official documents and beliefs that are held seriously enough to proclaim publicly.

Polls have shown that many Protestant ministers do not believe in the resurrection of Christ. One poll came back with the following percentages of ministers **not** believing in the literal, bodily resurrection of Christ: American Lutherans: 13%; Presbyterians: 30%; American Baptist: 33%; Episcopalians: 35%; Methodists: 51%.[10] In probably all of these cases, the ministers in question had to agree to the official doctrines of the denomination to be ordained. Obviously they were not sincere when they signed their ordination papers. What this means is that the doctrinal statements that churches have on file mean very little if the doctrines contained therein are never preached from the pulpit.

True orthodoxy is confessed publicly by those who truly believe and cherish the faith once for all delivered to the saints (Jude 3). Conversely, error that is proclaimed publicly is not sanctified by a private confession found on an official denominational document. If truth is important, it is important enough to be publicly proclaimed and defended. So to those who say to me, "you must go privately to people first and find out what they believe before you publicly disagree with them," I say, "I already know what they believe; they have published it in their books." It will not do to claim that one's public profession is not what he or she truly believes.

In the case of Rick Warren, we know what he believes; he has published his beliefs in a book and sold it to over 25 million people. One need not go on a pilgrimage to Saddleback Church to find out. What is published is an unholy mixture of human wisdom, bad Bible translations, misinterpreted and misapplied Scripture, approving citations of New Agers, mystics, an eroticist, a socialist, etc., combined with some of the truths of the gospel. This mixture purports to reveal God's purposes. But what it does is confuse the clear statements of God's purposes found in the Bible. I grant that privately Rick Warren holds valid, evangelical beliefs. However, the clear evidence is that his public teaching is different from his private beliefs. This was true of Peter until Paul corrected him. Rick Warren could yet turn away from his practice of obscuring his confession and become a bold preacher of the gospel.

The reason for the disjuncture between Rick Warren's public teachings and private confessions is likely found in his desire to create a version of Christianity that is acceptable to his target audience. Since he believes that people must be "wooed" into the kingdom of God by finding the key to attracting them, he has assured that clear, straightforward proclamation of the person and work of Christ cannot be the public message. The preaching of the gospel does not woo the world; it converts the elect.

Nevertheless, Warren's religious product, *The Purpose Driven Life*, has been produced and sold to millions. Its popularity is unabated several years after publication. There is something else important happening: With counsel from one of the world's top management gurus, Peter Drucker, Warren has given his Purpose Driven movement a brand identity that can be franchised and reproduced around the world. In the next chapter we will describe how the Purpose Driven franchise works.

The Purpose Driven Brand

The key idea behind the Purpose Driven church model is that the concerns and felt needs of unbelievers should determine the message and practice of the church. The church that is able to devise a mission statement and strategy that will result in a church that appeals to the target audience (the unchurched of a given community), and successfully markets the product (as epitomized by *The Purpose Driven Life*) to that audience, and converts many people from being unchurched to being active supporting members (people who sign a covenant to support the church and help market its product to others) is deemed "healthy" according to the protocol of the Purpose Driven movement.

Earlier we discussed the key problem that has faced the Church Growth movement since Robert Schuller became its practical founder in the 1960s and 1970s (i.e., the amount of talent, resources, and savvy required for a local pastor to successfully duplicate this model of "doing church"). Most pastors are starting with everything "wrong." Whether their churches are old line denominations or part of the evangelical movement of the 20th century, most were designed to care for the Lord's flock, not to appeal to the sensibilities of the unregenerate.

To convert a church from what it was to the new model takes a different set of skills than were required of pastors of traditional churches. What is found in society as well as in the business world is that some people are more talented than others in management skills, marketing, and finance. Since these are not skills normally associated with pastors, it is not surprising that many lack them.

Churches that exist as gathering places for the Lord's redeemed have certain characteristics. All Protestant churches traditionally were centered about the preaching of the Word. Those who bought into theological liberalism left this pattern, but evangelical churches were founded to be even more Bible-centered. Churches also emphasized the "means of grace" that include communion, baptism, and prayer besides the preaching of the Word. The rest of the typical church program was focused on training the children of believers in Christianity and supporting local and worldwide evangelism through missions. And sometimes churches reach out to the local community in other ways such as supporting food shelves and other programs to help needy people. No one expected that such churches would be particularly attractive to non-Christians because the church by definition was a gathering of the redeemed.

Robert Schuller's Crystal Cathedral was the first massively popular church to change this understanding of ministry. One of Schuller's oft quoted sayings is that his church is the last hope for people who have given up on religion—Schuller's church attracts a million visitors annually.[1] Anyone who has watched the "Hour of Power" broadcast understands that a local pastor could hardly duplicate what Schuller does. A few have learned from Schuller and been extremely successful themselves. Bill Hybels and Rick Warren come to mind. Both of them have huge successful churches with multi-million dollar programs. Both seek to help other local pastors duplicate their success. Nevertheless, the key hurdle to overcome if their church concept is to be replicated is the amount of talent and financial resources it takes to pull off the endeavor (ignoring for the moment the fact that the whole concept of changing the church to be attractive to the unregenerate is unbiblical). People with the talents of Schuller, Hybels and Warren are rare, whether in the secular world or in churches.

Rick Warren resolves this problem by taking a process that has worked for decades in the business world and applying it to Christianity. He has created a system where an ambitious person with ordinary talents can replicate Warren's process and get similar results. Warren has packaged Schuller's idea of a version of Christianity that appeals to unbelievers into a marketable product that can be purchased by pastors and churches. In so doing he has created a recognizable brand identity that the public will associate with something desirable. That brand is Purpose Driven. The massive popularity of *The Purpose Driven Life* has made the brand identifiable and desirable to the general public's religious consumers.

"Brand," by the way, is Warren's term, not mine. The mission statement from the Purpose Driven website specifically mentions the term "brand." It says, "To build health and balance within a local church by providing training, transferable products, and learning communities that leverage and extend the PD paradigm and brand to church leaders around the world."[2] The mission statement is a key component of being Purpose Driven. *The Purpose Driven Church* contains an extended section that explains the importance of a mission statement and how to compose one. Since Warren is so adamant about having a mission statement that clearly defines one's purpose, the mission statement above certainly defines Rick Warren's purpose in terms and concepts common to business management professionals. In this chapter, I will unpack this statement and show how Warren implements this vision in a way that helps ambitious local pastors with limited talent tap into Rick Warren's massive success.

Outcome Based Religion

The key to a successful mission statement is that its goals must be measurable, so the statement must be stated in terms of results. Using his local church as a model, Warren states, "It is stated *in terms of results* rather than in terms of activity."[3] Warren says of a mission statement, "Make it measurable. Otherwise your purpose statement is just a public relations piece."[4] From these comments we can assume that the Purpose Driven mission statement fits Warren's requirements for such statements and describes the outcomes he is looking for in specific, measurable terms.

These outcomes include providing training and transferable products, the existence of "learning communities," and the Purpose Driven brand identity being leveraged around the world to church leaders. This is designed to build "health and balance" in the local church. Let us see how each of these is measurable.

The training aspect is measured by Warren continually; he publishes the results. The Purpose Driven Web site states, "Over 300,000 church leaders in 22 languages have been directly trained, and there are now Purpose Driven congregations in every country of the world."[5] The Purpose Driven movement is constantly producing materials and holding seminars to train church leaders in Purpose Driven principles. How many attend, purchase Warren's curriculum, and implement his principles is measurable.

The "transferable products" include the items sold on the Purpose Driven Web site which lists 23 pages of products, many of which are DVDs or printed curriculums for establishing Purpose Driven small groups in your church. The items typically say, "Everything you need to start a new Purpose Driven® small group (or even ministry) in your home, class or church."[6] The products are packaged in bulk so that every member of a group can have one. They all promote the principles of the Purpose Driven approach and contain the brand identity. In addition, "transferable products" goes beyond the physical merchandise and includes the concepts, programs and campaigns themselves, measurable in the numbers of churches and groups embracing them. The Purpose Driven paradigm itself is a transferable product measured by how many new consumers adopt it as their own.

"Learning communities" are also measurable. Ideally, an entire church becomes a Purpose Driven learning community and consists of sub-learning communities as it implements Purpose Driven principles in every aspect of its ministry. The numbers of these communities and their health is measurable by Purpose

Driven standards. Rick Warren has established a "Church Health Award" to honor those who most ideally implement the principles of the Purpose Driven philosophy of ministry. I will comment on that in the next chapter.

Leveraging and extending the Purpose Driven paradigm is measurable in the number of churches who have a "paradigm shift." This means adopting an entirely different model of reality, or in this case a system of beliefs about what a church is and what it does. The old "paradigm" is the view that the church is a gathering of the redeemed, brought together by a work of God's grace. As we saw in Chapter 1, the Purpose Driven church is "driven" by the felt needs of unbelievers, or more appropriately in marketing terms, "religious consumers." The new "paradigm" church is one that gathers the maximum numbers of religious consumers and meets their felt needs, thereby maximizing customer satisfaction. The number of churches adopting the Purpose Driven paradigm is measurable.

Leveraging the Purpose Driven brand is also very much measurable in brand recognition—how many people are familiar with and know the brand's image. A brand is an identity that people associate in their minds with something that hopefully stands for quality and customer satisfaction. Zenith electronics showed the idea of brand value when they coined the slogan, "The Quality Goes In Before the Name Goes On." What association people have with a brand name is measurable. Brand recognition and image among targeted consumers ultimately give the brand its value. Corporate marketing executives seek this information to measure the success of their advertising campaigns and their influence on the consumer. Purpose Driven has recently achieved not only a highly visible brand identity, but one that is highly positive.

The primary target audience of the Purpose Driven paradigm and brand has been "church leaders." The reason for this is seen in the use of the term "leveraging." A lever is a tool that gives one an advantage whereby the effects of the force being applied are multiplied. When used in a business marketing context, leveraging is multiplying the effects of one's efforts or resources. Here is a definition of this usage: "As a frequently used business or marketing term, leverage is any strategic or tactical advantage, and as a verb, means to exploit such an advantage, just as the use of a physical lever gives one an advantage in the physical sense."[7] The idea is this: If you only have 10 pounds of thrust, you find a tool that multiplies it into 100 pounds of impact.

An example of how this works can be seen in an e-mail I received from one of my readers: "I have been attending [church name withheld] in PA for a while. The church bought every member (over 10,000 members) the book *The Purpose Driven Life*. This is what they now study, not the Bible." By selling one pastor on it, he ended up selling 10,000 books to one church. Now that is the ultimate in "leveraging!" For every one pastor who buys into the Purpose Driven paradigm and brand, dozens, hundreds, or thousands of others (depending on the size of the church) become customers without ever formally deciding for themselves on the benefits of the product. This is partly how Rick Warren's book became a best seller so quickly.

We have seen that everything in the Purpose Driven mission statement is designed to be measurable vis-à-vis an outcome that Rick Warren has chosen on purpose. The desired outcome is the multiplication of "healthy and balanced" Purpose Driven churches around the world. The movement and its leaders are the change agents who are redefining the church.

Achieving Health and Balance

The ultimate goal (outcome), according to the Purpose Driven mission statement, is to build "health and balance" in the local church. Rick Warren often emphasizes this, stating that balancing the "five purposes" of the church will make it so healthy that it cannot help but grow. Health, according to Rick Warren, will cause growth numerically in members and in income. He claims 20% more members and 20% more money are typical for those who participate in a Purpose Driven campaign. Using the analogy of living organisms such as the human body, Warren states: "Since the church is a living organism, it's natural for it to grow if it's healthy. . . . If a church is not growing, it is dying."[8] Since this is a key concept in the Purpose Driven movement, we need to understand what Rick Warren means by "health and balance."

On the surface, Warren's words and categories describing the healthy, balanced church seem so biblical that most evangelicals would never question it. The five purposes that are to be balanced are fellowship, discipleship, worship, ministry, and evangelism.[9] He claims that if these purposes are balanced that a healthy, growing church is a certain outcome. The problem is that he has his own Purpose Driven version of every one of these purposes that is significantly different from what the Bible means by these terms (the process of redefinition covers nearly every aspect of the church and her message). Being in a *Purpose Driven Life* study group is not fellowship as defined biblically. Having entertaining music is not worship. Having a P.E.A.C.E. program to solve global problems is not evangelism. Finally, committing one's time and money to further the Purpose Driven paradigm is not ministry (at least as any of these categories are defined biblically). Another example is the S.H.A.P.E. program. This is a huge part of Warren's program, and it amounts to studying one's self to find out one's spiritual gifts, heart, abilities, personality, and experiences.[10] Studying self, using such tools as the Myers Briggs indicator (part of the "P" in Warren's program), has nothing to do with discipleship or any of the other five purposes. But these are what the five purposes mean for those in Warren's program, and the outcomes that are measurable are judged according to Warren's version of these purposes, not by biblical standards.

The outcome of "health and balance" therefore is a code for replicating Warren's Purpose Driven model of church successfully. Pastors who are being sold the program need to look more carefully at what they are buying. This is not a program to expand evangelism, missions, worship, fellowship or discipleship as defined biblically; it is a program to expand the Purpose Driven brand and paradigm. It is designed to sell Rick Warren's version of these purposes to religious consumers (i.e., the unchurched), through first selling them to church leaders to create leverage.

Truncating the Work of the Church Through a Mission Statement

Warren teaches church leaders that they need a clear focused purpose that can be sold to the leadership and ultimately the membership of a local church. He writes:

> If you want to build a healthy, strong, and growing church you *must* spend time laying a solid foundation. This is done by clarifying in the minds of everyone involved exactly why the church exists and what it is supposed to do. There is incredible power in having a clearly defined purpose statement. If it is short enough for everyone to remember, your statement of purpose will yield five wonderful benefits for your church. [these are high morale, reduced frustration, concentration, cooperation, and evaluation][11]

In the business world, selling the "team" on this is called "vision casting." I discussed how this term is now used to promote secular marketing techniques to grow churches. Here is how Warren describes this idea, "Once you have defined the purposes of your church, you must continually clarify and communicate them to everyone in your congregation."[12] The best way to do this is not through complicated, theological teaching, but through slogans. Warren says, "Slogans, maxims, mottoes, and pithy phrases are remembered long after sermons are forgotten."[13] Having created a pithy, focused, easy to remember purpose statement, it must be stated over and over.[14] Warren is certainly the master of the slogan, a talent he shares with Robert Schuller.[15]

The purpose statement not only defines what the church does and where it focuses its energies, but just as importantly, it defines what the church **does not** do. Any proposed activity that cannot be justified by the mission statement is rejected on that grounds. For Warren, a healthy church is a focused church. It is the church leader's job to narrow the focus, communicate the focus, and create a structure that enables the church to implement the focus.

Rick Warren has been meeting with management guru Peter Drucker for over twenty years to discuss management ideas and to implement them in his understanding of the church.[16] The issue of focus is very important. This is what Drucker said, "So, I always advise my friend Rick Warren, 'Don't tell me what you're doing, Rick. Tell me what you stopped doing.'"[17] Drucker has helped Warren use cutting edge management ideas from the business world and implement them in his management of the local church. Warren has now taken those ideas and made a business system that can be implemented by church leaders all over the world to improve their own church management and bring their efforts and their budgets into alignment with Warren's Purpose Driven paradigm.

The key problem with the Drucker/Warren approach to church management is that it is designed for ambitious CEOs of large corporations who have corporate resources focused to achieve temporal goals, not eternal life. The pastor of a small church typically has to teach, preach, visit people, conduct weddings and funerals, counsel members, solve personal relationship problems, and run the organization. How does such a person step into the role of CEO, focused on one or two things, when there exists no staff and few volunteers? Not only that, but this new approach has changed the focus of the church from ministering to the flock to designing a version of evangelicalism that appeals to unregenerate religious consumers. How is the typical pastor supposed to embrace Purpose Driven while simultaneously caring for the needs of the flock?

It is important to realize, as we ponder these questions, that according to Rick Warren's own definitions, the pastors of most churches are failing. Moreover, by his definition, many of the Old

Testament prophets, such as Jeremiah, were also failures. He claims that if we were healthy and balanced we could not help but grow in attendance and income. Yet, most churches in America have stagnant or declining attendance. This means that most pastors do not have "healthy" churches according to Rick Warren's standards (in the next chapter I will show that Jesus Christ has entirely different standards). So not only are most pastors dealing with an unhealthy situation, but if they accept Warren's premise that everything the church does should be attractive to unbelievers, now they also face the daunting task of having to change everything they are doing. It is hard enough to write a solid, biblical sermon each week that brings the eternal truth of God's Word to the Lord's flock, but now that same sermon has to somehow sound exciting and appealing to those who do not even believe the Bible and have a distaste for the things of God.

The pastor who is considering a "paradigm" shift to Warren's definition of the church and ministry faces a daunting task indeed. He must quit doing most of what he has been doing (risking losing the people who have been attending). He must focus on making the church entertaining to unbelievers. He must design a focused purpose statement. He must sell the church on his new vision. He must learn how to dream up exciting slogans. He must create an entirely new organization that balances the five purposes of the church. In short he must learn how to be an ambitious CEO and corporate "vision caster," rather than denying himself to be a gospel preacher and shepherd of the flock. This looks to be just about impossible.

The Purpose Driven Franchise

The answer to the dilemma of how to implement the Purpose Driven paradigm utilizing hard working, dedicated persons with limited skill sets and limited resources is found in one of the truly ingenious business innovations of the twentieth century—the franchise. The franchise paradigm has made more millionaires of ambitious men with limited talent than any other business model in history.[18] Franchising is especially successful in the service industry where rapid expansion and market penetration are key goals. Returning to part of the Purpose Driven mission statement: "providing training, transferable products, and learning communities that leverage and extend the PD paradigm and brand," we can see the franchise idea. The key idea is to provide everything needed for a person with ordinary skills to capitalize on the success of the founder of the franchise. This includes everything from providing a quality product, product delivery, recognizable brand identity, and leadership training and support, to a repeatable, transferable system that will consistently work if used according to specifications. The franchise system enables ordinary people to share the success of extraordinary innovators who have created a new product. During a recent interview, Warren said that he is doing just that: "And we've actually created what we call clinic-in-a-box, business-in-a-box, church-in-a-box, and we are using normal people, volunteers."[19]

Warren stated the following during a transcribed interview with Peter Drucker:

> Rick: Well, one of our values is what I call "the good enough" principle. A person doesn't have to be perfect for God to use them. Because we want our church to be a model for other churches, we want average people doing average activities in order to get extraordinary results. Just like how the typical McDonalds is able to succeed while being staffed by high school students. Because the system works, it doesn't require unusual talent.[20]

As this statement shows, Rick Warren has created a franchise system whereby ordinary pastors are able to utilize Warren's "transferable products" to have their own Purpose Driven church without relying on their own limited managerial or creative talents to create it.

Purpose Driven is a marketable brand identity, especially since

The Purpose Driven Life has sold over 25 million copies and counting and Rick Warren has been regularly seen on national, secular news programs promoting Purpose Driven. As mentioned earlier, they claim to have trained 300,000 church leaders and established "Purpose Driven" congregations in every country of the world. The idea is that one can walk into any one of these churches and have a reasonable expectation of what he or she is going to find there. If that expectation is a positive one for the religious consumer, that is the mark of a successful religious franchise. There must be brand consistency and reproducible quality for the brand to maintain its value.

The following are a few of the ways that the Purpose Driven brand is helping ambitious, ordinary pastors replicate Rick Warren's success in creating a "healthy church" according to Warren's specifications.

Purpose Driven Campaigns

I have before me a glossy, full color ad that was sent to me by the Purpose Driven organization. It invites our church to join a "40 Days of Purpose" campaign that is led by Rick Warren. It offers three start dates: April 9, September 24, and October 8, 2005. It claims that 18,000 churches have already participated. It touts an average growth in worship attendance of 20 percent, and it claims to be a revival that is effective because of unified prayer, concentrated focus, multiple reinforcements, behavioral teaching, and exponential thinking. Those who join the campaign are given all the materials that Rick Warren produced for his church, including video lessons of Warren himself. All of the ministries of the church are told to participate. This is what it says:

> *40 Days of Purpose* will comprehensively reinforce the themes of the book by engaging your church on all levels, which multiplies exponentially the overall impact of the learnings. A mere book study will not give your church the excitement to get involved in ministry, the energy for evangelism, the increase in attendance and giving, the growth

in small groups, and the depth of discipleship that the *40 Days of Purpose* can achieve in 40 short days!"[21]

The campaign includes the opportunity to "downlink the Purpose Driven Life Simulcast via satellite." This is said about the downlink: "Our surveys show that churches viewing the planned satellite broadcast usually experience greater momentum out of the event." Pastors are offered a support infrastructure that includes weekly coaching e-mails, weekly conference calls, and a connection with an alumni or mentor church. Everything that is needed to use a 40-day campaign and become a Purpose Driven church is provided.

In order to feed off of the success of the 40 days of Purpose campaign, Warren has now produced a 40 Days of Community campaign that works the same way (church-wide), and has promised yet a third campaign that will emphasize global action. These campaigns are designed to help pastors tap into the success of the Purpose Driven brand identity and replicate Rick Warren's success in their own churches.

Small Group Resources

Rick Warren has devised a system where churches can multiply the numbers of their small groups and use these groups to grow the church. The Purpose Driven campaign ad claims an average increase of 102 percent in small groups formed for churches that participate. *The Purpose Driven Life* is touted as an excellent small group resource. In it, he urges people to start a study group using the book: "I *strongly* urge you to gather a small group of friends and for a Purpose Driven Life Reading Group to review these chapters on a weekly basis."[22] After the group spends 40 weeks on that topic, there is more: "After you have gone through this book together as a group, you might consider studying other Purpose Driven life studies that are available for classes and groups (see appendix 2)."[23] As I pointed out before, appendix 2 is all Warren material, like: *The Purpose Driven Life Journal, The Purpose Driven Life*

Scripture Keepers Plus; The Purpose Driven Life Album, The Purpose Driven Life Video Curriculum, etc.[24] There is much more than this available on the Purpose Driven Web site. Never again should a pastor have to wonder how to train people to lead small group Bible studies. A Purpose Driven church will never run out of small group resources produced by Rick Warren.

Online Sermons

One of the great problems created when a pastor adopts the Purpose Driven paradigm shift is the need to somehow make sermons interesting to unbelievers. The key message of the Bible which is redemption and atonement through the cross is repugnant to the unregenerate mind, as we discussed before. So week after week, a Purpose Driven pastor has to figure out pithy sayings, slogans, mottoes, aphorisms, and other clever verbal devices to captivate the minds of people who have no inclination to learn doctrine from the Bible. Very few pastors have the natural creativity and skill to do this. If one preaches biblical doctrine right from the Bible, there are many commentaries and interpretive helps available. But what do you do if you have to think of clever stories and entertaining ideas to inspire the "unchurched?"

The answer is the Web site pastors.com. There, Rick Warren offers a weekly sermon to those pastors who subscribe. Here is what is promised:

> Learn from a master communicator delivery, style, effect and pause to enhance your verbal communication; save time during your sermon preparation by using Rick's crafted outlines; help supplement your sermon preparation through highly researched material (Rick has over 30 people helping him research his weekly sermons.); keep a fresh flow of new ideas and insights pouring into your heart.[25]

Also available is the "Sermon Vault" with 23 years worth of sermons. The sermons from pastors.com are advertised as "seeker sensitive." Pastors receive CDs, presentations, and outlines of Rick Warren's sermons so that they can preach them in their churches.

Conferences and Training Seminars

Rick Warren's ministry has trained many pastors in his understanding of the church through conferences. Past conferences are available on DVD:

> The Purpose Driven Church Conference on DVD; Bring to your church the ground-breaking seminar that has trained over 250,000 pastors and lay pastors world-wide how to grow healthy churches. Rick Warren's new paradigm for church growth has changed the way thousands of churches reach the lost through evangelism, train its members, mature its believers, develop ministries, and live a life of worship.[26]

These conferences nurture the "learning communities" mentioned in the Purpose Driven mission statement. These trained leaders will help establish the "new paradigm," as Warren calls it. This new paradigm is a church designed to appeal to unbelievers through using Purpose Driven principles.

Brand Identity

These and other means are how Rick Warren is "leveraging" the Purpose Driven "paradigm and brand" around the world. The ambitious leaders who have bought the franchise, so to speak, are the change agents who are working to transform churches into the Purpose Driven model. The goal, if this movement is successful, is that people all over the world will be able to walk into a church that is Purpose Driven, and find the same quality of religious experience that Rick Warren is providing at his Saddleback Church. If this process works, it will be more than an establishment of a new denomination; it will be a transformation of many churches from many denominations into providers of a new religious product that satisfies the appetites of religious consumers of all backgrounds.

They can keep their denominational identity, but that identity will say more about their history or private beliefs than about their practice and public message.[27]

Pastors who become Purpose Driven become like branch managers of a franchise. As such, they need to do certain things to enjoy the success that the franchise promises. For one, they need to replicate the model of the founder of the franchise. For all the talk Rick Warren gives about the flexibility of his system, the literature that goes out touts the need to follow the pattern if one expects to enjoy the promised results. The stronger the brand identity, the more this is true because the identity creates expectations in the minds of consumers. Once a person has had a positive experience with the Purpose Driven brand, if he walked into a church that promised a Purpose Driven version of Christianity, he would expect the same quality of experience that he was used to. If the given franchise manager had decided to do things his own way and deviated from the Purpose Driven model, there would be few repeat customers. This provides strong incentive for conformity if success is the goal.

The brand identity is of little value unless the product is delivered consistently and in accordance with franchise specifications. No franchise can succeed that is not able to do this. It is *sine qua non* of being a franchise. The safest way to make sure this happens if you are a local franchise manager (Purpose Driven pastor) is to have one of the 40 day campaigns happening regularly, with sermons downloaded from pastors.com in the interim. This guarantees a homogeneous, quality product consistent with the global brand.

Another key to cashing in on brand identity is that the franchise manager must not deviate from the corporate mission and procedures. The mission and the procedures to fulfill it are "created and tested by experts" or the brand would not be successful. Each evolution and new product introduction is carefully researched and tested in focus groups before being introduced to the franchises. Managers who are unconvinced of what the franchise promises have another option—develop their own brand and do not buy into the franchise. If you are going to have a Purpose Driven church, you do not go to some other model to determine your mission and protocol. All the potential problems and issues have already been identified by others years ago, and procedures have been put in place to deal with them. The brand works because of this, and ambitious managers who value success will consistently follow corporate protocol because they believe it will deliver what it promises.

Every manager of a franchise with a brand identity is responsible to motivate a team to insure the success of the franchise. This means being able to understand and articulate the corporate mission, believe in that mission, and motivate others to do the same. The success of the local expression of the franchise is largely dependent on the ambition, quality, and enthusiasm of the members. The more fully every member is onboard with the vision, the more successful the franchise will be. This also means that every member must embrace the mission and be dedicated to its success. The negative side of this is that non-team players who fight the mission must be identified and either converted to team players or removed.

Dealing with Problem People

One big problem with buying into the Purpose Driven franchise and adopting the paradigm shift that Rick Warren has identified is that some long-time church members will resist this change. Some, including people who have been key, faithful leaders, will cling to the idea that the Bible should be preached, doctrine taught, and the gospel presented in the way it was preached by Christ and His apostles. These people have to be dealt with or the franchise cannot work as designed and deliver on its promises. They will undermine the unity of purpose that is necessary for the church to be Purpose Driven.

I have received many e-mails from such "problem" people. They see the changes in a different light from those who have adopted the new paradigm. They are alarmed that the Bible is being removed from the pulpit and from Bible studies, and they see this movement as apostasy and not revival. This is a serious problem that leads to division in churches. Here is an e-mail that is typical of many:

> My church is just now finishing up the 40 Days of Purpose program. They seem to all be eating up everything Rick Warren has to say. My pastor and other leaders in my church have dismissed my concerns about the book and program (most of which you addressed in your article). When I told my pastor that if human measurable experiences are more important that the truth, I would need to find a new church home. He asked me to reconsider leaving. He did not defend Warren. He did not defend the program. He did not even defend himself and say that God's truth does matter. Instead he asked me to reconsider leaving. I have asked him to correct me if I am wrong, but he has not responded. . . . I am afraid that nearly every church in America (or at least those in my area) has fallen for the self-centered, pragmatic Purpose Driven sales pitch. I have come to the conclusion that Warren is preaching a different gospel, and I am astonished and in anguish over what it is doing to those I love. I am amazed at the lack of discernment in what I thought was a Bible-believing church.

The reason people are feeling disenfranchised from their congregations is that when a church becomes Purpose Driven, it changes the very core of its identity. The change from existing to feed Jesus' flock to existing to feed the appetites of religious consumers is drastic and systemic.

Typically, those who cannot be convinced of the validity of the Purpose Driven paradigm are either asked to leave or made so uncomfortable that they willingly leave. It is not possible that people who reject the Purpose Driven philosophy can be seamlessly integrated into the new franchise. It would be like McDonalds hiring a cook who refused to cook hamburgers. The entire "team" has to be willing to follow the franchise protocol. Those who refuse cannot co-exist on the team.[28]

In some cases, the response of church leaders to those who resist becoming a Purpose Driven church has been harsh. In one case, published in a newspaper, 165 members were thrown out of a church because they resisted the change to becoming seeker oriented.[29] According to ousted members, the pastor was promoting Rick Warren's Purpose Driven program. The only way for the disfellowshipped members to be received back was by signing a "covenant of unity."[30] This is a requirement that Rick Warren makes of all members of his church as well: "At Saddleback Church, every member signs a covenant that includes a promise to protect the unity of our fellowship."[31] Those who do not promote "harmony and unity" are warned and then removed on grounds of being divisive.[32]

While to some this may sound biblical, it is not. There is nothing in these unity covenants that has to do with "the unity of the faith" as defined biblically. This is about the unity of the local organization under the pastor, as we discussed in an earlier chapter. What this does show is the guarding of the integrity of the Purpose Driven brand and paradigm. No franchise can succeed unless the team members, under the direction of the franchise manager, are fully committed to the brand specifications and corporate protocol of the franchise. That is why those who resist the leadership of the church that is becoming Purpose Driven have to be removed from fellowship. Their continued resistance could sabotage the process of the change agents and the franchise may fail to deliver on its promises.

Because Warren has been so successful at selling his franchise to ambitious pastors, many of those who "resist" end up with nowhere to find biblical fellowship. Here is another e-mail typical of so many I have received:

We were labeled critical and divisive and negative in our Southern Baptist church for pointing out the watered-down gospel and twisting of Scripture in the book *The Purpose Driven Life*. Despite the concerns we raised, our church pressed ahead with their 40 day journey earlier this year and we found it too difficult to attend church over that period, where all the ministries of the church were geared to that study over that time. We have found the lack of discernment very alarming. Someone has said that it is not that we are losing the lost, it's that we're not reaching the reached. We are shocked at the weak teaching of Scripture we are seeing, the lack of discernment, the ignorance of truth versus error, and the willingness to jump unquestioningly on every popular "Christian" bandwagon that comes along. We are very discouraged as we know of no solid, Bible-honoring, discerning church in our area and wonder what those of us who see these problems are to do.

It is very difficult to answer people who long for a gospel preaching, Bible teaching fellowship and are unable to find it anywhere in their town or city. The Purpose Driven "reformation" has been so successful that churches that have not been "reformed" are few and far between. It would be like a town in which a single franchise took over every single restaurant and you were allergic to the food from that franchise.

Once the pastor has bought into Warren's brand and paradigm and convinced key leaders to do the same, it is very unlikely that resisters within the congregation will be able to stop the conversion to the new model of church. The pastor is already committed to riding out such opposition and furthermore is convinced that he is a noble-minded servant of God in doing so. Rick Warren predicts this type of confrontation and offers these managers proven tools and procedures to overcome this obstacle.

Conclusion

Rick Warren is very good at what he does. His system is the best one ever developed to help ordinary church leaders join the Church Growth movement without having to have massive resources and specific talents to do so. If a pastor truly wants to create a church that is attractive to the world, the easiest way to do so is to buy into the Purpose Driven franchise. Thousands of pastors and churches have already joined and more are doing so all the time.

This means that there are fundamental questions that must be answered: Does God want His church to be attractive to the world and its worldly ideals? Must our message appeal to the unregenerate mind? Must our worship be entertaining to a worldly target audience? Must we grow in numbers and money to be pleasing to God? If we are one of the 80 percent of churches in America with stable or declining attendance, are we indeed "failing" as the Church Growth experts define us?

I hope my readers see what is going on. These change agents make all the definitions, compare us to the church as they define it, declare us failures, then offer us "success" if we join their programs. Dear fellow Christians and specifically church leaders, this is American marketing pure and simple: Define a problem so that you convince nearly everyone they have it, then sell them the solution. In this case the goal may not be to make money. In Rick Warren's case, I do not think he wants money for his own benefit; I think he wants his "reformation" to succeed and go down in history as a reformer like Martin Luther. He wants to create a version of Christianity that the world loves.

To help my readers resist the lure of this movement, I will provide a discussion of the seven churches in Revelation in the next chapter. The only real "franchise owner" of the church is Jesus Christ. Only He can tell us authoritatively what a "healthy" church looks like. We shall see that it does not look like a Purpose Driven one.

Who Determines "Church Health," Jesus Christ or Rick Warren?

We saw in the last chapter that the Purpose Driven movement is designed along the lines of a franchise. Now if the church is thought of as a franchise, then Jesus Christ, not Rick Warren, is the founder, CEO and owner of 100 percent of the outstanding shares of the franchise. Since this is His role, only Jesus Christ can authoritatively declare the corporate policies and procedures that are binding on the corporation (continuing the analogy). Likewise, only Jesus can declare a local franchise holder "healthy" or "unhealthy" based on His unchanging purpose for His church.

But Rick Warren has stated his vision for those who join his franchise: "Our vision is to see healthy, balanced congregations producing Purpose Driven lives of all ages everywhere."[1] And, as mentioned earlier, he has declared his movement to be a new reformation of the church: "Saddleback Church is now but one among thousands of Purpose Driven churches—the vanguard of a new reformation."[2] So, for the franchises of the new reformation—the churches who most successfully copy Rick Warren's pattern—he has created a "Church Health Award."[3]

Rick Warren has declared the terms and conditions for being "healthy" in his corporate mission statement. Here is an important question: Are Rick Warren's standards for a Purpose Driven church the same as Jesus Christ's revealed will and purpose for His church? If they are the same we have no problem. If, however, they are different we have a significant problem because a fallible man is setting standards that are different from the ones set once for all by the true Head of the church, Jesus Christ. Let us consider first what Jesus Christ has given us.

Jesus has already spoken about what He approves and disapproves in churches. We do not have to guess what Jesus thinks about these matters; it is revealed in the New Testament.

The Seven Churches in Revelation

In the Book of Revelation, Jesus addresses seven churches in Asia Minor. These churches are presented in the order of their geographical location, going from Ephesus to the south, then northward, back south and then east.[4] Though some have held that the churches are representative of stages of church history, there is nothing in the context to support this theory. These were literal churches that existed at the time John wrote the book of Revelation. I believe that Jesus addressed these churches at that time so that for all subsequent generations of church history, we would know what Jesus commends and what Jesus condemns in His churches. Lenski comments, "They are typical of the conditions obtaining in the churches of all time irrespective of the number that at any time may belong to one type or to another."[5] I agree with this.

The material in Revelation 2 and 3 provides for us a precious opportunity to find out what Jesus, the true owner of His churches, uses as criteria for evaluation. Please note that what modern marketing experts deem healthy is of no significance in the eyes of Christ. The seven churches reveal the virtues and vices of all churches throughout the church age. We can learn from these churches and thereby "Hear what the Spirit says to the churches."[6] We need to listen to what God says is in these passages, because He is giving us an opportunity to correct what is wrong before Christ comes in judgment. There is no reason to be in the dark about what Jesus approves or condemns.

For those interested in a deeper study of these chapters, I provide a detailed analysis in appendix 2. The analysis is the exegetical work that verifies what I present in summary form in the remainder of this chapter and apply to Warren's church health standards.

The Key Virtues According to Jesus
Overcoming

The messages to the seven churches contain seven promises to overcomers. The promises have to do with eternal life, escaping punishment, ruling with Christ, and having a new name[7] and are summarized at the end of Revelation, *"He who overcomes shall inherit these things, and I will be his God and he will be My son"* (Revelation 21:7). Nothing is more important than being an overcomer. Let us discuss this matter first and then survey Jesus' assessment of the virtues and vices in His churches.

An overcomer is one who has maintained his confession in the face of persecution and/or temptation. Some in the church had so compromised with the world they avoided persecution or rejection. Though they appeared successful, powerful, and popular, they were rebuked by Christ. Others, though small in number, lacking in power and persecuted by both pagans and Jews, maintained their confession and refused to compromise. These are the ones who are overcomers. The key to overcoming is confession at any cost. Any church that fails at this point is not numbered among the overcomers, no matter how successful or popular it may be.

The Revelation contains a passage that describes the essence of being an overcomer: *"And they overcame him because of the blood of the Lamb and because of the word of their testimony, and they did not love their life even to death"* (Revelation 12:11). It was Satan, the "accuser of the brethren," who was thus defeated. Satan holds people in bondage, not because of his great power, but because of their sins before God. If their sins remain unforgiven, then people remain in his power.

The blood atonement is absolutely necessary for anyone to be an overcomer. The blood of Christ was poured out "once for all"[8] to avert God's just wrath against sin. People need to know that they have offended a Holy God and that they are facing God's wrath.[9] Without the blood atonement that is provided by Christ for all who repent and believe the gospel, there is no escape from the wrath of God. The "blood of the Lamb" is not a phrase, the utterance of which will scare away Satan, but it is the once for all shed blood of Christ that simultaneously delivers sinners from God's wrath and from Satan's bondage.

As we have said previously, Warren fails to preach the blood atonement in his public confession, and he fails to include it in the gospel as presented in *The Purpose Driven Life*. This glaring omission is a huge void to those who so badly need to become overcomers. This is unacceptable.

The "word of their testimony" concerns the confession of the Christian. Those who willingly and openly confess Christ are never popular in the world and are often persecuted. They are not just "confessing," in the sense of "saying something nice about Jesus," they are confessing the uniqueness of Christ, the deity of Christ, the humanity of Christ, the sinlessness of Christ, the cross of Christ and the resurrection of Christ. This type of confession brings division between true Christians and nominal Christians. The word "testimony" is *marturia* in the Greek, from which we get our word "martyr." Many who "testified" were killed for their confession of Christ. This is expressed in the phrase, *"did not love their life even unto death."* Nothing is more important to overcomers than their relationship with Christ which is based on His shed blood, expressed in their confession, and demonstrated in their willingness to lay aside their own self-love.

Perseverance

Four times in the addresses to the churches, Jesus commends perseverance. And later in Revelation there is a description of perseverance: *"Here is the perseverance of the saints who keep the commandments of God and their faith in Jesus"* (Revelation 14:12). Those who persevere have genuine faith, and this faith is demonstrated in obedience. This is a virtue that shows a genuine work of grace in one's heart: *"And* the seed in the good soil, these are the ones who have heard the word in an honest and good heart, and hold it fast, and bear fruit with perseverance" (Luke 8:15). Perseverance is shown by how one reacts to trials: "*Therefore, we ourselves speak proudly of you among the churches of God for your perseverance and faith in the midst of all your persecutions and afflictions which you endure*" (2 Thessalonians 1:4).

Rejecting and Hating False Doctrine

Jesus commends those who refuse to tolerate false prophets, false apostles, and false teaching. That Christ's apostles were like this is seen in the many warnings against false teaching found in the New Testament. Local churches are responsible to stand for sound doctrine and to correct false doctrine. Paul laid down this standard for elders: "*Holding fast the faithful word which is in accordance with the teaching, that he may be able both to exhort in sound doctrine and to refute those who contradict*" (Titus 1:9). Paul also predicted a time when many will refuse to embrace sound doctrine or correct false doctrine: "*For the time will come when they will not endure sound doctrine; but wanting to have their ears tickled, they will accumulate for themselves teachers in accordance to their own desires*" (2 Timothy 4:3).

Being Faithful When Weak

The two churches that were only commended and not rebuked were small and lacked influence. The church in Smyrna was poor and suffering. The church in Philadelphia had but "little power." But those highly commended, small, non-influential churches were faithful to Christ and would not let anything allow them to deviate from their confession of Christ. They faithfully used the "keys" to show people the way of entrance into the Messianic kingdom.

The Worst Vices According to Jesus
Lack of Love

The Ephesian church, though commended for orthodoxy, was rebuked for a lack of love. This has many applications in churches today. Some have hung onto orthodoxy in spite of their spiritual coldness. They, perhaps, consider orthodox truths worth fighting for because of sectarian considerations. "Dead orthodoxy" is the term usually used to describe a group that would never tolerate tampering with their historical, doctrinal formulations or statements, but who show little evidence of the love for God and neighbor that is the true keeping of the commandments. Such orthodoxy could possibly be no more than mental assent to truths that are not fully grasped by life-changing faith. We need to remember Paul's admonition to *speak the truth in love.*[10] I believe that in the case of those who defend orthodoxy but demonstrate little love for God and neighbor, the problem is not orthodox truth, but a lack of a genuine, vital faith in Christ.

Warren's P.E.A.C.E. plan and other Purpose Driven projects surely emphasize showing love in tangible ways. These are activities we all should do. However, good deeds, in the absence of clear gospel preaching, do not distinguish one from a Gandhi who did good deeds, with no gospel preaching.

Toleration of False Doctrine

One church tolerated the teaching of the Nicolaitans and another the teaching of a prophetess of the ilk of Jezebel. We live in a time where tolerance is considered the ultimate virtue. Jesus denounced such tolerance as spiritual wickedness. In too many churches today, everything is tolerated except sound doctrine! We need to listen to what Jesus has already said about this matter before it is too late.

The Purpose Driven movement that defines "healthy churches" is seriously lacking in its teachings and procedures when it comes to correcting false doctrine. In more than two years of research and careful study of Warren's two popular books, I have seen nothing that emphasizes correcting false doctrine. And given the associations that Rick Warren uses to further his movement, it seems unlikely we will hear Warren correcting anyone's false doctrine publicly (whether he does privately I do not know). This shows a major departure from Jesus' practice. Jesus commends those who rebuke false teachers and rebukes those who tolerate them. Rick Warren gives tacit approval to false teachers by citing them approvingly in *The Purpose Driven Life*.

Compromise with the Pagan Culture

The sharp rebuke about the teaching of Balaam and the tolerance of Jezebel shows the danger of compromise with the pagans. The Lord sternly rebuked the churches who found it convenient to retain pagan practices and thus keep their wealth and avoid persecution. Those churches learned what many today know so well—the more you blur the line between the pagan culture and the church, the more people you attract to your church. The world will never reject or persecute a version of "Christianity" that reflects its own wants, needs, and values. A non-confrontive "gospel" is a popular gospel. The world will reward what it favors and persecute what it hates. As we have shown, this is precisely what the Purpose Driven movement has done—it has created a gospel the world loves.

Deluded Self-satisfaction

The church in Laodicea thought she had it all. Like the city in which she was located, this church had the same signs of "success:" power, wealth, influence, and a strong self-confidence. Her true spiritual needs were many, but she was unaware of them. This happy ignorance of spiritual poverty brought on the most stunning rebuke Jesus offered any of the churches. If there is any church that epitomizes the condition of many churches in America today, this is the one. We have it all: power, money, popularity, success, influence, and often the accolades of the society around us. But what does Jesus think?

What is not Important: Size or Growth

The churches that were praised by the Lord and not rebuked were small churches. Clearly, Jesus is not impressed with large numbers. More significantly, He never addresses church growth.

How big these churches were, compared to earlier times in their history, was of no consequence to Jesus. Sometimes under severe persecution churches shrink because only those who are "over-comers" are willing to remain and pay the price. When Christianity is popular, churches grow for reasons other than true conversions. Therefore, what is essential is maintaining the true confession of the church regardless of whether it is being received or rejected. The only way to become an overcomer is through the blood of the Lamb. If the blood atonement is not proclaimed, the church can-not possibly overcome. Size or growth in numbers of people is not important. If the church is a confessing church, God will add to it those who are being saved. Noah was faithful to God and preached 100 years with no converts. Jonah was an unwilling preacher and God saved an entire city through his preaching. Noah is com-mended in the Bible, and Jonah is portrayed in a bad light. We need to rid ourselves of thinking about numbers.

Rick Warren's "Healthy Church"

Now, let us compare the criteria Rick Warren and his Purpose Driven reformation have set for health with the standards that the true owner of the church, Jesus Christ, has established. Rick Warren has defined his criteria and publicly commends those who are exemplary at being Purpose Driven.[11] Given what we have learned from Jesus' assessment of His churches, would He deem these churches "healthy"? I think not. Let me explain.

Rick Warren claims that doctrine is so unimportant that God will not even ask about it.[12] Jesus made doctrine very important and rebuked those who tolerated false doctrine. Four times the term "doctrine" appears in *The Purpose Driven Life*, as I mentioned before, and all four times its importance is downplayed. The Purpose Driven Web site consistently assures pastors that they can be Purpose Driven without changing their particular doctrines or tra-ditions.

Rick Warren's Purpose Driven life never explains the blood atonement in the context of the gospel or salvation. However, to

Jesus it was of greatest importance that those in His churches become "overcomers." As we saw, this is only possible through the blood of the Lamb. Since Warren's readers and followers hear little if anything from him about the blood atonement or the wrath of God against sin, they have no way to become overcomers. It is not possible to have a "healthy church" by Jesus' standards without the blood atonement and straightforward, public confession of the gospel. But these matters are where Rick Warren and his Purpose Driven movement are at their weakest. Warren does not proclaim the blood atonement when he has his biggest audiences, and he obscures the gospel message to make it sound appealing to the pagans.

The church leaders who follow Rick Warren are told that if they follow his campaign and are typical of other churches that do, they will grow 20 percent in attendance and 20 percent in money. Jesus doesn't care about attendance or money. Those who follow Rick Warren are investing in that which does not matter.

Rick Warren sets up his Purpose Driven movement as a tool for others to use if they wish to be "healthy." He consistently points to the success of Saddleback Church as a positive role model. His positive self-assessment rivals that of the Laodicean church. He tells his followers of his many achievements as proved by numbers and the accolades of man. Jesus called another church like that "lukewarm," and threatened to spew it out of His mouth. Recently, in interviews with the secular media, Warren told how much money he has given away.[13] The world loves people who give away their money. It is a good thing to be generous and give to the poor. It is a bad thing to make that something which finds favor in the eyes of man (see Matthew 6:1-4). Rather than impressing the pagans with his good deeds, he should be contending with them about the truth of the gospel.

Rick Warren compromises with the pagans like the churches did whom Jesus rebuked. Warren uses pagan principles in his S.H.A.P.E. program.[14] He teaches pagan "prayer" practices such as "breath prayers" and other mystical practices.[15] He has consulted other pagan compromisers such as Robert Schuller and Ken

Blanchard.[16] He integrates pagan teachings into his key religious product, *The Purpose Driven Life*, making it appear that the Bible and the pagan world are compatible in their beliefs.

Rick Warren ultimately fails to "confess" in a manner that would set his teaching apart from the beliefs of the world. His non-offensive gospel is a hybrid version that appeals to the world. He has opened the wide gates of compromise and obscured the narrow gate that leads to salvation. There is no such thing as a non-confessing overcomer.

What is most unhealthy about Warren's Purpose Driven movement is a glaring failure to do what Jude tells us to do: *"Beloved, while I was making every effort to write you about our common salvation, I felt the necessity to write to you appealing that you contend earnestly for the faith which was once for all delivered to the saints"* (Jude 1:3). Churches in Revelation were rebuked for "tolerating" false teachers. Jude goes on and says, *"For certain persons have crept in unnoticed, those who were long beforehand marked out for this condemnation, ungodly persons who turn the grace of our God into licentiousness and deny our only Master and Lord, Jesus Christ"* (Jude 1:4). Those who teach error are to be rebuked using sound doctrine (Titus 1:9).

What Warren does that is alarming is to cite false teachers approvingly without qualification. These teachers are so false that many of their ideas are damnable (for example, the writer of erotica he cites). By using their ideas, even some perhaps innocuous, and integrating them with his Christian material, he gives the impression that the false teachings espoused by these people are compatible with biblical Christianity. But the Bible requires that, on the contrary, false teachers be publicly rebuked. Their ideas are at war with the gospel. How can they be integrated as they are in *The Purpose Driven Life* without so much as a qualification in a footnote? It is not made clear anywhere that Warren has serious disagreements with them. This is toleration that Jesus condemns. How many people are on their way to Hell believing the New Age, and yet Warren fails to warn them?

I appeal to Rick Warren and his Purpose Driven followers to

change this policy. They need to publicly and forthrightly rebuke error, falsehood, and false doctrine. There are many false teachers cited in *The Purpose Driven Life*. I appeal to Rick Warren to publicize just as widely what is wrong with the false teacher's beliefs and publicly rebuke them for teaching as they do. Any less than this is "tolerating" false teachings like those who tolerated Jezebel.

True Health Comes from Submitting to Christ and His Word

The church belongs to Jesus, not to man. Jesus, as the head of the church, will ultimately judge His church. In order to make it possible to repent before it is too late, Jesus gave us the seven inspired messages to the seven churches so that we might know what He commends and what He condemns. The great danger for each of us is self-delusion. We tend to not see ourselves realistically. Instead we think that surely we epitomize the virtues and avoid the vices. The only way to avoid such self-delusion is to carefully and objectively study what Jesus has said. Having made such a study, we need to look at ourselves and our churches, humbly asking how these things apply to our own situation.

We are getting a lot of bad advice from the contemporary, evangelical culture. This bad advice virtually ignores everything Jesus said was important to Him in His churches. What He cares about is deemed irrelevant for popular, "healthy" churches today. Let us consider the words of our Lord as spoken to the Laodicean church: *"Those whom I love, I reprove and discipline; be zealous therefore, and repent"* (Revelation 3:19).

Rick Warren has a big audience. He likely has a bigger audience than any other evangelical today. If he would become a confessor who publicly contended for the faith, who declared God's wrath against sin, clearly described the person and work of Christ, preached publicly the need for the blood atonement, and called his hearers to repent and believe the gospel, then he would be an overcomer as described by Jesus in Revelation. As it is, he has redefined nearly every important aspect of Christianity (at least in the version presented to the public) and created a Christianity that the world loves.

Since he has done this, his church health award is dangerous. The key Purpose Driven principles and protocols are very different from those in the New Testament that describe a church pleasing to Jesus Christ. If those of the New Testament prevail, the result is a church that is pleasing to Christ. If those of Rick Warren prevail, the result is a church popular with religious consumers in the world, but which is much different from Jesus' "little flock." Since his "reformation" (along with others such as Robert Schuller's and C. Peter Wagner's) is apparently prevailing, we are facing a choice. We can either please Jesus Christ and "fail" in the eyes of our contemporary religious peers, or we can join the "reformation" and enjoy the accolades of men like Rick Warren. We cannot have both.

Warren has so redefined the major issues (the gospel, the Bible, the church, fellowship, worship, discipleship, evangelism, and missions), that he has effectively redefined Christianity. The new version of Christianity is popular with the world. This version has avoided the outcome that Jesus predicted to His disciples: *"If you were of the world, the world would love its own; but because you are not of the world, but I chose you out of the world, therefore the world hates you"* (John 15:19). The world loves a P.E.A.C.E. plan which promises to solve the problems they want solved. The problem is that the world hates the gospel of Jesus Christ. May we boldly proclaim that gospel so that God will use it to save some from His coming wrath. May we shun the lure of popularity and success offered by Warren's redefined Christianity. It is so much better to be pleasing to Jesus Christ.

"It is better to take refuge in the Lord Than to trust in man" (Psalm 118:8).

Conclusion

Redefining Christianity

In this book, I have detailed the process that the Purpose Driven movement has followed to create a version of Christianity that the world loves. Included has been a description of how they package it and market it to religious consumers—a process that is succeeding. The Purpose Driven Web site states, "Peter Drucker called him [Warren] 'the inventor of perpetual revival' and Forbes magazine has written, 'If Warren's church was a business, it would be compared with Dell, Google or Starbucks.'"[1] Businesses succeed because they satisfy customers. Warren's customers are people in the world—the "unchurched" to use his terms. What I have shown is that Warren has created a version of Christianity the world loves through a process of redefinition.

This redefinition is thorough in that everything important to historical Christianity has been touched in the process. The gospel has been smoothed out through removing or obscuring its greatest offense—the need for Christ's blood atonement to satisfy God's wrath against sin. The Bible has been misused to make it appear to agree with worldly wisdom. The hard truths of Christianity that have offended non-Christians for centuries have been relegated to the file cabinet where they collect dust. And, finally, the mission of the church has been redefined in ways that make it attractive to the world. Rick Warren, the architect of the process, dubs it a "reformation."

The P.E.A.C.E. Plan

Warren wants to reform what the church does. What will this new "reformed" church look like? No complete picture has been presented yet, but the centerpiece of his reformation is the P.E.A.C.E. plan. The details of this plan are still being worked out, but so far we know that the objective of the plan is to mobilize "a billion foot soldiers"[2] to wipe out the "five giants:" spiritual emptiness, lack of servant leaders, poverty, disease, and ignorance.[3] To work together, share our resources, and mobilize the masses to solve these world problems will be the new mission of the church, if this planned reformation succeeds.

The needs are couched in terms the world would accept as true needs, and would be very happy to have solved. In an interview on *The Pew Forum on Religion and Public Life*, Warren discussed his P.E.A.C.E. plan in a way that is very revealing:

> And we've actually created what we call clinic-in-a-box, business-in-a-box, church-in-a-box, and we are using normal people, volunteers. When Jesus sent the disciples—this will be my last point—when Jesus sent the disciples into a village, he said, "Find the man of peace." And he said, "When you find the man of peace, you start working with that person, and if they respond to you, you work with them. If they don't, you dust the dust off your shoes; you go to the next village." Who's the man of peace in any village—or it might be a woman of peace—who has the most respect, they're open and they're influential? They don't have to be a Christian. In fact, they could be a Muslim, but they're open and they're influential and you work with them to attack the five giants. And that's going to bring the second Reformation.[4]

Let us unpack this paragraph. The "in-a-box" terminology is from business jargon and it denotes a franchise. It means a reproducible and transferable package of processes and products that

can be used by ordinary people to replicate the success of the inno-
vator who created the system. Burger King is a "hamburger restau-
rant-in-a-box." As we have shown, the Purpose Driven church is a
franchise system; it is "church-in-a-box." Notice he says, "We are
using normal people." That is the genius of a franchise; a person
with normal talents can utilize a system created by a much more
talented person and share in its success. Warren wants to create a
worldwide system of franchises that will be utilized by ordinary
people to wipe out the world's biggest problems.

Warren's interpretation of Jesus' instructions to find a "man of
peace" gives them a unique spin. This needs closer scrutiny. Here is
the passage to which he is alluding:

"And whatever house you enter, first say, 'Peace be to this house.'
And if a man of peace is there, your peace will rest upon him; but if
not, it will return to you" (Luke 10:5, 6).

Though Luke was written in Greek, the concept of "peace,"
first as a greeting and then as a hoped-for reality through the
promises of God, is Hebrew. It draws on the concept of *shalom* as
being "ultimate well-being." This well-being, according to the
Hebrew Scriptures, was only true for those who were in the right
covenant relationship with God—there is no peace for the wicked
(Isaiah 48:22). In Luke 2:14 a multitude of angels announced
peace: *"Glory to God in the highest, And on earth peace among men with*
whom He is pleased" (Luke 2:14). Isaiah 9:6 prophesies of Messiah,
calling him "Prince of Peace." The idea is that true well-being
(peace) only comes through being right with God. Messiah came to
bring this peace to those who believe in Him.

The phrase "man of peace" is literally "son of peace" in the
Greek. This is a Hebraic expression meaning "characterized by." In
that context, when Jesus sent the disciples out ahead of him in
Luke 10 (see verse 1) as lambs among wolves (verse 3) because "the
harvest is plentiful and laborers few" (verse 2) the "man of peace"
is the one who is willing to put his trust in Messiah as the "Prince

of Peace." One cannot be a "son of peace" in the Hebrew under-standing of peace if he rejects the terms of the covenant.

With this understanding of Luke 10:5, 6 in context, let us return to Warren's statement: "They don't have to be a Christian. In fact, they could be a Muslim, but they're open and they're influen-tial and you work with them to attack the five giants. And that's going to bring the second Reformation"[5] This is not even close to what Luke 10:5, 6 are about. The mission was the announcement of Messianic salvation; the kingdom was near (Luke 10:9) in the Person of Messiah, the rightful King. The "son of peace" was not a person willing to cooperate to solve the world's problems, but a per-son who was willing to embrace the Prince of Peace on His terms.

Muslims reject the claims of the gospel forthrightly. So how can a Muslim be the "son of peace" simply because he is influential and willing to attack illiteracy, sickness, world hunger, etc.? Furthermore, how can the church have a valid "reformation" work-ing with unconverted Muslims to solve the world's problems? What he is proposing is a franchise system to solve problems so well designed that it will work whether those running it are Christian or not. It has to be that way because there are not a bil-lion truly regenerate Christians in the world. The foot soldiers for the "gospel" will consist of many pagans!

The P.E.A.C.E. plan is another piece of the redefinition process Warren uses to ultimately redefine Christianity. For example, Darrell Dorr describes how this process is to work according to Acts 1:8:

> Building on the sequence in Acts 1:8, Warren explains that Purpose Driven is seeking to progressively move the church from self-centeredness to unselfishness. If *The Purpose Driven Life* retools your life in "Jerusalem," and *The Purpose Driven Church* immerses you in community with your "Judea and Samaria," the P.E.A.C.E. aims to launch church-based, short-term small groups to the "uttermost parts" as catalysts for long-term, cross-cultural mission."[6]

That sounds wonderful, except for one problem: Neither Acts 1:8 nor the sequence of what God did in Acts has anything to do with solving the worlds five giants. Here is what it says: *"But you shall receive power when the Holy Spirit has come upon you; and you shall be My witnesses both in Jerusalem, and in all Judea and Samaria, and even to the remotest part of the earth"* (Acts 1:8). If an unconverted Muslim can be the "son of peace" who helps launch a "clinic-in-a-box" or one of the other franchises, then this process of creating a new reformation is not based on the power of the Holy Spirit! Furthermore, it says, "You shall be My witnesses." A witness testifies about the Person and work of Christ. We are not in the dark about how this happens. It started in Jerusalem when Peter preached his sermon and God converted people. His sermon and God's actions resulted in a church that fellowshipped around the apostle's teachings (Acts 2:42). It should be apparent that Acts 1:8 has no similarities to the P.E.A.C.E. plan.

A Work of the Holy Spirit

The use of Acts 1:8 minus the need for the Holy Spirit and the content of what it truly means to be Christ's witnesses underscores a key problem I see with Warren's redefined Christianity. Management guru Peter Drucker calls Warren the "inventor of perpetual revival." How does a man "invent" a revival? Warren is not the first to try. Charles Finney was the first to disconnect revival from a sovereign work of the Holy Spirit:

A revival is not a miracle according to another definition of the term "miracle"—something above the powers of nature. There is nothing in religion beyond the ordinary powers of nature. It consists entirely in the right exercise of the powers of nature. It is just that, and nothing else... A revival is not a miracle, nor dependent on a miracle, in any sense. It is a purely philosophical result of the right use of the constituted means—as much so as any other effect produced by the application of means.[7]

Finney, in spite of his horribly unbiblical theology, was accepted in his 19th century generation because he was successful and promised techniques that would cause the millennium to come sooner rather than later (he was post-millennial in his theology). Today Warren is just as popular if not more so, in spite of similar problems with his publicly professed teachings.

What is different today is that Warren has technology available to him that Finney did not. Finney was hoping to bring in a millennium in America.[8] Warren wants to solve the world's problems. However, he defines the problems for the church to solve in terms that need no supernatural work of God. People can and do feed the hungry without a work of God through the Holy Spirit. People can train leaders and fight illiteracy without being Christian or depending on God. Warren's P.E.A.C.E. plan perfectly fits Finney's definition of a "revival;" and it is surely a revival that a man can invent and implement.

What he "invented" was how to harness the latest technology, marketing strategies, management systems; couple those with a message that appeals to the unregenerate mind; then put the whole thing "in-a-box" and replicate it around the world. This revival bears no resemblance to what happened in Acts. What happened in Acts was a work of the Holy Spirit through the means of uncompromised gospel preaching. The P.E.A.C.E. plan does not depend on the Holy Spirit but on the wisdom of man.

Part of the reason this is such a problem is that Warren's five giants do not include the ultimate GIANT, which is the great grandfather of all giants—the wrath of God directed against the sins of mankind that has been building up, gathering interest, and is about to boil over in cataclysmic, worldwide judgment. If nothing is done about the real GIANT these others will become midgets in comparison; they are only temporal problems. Tackling the GIANT most definitely takes a supernatural work of the Holy Spirit. It takes gospel preaching and Bible teaching to bring the true work of the Holy Spirit to bear on the GIANT that is facing a lost world.

Jesus said, *"And He, when He comes, will convict the world concerning sin, and righteousness, and judgment"* (John 16:8). The Holy Spirit does this through the means of clear, unadulterated gospel preaching. A supernatural work of God is necessary because of a veil of blindness that covers the eyes of the lost that only the Holy Spirit can remove (see 2 Corinthians 3:12-17). Because people are in spiritual darkness, having their minds blinded by Satan (2 Corinthians 4:4), Paul conducted his ministry in a way that would maximize the work of the Holy Spirit. The Holy Spirit inspired the Scriptures. The Scriptures are the very words of God. The word is called "the sword of the Spirit" (Ephesians 6:17). It is a sharp, two-edged sword that can divide the thoughts and intent of the heart (Hebrews 4:12). There is no greater way to bring the power of the Holy Spirit to bear on man's greatest problem (his sin and God's wrath against it) than to preach God's Word forthrightly.

These facts explain why Paul refused to adulterate his teaching:

But we have renounced the things hidden because of shame, not walking in craftiness or adulterating the word of God, but by the manifestation of truth commending ourselves to every man's conscience in the sight of God. And even if our gospel is veiled, it is veiled to those who are perishing, in whose case the god of this world has blinded the minds of the unbelieving, that they might not see the light of the gospel of the glory of Christ, Who is the image of God. For we do not preach ourselves but Christ Jesus as Lord, and ourselves as your bond-servants for Jesus' sake. (2 Corinthians 4:2-5).

The ONLY reason Paul's message was veiled was the spiritual blindness of the hearers. He showed that he believed that only the Holy Spirit could take away the veil, and that the means He would use is the unadulterated preaching of the word that He inspired. Therefore Paul renounced "craftiness." Why? Because the preacher would be tempted to change the message so that it would sound more appealing—then people would accept him and his message. As we have shown using many examples, Warren has craftily adulterated biblical passages to create a message that people will love and appreciate *while the veil is still there!* That way no one has to rely on the Holy Spirit to supernaturally remove it.

The Scriptures, being the very voice of the Holy Spirit to men, must always be handled with a holy sense of awe and the utmost respect for the meaning of the text. The most powerful work of the Holy Spirit that the preacher can bring to the lost is the pure message of the gospel supported by the clear proclamation of God's word, both law and gospel. Finney and Warren are wrong. Revival is not a use of natural means nor is it invented by human ingenuity. It is God sovereignly and supernaturally working to convict the world of sin, righteousness, and judgment, and thus convicting spiritually blind sinners that they have offended the holy God of the universe. Those smitten with conviction have their eyes opened to their lost and sinful condition. They then see what had previously been veiled to their sin-hardened minds—their need for Jesus' blood that paid the full penalty to avert God's wrath. Then they can heed the call to repent and believe the gospel. This all is a work of Holy Spirit.

There is a warning in the Bible: *"Do not quench the Spirit"* (1 Thessalonians 5:19). Any veiling, adulterating, or crafty manipulation of a biblical text for the sake of gaining the approval of those who have not been convicted by the Holy Spirit, is "quenching the Spirit." Any modifications made to the message, any lack of forthright, valid applications of the message, or any additions from human wisdom and tradition, detract from the work of the Holy Spirit. It is like taking the sword of the Spirit and turning it into a rubber knife that kids play with. In that condition it will neither wound nor heal; it can only amuse.

After extensive research into the Purpose Driven movement, I can come to no other conclusion—this is precisely what has happened. Now they think they can slay the giants of the world with their rubber play knives, the weapons of the "church-in-a-box," when the GIANT who can only be slain with the Sword of the Spirit is not even addressed. More than the Great Commission has been redefined, but Christianity itself.

A Loving Appeal to Rick Warren

Pastor Warren, I believe you are an evangelical, one with an evangelical heritage that goes way back, much farther than mine. I was a latecomer, having been saved from liberalism when I was 20. I do not assume that you are motivated by money—I am quite sure you are not. I believe you sincerely want to spread your version of evangelicalism throughout the world. I believe you sincerely want to make a worldwide version of Christianity that will indeed wipe out world problems and spread Christendom where it has not been. I believe that you sincerely believe the truths in your statement of faith.

The problem is with what you proclaim and what you add to those beliefs. By muting the most important ones in public proclamations and by adding of ideas from the wisdom of man you have made the message of *The Purpose Driven Church* very different from historical, evangelical preaching.

My appeal is very simple. Pastor Warren, you have the biggest audience right now of any evangelical on the planet. You have the most influence. You have the tools, the resources, the education, and the scholarly ability to understand, proclaim and expound the truths of the gospel and God's word. Please use them! We need you to use them. Take up the Sword of the Spirit and mobilize people to slay the GIANT of people abiding under God's wrath, not knowing it, and living in a world that is on a slippery slope toward judgment. That is the weapon most of your evangelical forefathers used.

In conjunction with that, please repent of the practice of putting out material that obscures, confuses, and ultimately redefines all the important aspects of Christianity. Join those who are fully willing to accept these truths: *"They are from the world; therefore they speak as from the world, and the world listens to them. We are from God; he who knows God listens to us; he who is not from God does not listen to us. By this we know the spirit of truth and the spirit of error"* (1 John 4:5, 6). None of us who are evangelical need the world to love us or our message. Nor do we need the help of those in its sinful grips to fulfill our calling. We need boldness to proclaim what they hate, but what we know God will use to rescue some of them. May the Lord grant you that boldness to preach the gospel and the grace to return to His definition of Christianity.

Appendix 1

The Invisible and Visible Church

The Invisible Church

At the time of the Reformation, the Reformers made a distinction between the visible and invisible church. Though this distinction could properly be made between the church triumphant (all believers who have gone before us and are in Heaven) and the church militant (those alive now and in the battle), it was used by the Reformers in a different manner.[1] Louis Berkof describes the reason for the terminology:

> It [the distinction between the visible and invisible church now on earth] stresses the fact that the church as it exists on earth is both visible and invisible. This church is said to be invisible, because she is essentially spiritual and in her spiritual essence cannot be discerned by the physical eye; and because it is impossible to determine infallibly who do and do not belong to her. The union of believers with Christ is a mystical union; the Spirit that unites them constitutes an invisible tie; and the blessing of salvation, such as regeneration, genuine conversion, true faith, and spiritual communion with Christ, are all invisible to the natural eye; and yet these things constitute the real *forma* (ideal character) of the church.[2]

Before the Reformation, the Roman church saw its ecclesiastical system as the church. As the Roman church gained influence over nations and kingdoms, she believed that thereby the church was growing. Berkof describes the issues at the time of the Reformation that led to this terminology:

> The Bible ascribes certain glorious attributes to the church and represents her as a medium of saving and eternal blessings. Rome applied this to the church as an external institution, more particularly to the *ecclesia representative* or the hierarchy as the distributor of the blessing of salvation, and thus ignored and virtually denied the immediate and direct communion of God with His children, by placing a human mediatorial priesthood between them. This is the error which the Reformers sought to eradicate by stressing the fact that the church of which the Bible says such glorious things is not the church as an external institution, but the church as the spiritual body of Jesus Christ, which is essentially invisible at present, though it has a relative and imperfect embodiment in the visible church and is destined to have a perfect visible embodiment at the end of the ages.[3]

Various Scriptures show that this distinction is valid. In the following passage from Ephesians, Paul is not speaking of a visible congregation, but those who are cleansed by Christ whoever they are:

> *Husbands, love your wives, just as Christ also loved the church and gave Himself up for her; that He might sanctify her, having cleansed her by the washing of water with the word, that He might present to Himself the church in all her glory, having no spot or wrinkle or any such thing; but that she should be holy and blameless.* **(Ephesians 5:25-27).**

This "church" cannot be seen now, nor can this one: *"To the general assembly and church of the first-born who are enrolled in Heaven"* (**Hebrews 12:23a**). The church is a spiritual building: *"You also, as living stones, are being built up as a spiritual house for a holy priesthood, to offer up spiritual sacrifices acceptable to God through Jesus Christ"* (**1 Peter 2:5**). As such it is invisible.

We cannot be certain who make up the invisible church, but the Lord knows: *"Nevertheless, the firm foundation of God stands, having this seal, 'The Lord knows those who are His,' and, 'Let everyone who names the name of the Lord abstain from wickedness'"* (**2 Timothy 2:19**). This passage shows the idea of the visible and invisible church. Those who make up the visible church (who name the name of the Lord) are instructed to abstain from wickedness. Not everyone who "names the name of the Lord" is truly regenerate. Some will say, "Lord, Lord" and He will answer, "I never knew you" (see **Matthew 7:22, 23**). We cannot have absolute knowledge of who truly knows the Lord, but God does. No matter how strict a local church's membership requirements may be, there is no certainty that someone who has all the external evidences of being a Christian may join who may not truly know the Lord. Thus the invisible church is hidden in the visible one. John says this: *"They went out from us, but they were not really of us; for if they had been of us, they would have remained with us; but they went out, in order that it might be shown that they all are not of us"* (**1 John 2:19**). Before they went out, they were part of the church and appeared at the time to be Christian. Later it became evident that they were not.

The Visible Church

The visible church consists of people who have professed faith in Christ and have agreed to live accordingly. Berkof makes some important clarifications:

> It is possible that some who belong to the invisible church never become members of the visible organization, as missionary subjects who are converted on their deathbeds, and

that others are temporarily excluded from it, as erring believers who are for a time shut out from the communion of the visible church. On the other hand there may be unregenerate children and adults who, while professing Christ, have no true faith in Him, in the church as an external institution; and these, as long as they are in that condition, do not belong to the invisible church.[4]

Since humans cannot infallibly know who the elect are, churches must receive those who profess Christ, confess belief in true biblical doctrines, and are willing to live lives in accordance with the teachings of the Bible. This is good and proper. However, we cannot be sure that every member of the external organization is also a member of the invisible church, the true body of Christ. Anyone can see who belongs to the visible church. Membership numbers can be tracked. Attendance at worship services can be monitored.

It should be noted, however, that a visible "church" must corporately confess the essential truths of the gospel to be a church and not merely a religious institution. This is necessary because at this point in history there are Mormon "churches," New Age "churches," Universalist "churches," and other such groups that deny the biblical doctrine of Christ. Such groups should not be considered visible churches nor should it be expected that the invisible church is within them.

This leads us to some issues that will help explain some of the current confusion. Visible churches that at least superficially confess the key doctrines of the Bible are massively diverse. Every major Christian denomination confesses these doctrines in their official documents. Even when the modernist movement swept through most of the main line Protestant church during the late 19th century and early 20th century, not one of those denominations officially denied their historical creeds.

This means that visible churches exist that contain the light of the gospel in their hymnals and creedal confessions if not in their pulpits. Inasmuch as some light is there, these churches may contain a few of the invisible church. However, if the Word is not purely taught and the gospel not clearly preached, people are much less likely to be converted. Those who attend have to find the gospel hidden within an organization that no longer has it on its agenda. This is difficult but not impossible.

Martin Luther, though writing scathingly against the Pope and Rome, confessed that inasmuch as the Roman church had the Word and sacraments, there existed within it some of the invisible church:

> But it is God, who by His wonderful almighty power, despite the great abomination and harlotry of the devil, preserves among you [Rome] through Baptism some infants and a few older persons, only alas too few who, when dying, hold to Christ, of whom I have known many. Therefore, the true ancient church with its Baptism and God's Word remains with you, and your idol the devil, cannot altogether destroy it [the true church] despite so much new idolatry and your satanic harlotry.[5]

Though Luther lambasted the Roman Catholic Church with amazing vitriol and stinging rebuke, he confessed that there was still enough light of truth within her that some were saved in spite of her unbiblical innovations.

Likewise today, with the huge variations of visible congregations and denominations, we must confess that if some light of the gospel is present, howbeit dim and hidden, there will be some who believe and are graciously added by God to the invisible church. This, however, never justifies false teaching, unbiblical innovations, and the failure to preach the gospel. For example, those congregations who adopted modernism in the early 20th century and denied the authority of Scripture still contained some of the invisible church who had true faith in the gospel. Those persons were sorely grieved and many eventually left to join newly formed congregations and denominations where the evangelical faith was publicly taught and confessed. Yes, one can be saved in a visible church that has mostly gone astray; but it does not follow that such a person should stay and support false teaching. Today the seeker movement, including the Purpose Driven version of it, is creating a similar situation.

Appendix 2

The Churches of Revelation

The Church in Ephesus

Jesus begins His address to the church in Ephesus with a commendation: "*'I know your deeds and your toil and perseverance, and that you cannot endure evil men, and you put to the test those who call themselves apostles, and they are not, and you found them to be false; and you have perseverance and have endured for My name's sake, and have not grown weary*" (Revelation 2:2, 3). Contrary to what some people think, this is a commendation. They had obeyed Paul's former words precisely: "*Be on guard for yourselves and for all the flock, among which the Holy Spirit has made you overseers, to shepherd the church of God which He purchased with His own blood. I know that after my departure savage wolves will come in among you, not sparing the flock*" (Acts 20:28, 29). Jesus commended them for obeying the words of Paul and guarding the flock against false "sent ones" (apostles).

This church had a long history of apostolic teaching, beginning with Paul himself (see Acts 20:18-35 for Paul's address to the Ephesian elders which describes his previous ministry there). Timothy was told to correct false doctrine in Ephesus: "*As I urged you upon my departure for Macedonia, remain on at Ephesus, in order that you may instruct certain men not to teach strange doctrines*" (1 Timothy 1:3). John was likely in Ephesus before his exile to Patmos. Never has there existed a church that had a history of greater leadership:

Paul, Timothy and John. This apostolic teaching had born the good fruit of discernment. They refused to tolerate evil men or false apostles.

Given this backdrop, Jesus' rebuke is stunning: *"But I have this against you, that you have left your first love. Remember therefore from where you have fallen, and repent and do the deeds you did at first; or else I am coming to you, and will remove your lampstand out of its place— unless you repent"* (Revelation 2:4, 5). How could it be that a church that had profited from the ministries of Paul, Timothy and John be so severely rebuked? This shows how quickly a church can fall from the fervency of love for God and neighbor that characterizes those who have been truly converted! Here we have a church that defends herself against false apostles and endures for the sake of Christ, but has left her first love.

Some have used this passage to warn about those who correct error. They suggest that somehow the process of withstanding evil and error makes a person unloving. There is nothing in the text that says this. The word *"but"* in the Greek is a strong adversative. That means that the rebuke is in stark contrast to the commendation. The praise and rebuke are both strong. The idea is that the church **should** reject false teachers and practicers of evil **and** have a strong, heartfelt love for God and neighbor (see Matthew 22:37-40). This "first love" that had characterized this church earlier in its existence is love that is demonstrated through action. We know this because Jesus said, *"do the deeds you did at first."* In the New Testament, love for God is shown by one's love for the brethren (1 John 4:20, 21). Love for one's neighbor is shown by the one who takes concrete action to help those in need (Luke 10:27-37). Love for the truth is shown by correcting those who fall into error: *"My brethren, if any among you strays from the truth, and one turns him back, let him know that he who turns a sinner from the error of his way will save his soul from death, and will cover a multitude of sins"* (James 5:19, 20).

Correcting error and showing love to God and neighbor are not mutually exclusive. Perhaps the tendency is for those who battle false teaching and practices to become battle "hardened" and unloving. George Eldon Ladd comments, ". . . their struggle with false teachers and their hatred of heretical teaching had apparently engendered hard feelings and harsh attitudes toward one another to such an extent that it amounted to a forsaking of the supreme Christian virtue of love."[1] Those of us in discernment ministries do well to ask God to graciously preserve us from becoming this way and to kindle the flame of Christian love that is expressed in practical ways.

Jesus has a further commendation for the church at Ephesus: *"Yet this you do have, that you hate the deeds of the Nicolaitans, which I also hate"* (Revelation 2:6). No one knows exactly who the "Nicolaitans" were, but clearly they were a heretical sect. It is noteworthy that the Nicolaitans who were hated by the Ephesian church were embraced by the church at Pergamos (Revelation 2:15). Jesus' words to the church at Ephesus show that it must be possible to simultaneously hate the deeds of evil doers and love God and neighbor. We can hate the wicked deeds of those around us yet lovingly preach the gospel to them, hoping that God grants repentance (2 Timothy 2:24-26).

The Church in Smyrna

The short message to the church in Smyrna contains no rebuke, only commendation. Smyrna was a very wealthy city that is not mentioned elsewhere in Scripture. It was known for its wickedness and opposition to the Christian gospel.[2] In this wealthy and wicked city existed a small, poor, persecuted church: *"I know your tribulation and your poverty (but you are rich), and the blasphemy by those who say they are Jews and are not, but are a synagogue of Satan"* (**Revelation 2:9**). The term for "poverty" here means "abject poverty."[3] They were likely in this condition because of the extreme persecution they were under. They may have been deprived of jobs or perhaps their goods plundered (Hebrews 10:34). Whatever the cause of their physical poverty, they were spiritually rich in the sight of Christ.

Not only was there pagan persecution of these Christians, but there was Jewish persecution as well. These persecutors were Jews

by birth but because they rejected Messiah and persecuted His fol-
lowers. Jesus said that they were of the "synagogue of Satan." When
Jesus said they were not Jews, He did not mean they were not
descendants of Abraham, Isaac, and Jacob, but that they were not
fulfilling their spiritual calling. The term "Jew" comes from
"Judah" which means "praise." These Jews who persecuted
Christians in Smyrna were not bringing praise to God (See
Romans 2:28, 29), thus the strong words from Jesus.

Jesus then tells the Smyrna Christians that they would be going
through more suffering, imprisonment, and tribulation (Revelation
2:10, 11). He promises them the crown of life and that as overcomers
they would not be hurt by the second death. In Revelation those who
"overcome" are those who do not compromise with the world, who
are willing to suffer for their faith, who confess Christ and refuse to
deny him under persecution, and who resist false teachings. The little, poor church in Smyrna was a church of overcomers. As such they
are pleasing to Jesus and receive no rebuke, only commendation.

The Church in Pergamum

Pergamum was a prominent city that from an early time supported the cult of emperor worship.[4] The city was famous for the
various pagan gods, one of the more famous being Asclepius who
was a serpent god of healing.[5] Thus Jesus says this about the
dwelling place of this church: "*I know where you dwell, where Satan's
throne is; and you hold fast My name, and did not deny My faith, even in the
days of Antipas, My witness, My faithful one, who was killed among you,
where Satan dwells*" (Revelation 2:13). Perhaps "Satan's throne" is a
reference to the famous serpent god Asclepius. There were many
pagan temples and pagan cults operating in Pergamum; yet there
was a Christian church there.

The church in Pergamum was commended for holding fast,
not denying the name of Christ, and for having a martyr who stood
up for the Christian faith. In the Greek, Jesus said that they, "did
not deny the faith of Me." The definite article would indicate the
content of the body of Christian truth.[6] Here was a little church

existing in a horrible, hostile, pagan environment which held firm in her faith and confession even under persecution. But there was trouble as well.

Jesus further said to the church in Pergamum: *"But I have a few things against you, because you have there some who hold the teaching of Balaam, who kept teaching Balak to put a stumbling block before the sons of Israel, to eat things sacrificed to idols, and to commit acts of immorality. Thus you also have some who in the same way hold the teaching of the Nicolaitans"* (Revelation 2:14, 15). The doctrine of Balaam is a reference to Numbers 31:16. Though Balaam failed to curse Israel as Balak had requested earlier in Numbers, Balaam came up with a better plan. The problem was that God had blessed Israel and Balaam could not change that (Numbers 23:20). So Balaam came up with solution. He knew that if Israel would compromise with the pagans in their religious practices they would put themselves under God's curse. That is just what they did as recorded in Numbers 25:1-3. The teaching of Balaam was to promote compromise with the religious practices of paganism. In the case of Pergamum, it was to participate in the pagan religious services which included eating meat offered to idols and committing fornication.[7] Some members of the church had listened to this teaching and claimed the liberty to participate. Those who did probably found it much easier to fit in with the citizens of the city and avoid persecution.

As mentioned earlier, whatever the doctrine of the Nicolaitans was (possibly the passage here is linking the Nicolaitans with Balaam, implying they taught the same thing[8]), Christians in Ephesus hated it and some in Pergamum embraced it. The former were commended and the latter rebuked.

This church likely had two types of members within: those who confessed the faith and resisted the world who were persecuted and even martyred and those who compromised with the pagans for their own pleasure. This means that biblical church discipline was not being practiced. They tolerated what they should not have.

The Church in Thyatira

Thyatira was a wealthy city known for its trade guilds, fabric industry, and purple dye.[9] Outside of Revelation, the only mention of this city concerned the fact that Lydia, a key person in the church of Philippi, was a seller of purple from Thyatira (Acts 16:12-15). That Acts mentions the selling of purple and Thyatira shows the historical accuracy of the Bible. The trade guilds and wealth that accompanied them most certainly contributed to the serious problems in the Thyatiran church. Those who belonged to the guilds were expected to participate in common meals dedicated to pagan deities.[10] These meals often ended in what Ladd calls, "unbridled licentiousness."[11] Thus the members who became Christian would likely be faced with a very difficult choice between retaining their economic prosperity or maintaining the purity of their Christian faith. Jesus' message to the church shows that they chose the former with the blessing of a false prophetess called "Jezebel."

The church in Thyatira receives a brief commendation followed by a lengthy, stern rebuke. Here is the commendation: *"I know your deeds, and your love and faith and service and perseverance, and that your deeds of late are greater than at first"* (Revelation 2:19). That these qualities existed would not seem remarkable if it were not for the fact of the scathing rebuke that follows. The church was progressing in the key Christian virtues of faith and love which were being manifested in Christian service. One would think that this was an exemplary church if no more were said. It is noteworthy that this church had the type of love that the Ephesian church lacked. From what follows we see that the condition of this church is the opposite of that in Ephesus. Thyatira had love but tolerated false teaching; whereas Ephesus did not tolerate false teaching but lacked love.

Jesus goes on to rebuke the church of Thyatira for tolerating a false prophetess: *"But I have this against you, that you tolerate the woman Jezebel, who calls herself a prophetess, and she teaches and leads My bond-servants astray, so that they commit acts of immorality and eat things sacrificed to idols"* (Revelation 2:20). These sinful acts were likely linked to the pagan feasts of the trade guilds. In 1 Corinthians Paul allows eating meats offered to idols if the meat were merely bought in the marketplace (1 Corinthians 10:25). In a city like Thyatira, any meat found in a marketplace would likely have been offered to idols. However, Paul forbids eating such meat in connection with the idol worship itself: *"But if anyone should say to you, "This is meat sacrificed to idols," do not eat it, for the sake of the one who informed you, and for conscience' sake"* (1Corinthians 10:28). Also, since the eating of the meat is coupled with immorality, the evidence points to participation in the pagan feasts.

The problem was that several lusts were being fulfilled with prophetic endorsement: the lust for money and prestige and the lust for immorality. Ladd writes, "The reason why the problem assumed such acute form in Thyatira was that membership in the trade guilds involved participation in pagan meals and often led to immorality."[12] In the gospels, Jesus required people to lay aside everything for His sake, to take up their cross and follow Him. The church in Thyatira gave no heed to that part of Jesus' message. They enjoyed their relationship with the world too much.

Jezebel, who encouraged these sins, is likely a real person in Thyatira who is called Jezebel because of her spiritual relationship to the Jezebel of the Old Testament. The Old Testament Jezebel attempted to integrate Baal worship into the practices of Israel. She hated the prophets who pointed out her sin and killed as many of them as she could, though God spared Elijah from her.

Another aspect of the problem in Thyatira is revealed in this verse: *"But I say to you, the rest who are in Thyatira, who do not hold this teaching, who have not known the deep things of Satan, as they call them— I place no other burden on you"* (Revelation 2:24). Jezebel's teaching is called, "the deep things of Satan." It is not clear from the grammar whether this is irony (they claim to know deep things of God but these are actually from Satan, so Ladd) or a literal claim (that they gain some benefit from knowing details of the Satanic system, so Lenksi). In either case, there is a spiritual side to this immorality. They had a sensual spirituality that they actually thought made them superior.

Jesus addressed a remnant, "the rest" who have not known the supposed superior spirituality advocated by the prophetess. That He placed no other burden is possibly a reference to the determination of the Jerusalem council which forbade fornication and eating things strangled. The remnant was to not listen to Jezebel and refuse to participate in the pagan feasts or seek the secret, "deeper" spiritual knowledge that the others claimed. Thus their faith, love and service would be unsullied and praiseworthy.

The Church in Sardis

Jesus called the church in Sardis "dead": "*I know your deeds, that you have a name that you are alive, but you are dead*" (Revelation 3:1b). This alarming diagnosis from the Lord shows that what others think of a church has no bearing on what God thinks of it. Those who are clamoring for recognition from Rick Warren and other purveyors of Church Growth should take careful note of this. It is one thing to be popular with man, quite another to please the Lord.

This was a church that had a reputation ("name") of being an "alive" church. However they were spiritually asleep: "*Wake up, and strengthen the things that remain, which were about to die; for I have not found your deeds completed in the sight of My God*" (Revelation 3:2). There is no indication that this church was persecuted or that she embraced false doctrine. The church was satisfied to be known as alive by others and to be content with her peaceful situation. The incomplete deeds show a lack of living out all the implications of the gospel. Had this church been fervent and faithful in its response to the gospel and outreach with the gospel, she would likely have faced the hostility of the pagan world. She had found favor with the world by not fully teaching and practicing the implications of the gospel.

The church at Sardis coexisted in the city with the cult of Cybele,[13] a pagan goddess whose worship included horrid and disgusting practices.[14] Also, later in Sardis a large synagogue was built which has been excavated and is very impressive.[15] What is interesting about the church at Sardis is what is lacking compared to several of the other churches: compromise with the pagans and hostility from the Jews. There are possible reasons for this. For one, the practices of the cult of Cybele involved self-mutilation and other revolting practices that were unlikely to be attractive to outsiders (unlike the feasts and immoral parties of Thyatira). For another, the outwardly popular but inwardly dead church at Sardis was unlikely to have been bold enough to preach the gospel to the Jews and pagans and thus bring persecution. They were content to have the name of being alive and relative peace with the society around.

Jesus further said, *"Remember therefore what you have received and heard; and keep it, and repent. If therefore you will not wake up, I will come like a thief, and you will not know at what hour I will come upon you"* (Revelation 3:3). They were to call to mind the truths of the gospel that had caused the church to come to be in the first place. They were to repent of their satisfaction of being popular with man, "alive" in reputation, and return to the only thing that can truly make anyone alive which is the work of the Holy Spirit through the gospel to regenerate sinners. George Eldon Ladd comments, "Here is a picture of nominal Christianity, outwardly prosperous, busy with the externals of religious activity, but devoid of spiritual life and power."[16]

Revelation 3:4, 5 shows that there was still a faithful remnant in Sardis. Often when a church comes to exist for other reasons than why it existed in the first place, there remain people who truly know the Lord. Such individuals often know that something is wrong but are not sure what to do. Jesus comforted them with the promise of white garments and their names in the book of life.

The Church in Philadelphia

The Lord had no words of rebuke for the church in Philadelphia. This church was under Jewish persecution as shown by the reference to the "synagogue of Satan" (discussed in the section about the church in Smyrna). Lord gives them this commendation: *"I know your deeds. Behold, I have put before you an open door which no one can shut, because you have a little power, and have kept My Word, and have not denied My Name"* (Revelation 3:8). To understand the church we need to understand the phrase, "a little power." The NIV and ESV translate this, "I know you have little strength" and "I know you have but little power" respectively. Ladd also translates it that way and comments, "The emphasis is not on the little strength that the church possess, but upon the fact that she has only a little strength. Apparently this church was small, poor, and uninfluential."[17] Like the church of Smyrna who was also commended only, Jesus did not see poverty or lack of size as a sign of malaise.

The key of David mentioned in verse 7 and the open door in verse 8 concern the means of entrance into the Messianic kingdom. This small, poor church had in its possession the keys to the kingdom. The only means of entrance to the Messianic kingdom is through the gospel of Jesus Christ. Ladd comments on this, "The thought may well be that though the church is small and weak, Christ has set before her a great opportunity to make the gospel known."[18] Perhaps compared to the prospering synagogue, the church seemed to have little going for it. But those in the synagogue did not have the key of David (an allusion to Isaiah 22:22) because the Son of David is Jesus the Messiah and He gave the key of entrance to the Davidic kingdom the church (Matthew 16:16). The open door given to the church cannot be shut by man because the church has entrance through the gospel.

The commendation is that they have "kept My Word" and "not denied My Name." They not only had the keys, they were using them. They actively confessed Christ and His gospel even in the face of persecution. The pattern emerging from the commendations in the letters to the churches is that nothing is more important than confessing. This is probably because of the persecution in the first century. A church like Sardis could avoid conflict with the pagan society by keeping quiet and not actively confessing the gospel before the pagans. Confessors were often martyred as we saw in Smyrna and Pergamum. Confession offended the Jews and the Pagans because it meant telling them that unless they repented and believed on Christ, they would perish under God's judgment. The church in Philadelphia was poor and small, but they confessed, thus using the keys of the kingdom. Today as well, as the church exists in an increasingly pagan society, the key virtue that we desperately need is clear and forthright confession of the gospel.

The Church in Laodicea

The church in Laodicea is the most famous one in the minds of most Bible believing Christians because of two famous passages, the one about being lukewarm and the one about Jesus standing at the door and knocking. It is interesting that both of those passages are usually misunderstood or misused. The church in Laodicea was rebuked only and received no commendation. The one "attribute" that this church possessed was a positive self image: *"Because you say, 'I am rich, and have become wealthy, and have need of nothing,' and you do not know that you are wretched and miserable and poor and blind and naked"* (Revelation 3:17). The Laodicean church boasted of being healthy and prosperous. Ladd translates this, "I have gotten riches" pointing out that they did trust their own successful efforts.[19] They were a strong, wealthy, successful church, at least in their own eyes. This attitude reflects the local attitude of the city, which was a very wealthy city that prided herself in having been rebuilt after an earthquake with no outside help.[20]

The Laodicean church was self-deluded. Perhaps the most dangerous time for the church (as is borne out by church history) is when the church is wealthy and successful. It does not necessarily follow that an outwardly successful church must of necessity be one that has compromised. We need more information before we can make such an assessment (like whether the law and the gospel are being preached without compromise). However, the key problem is the **thinking** that because we are successful, therefore we must be pleasing to God. The Laodicean church makes it clear that such thinking can be the result of tragic self-delusion. This shows how badly we need objective criteria from God Himself to determine if what we are doing is pleasing to Him. That is why only Jesus can judge the "health" of a church and that we need to learn from the criteria he uses as shown here in Revelation.

Here is what Jesus said to this seemingly "successful" but self-deluded church: "*I know your deeds, that you are neither cold nor hot; I would that you were cold or hot. So because you are lukewarm, and neither hot nor cold, I will spit you out of My mouth*" (Revelation 3:15, 16). The common interpretation of this is that cold signifies the lost or spiritually dead, the hot signifies fervent Christians, and the lukewarm are complacent Christians.[21] However, the passage is more likely a reference to local water supplies. Just north of Laodicea was Hierapolis, famous for its hot springs that were deemed medicinal.[22] Colossae was known for cold pure waters.[23] Laodicea did not have a suitable water supply: "The city's lukewarm, mineral-laden water was suitable only as a means to induce vomiting."[24] So the cold water was useful as was the hot water, but the Laodicean water was useless. The church was being rebuked for the spiritual uselessness of her "deeds." Jesus was saying that the deeds of the Laodicean church were as nauseating to Him as their own local water was to them. What a graphic and stunning rebuke!

Jesus instructed this church, "*I advise you to buy from Me gold refined by fire, that you may become rich, and white garments, that you may clothe yourself, and that the shame of your nakedness may not be revealed; and eye salve to anoint your eyes, that you may see*" (Revelation 3:18). Jesus spoke to their real needs which were many, not to their "perceived needs," which were none. As we have seen, the Purpose Driven movement is concerned with perceived needs, which Jesus saw as self-deluded.

Refined "gold" would be spiritual wealth that has been through the refiner's fire of testing and discipline.[25] White garments are the righteousness of Christ which, if they had received it by faith, would cover the embarrassment of their spiritual nakedness. The eye salve is another local allusion. Laodicea was famous for producing eye salve that was said to have curative power.[26]

They were spiritually blind and did not know it. Here was a church with a total lack of discernment, particularly concerning their own condition. Their wealth and success had blinded their eyes to their beggarly spiritual reality.

There is another passage in Jesus' address to this church that needs comment in regard to the virtues and vices of churches. It is this famous passage: *"Behold, I stand at the door and knock; if anyone hears My voice and opens the door, I will come in to him, and will dine with him, and he with Me"* (Revelation 3:20). This passage is not an evangelistic verse about a sinner asking Jesus into his or her heart as it is so often misused. It is an ironic rebuke to the Laodicean church. Dining should be understood in the context of Jewish table fellowship. Jesus used this concept to rebuke others who, like these Laodiceans, were self-sufficient and blind to their spiritual condition. For example He said this to His Jewish brethren who were not believing in Him: *"There will be weeping and gnashing of teeth there when you see Abraham and Isaac and Jacob and all the prophets in the kingdom of God, but yourselves being cast out. And they will come from east and west, and from north and south, and will recline at the table in the kingdom of God"* (Luke 13:28, 29). When we receive communion in the manner the Lord prescribed we, *"proclaim the Lord's death until He comes"* (1 Corinthians 11:26b). True Christian fellowship is centered about the person and work of Christ, and His spiritual presence in our midst. In Laodicea, the Lord Himself was excluded from their table fellowship. He asked to be brought back in. Mounce comments, "In their blind self-sufficiency they had, as it were, excommunicated the risen Lord from their congregation."[27]

Endnotes

Introduction
[1] http://www.rna.org

[2] http://www.rna.org

[3] http://www.fortune.com/fortune/articles/0,15114,1118645,00.html

[4] http://www.fortune.com/fortune/articles/0,15114,1118645,00.html
Will Success Spoil Rick Warren; in Fortune; Oct 31, 2005.

Chapter 1
[1] Rick Warren, *The Purpose Driven Church*, (Grand Rapids: Zondervan, 1995) 29, 30.

[2] Donald A. McGavran, *Understanding Church Growth*, revised and edited by C. Peter Wagner, (Grand Rapids: Eerdmans, 3rd edition, 1990) C. Peter Wagner's introduction, xi.

[3] Ibid. viii.

[4] Donald A. McGavran and Winfield C. Arn, *Ten Steps for Church Growth*, (San Francisco: Harper and Row, 1997). McGavran discusses "excuses, rationalizations, and defensive thinking" as major causes of non-growth. 2.

[5] McGavran, *Understanding*, 165.

[6] Warren, *Church*, 169.

[7] McGavran, *Understanding* 233.

[8] Ibid. 227.

[9] Warren, *Church*. 219, 253.

[10] Ibid. 253.

[11] From the 40 Days of Purpose campaign promotion for September and October 2005.

[12] To be fair to the seminary, they were not entirely to blame. The large growing churches that were hiring seminary graduates placed little or no premium on theological knowledge. The seeker sensitive approach marginalized the need for high level theology.

[13] The seminary in question is Bethel Seminary in Arden Hills, MN and my friend is Ryan Habbena who is an assistant pastor with our church.

[14] Robert Schuller, *Your Church as a Fantastic Future*, (Ventura: Regal Books, 1986) 29.

[15] Ibid. 30.

[16] Ibid. 115.

[17] Robert Schuller, *Self-Esteem: The New Reformation*, (Waco, Word Books, 1982). This book called for the church to be "reformed" by integrating psychology and religion to promote high self esteem.

[18] http://www.crystalcathedral.org/rhsi/rhsi.about.html (as of March, 2005) claims Bill Hybels, John Maxwell, Bishop Charles Blake, Rick Warren, Walt Kallestad, Kirbyjon Caldwell, as alumni. Schuller praises these leaders, saying, "The students outran the master and I'm proud of them - and you can do it, too!"

[19] Warren, *Church*, 196.

[20] Ibid. 197.

[21] Ibid. 226.

[22] Ibid.

[23] Ibid. 227. Italics added by Warren.

[24] Ibid.

[25] Ibid.

[26] Ibid. 219.

[27] Ibid. 295.

[28] Ibid. 222.

[29] Ibid. 228.

[30] Robert Schuller, *The Be Happy Attitudes*, (Waco: Word, 1985).

[31] Craig L. Blomberg, *Matthew* in *The New American Commentary*, (Nashville: Broadman, 1992); 97.

[32] Warren, *Purpose Driven Church*, 228.

[33] Ibid.

[34] Ibid. 229.

[35] Rick Warren, *The Purpose Driven Life*, (Zondervan: Grand Rapids, 2002) 20.

[36] Warren, *Church*, 164.

[37] Ibid. 231.

[38] Ibid.

[39] Ibid. 232.

[40] Ibid.

[41] Ibid. 233.

[42] R C H Lenski, *1-2 Corinthians in Commentary on the New Testament* (Peabody, MA: Hendrickson, 1998; reprint, Minneapolis: Augsburg, 1966), 1239.

[43] Warren, *Church*, 253.

[44] Warren has determined through surveys that most unbelievers, if they were to visit a church, would do so on Sunday; ibid. 245.

Chapter 2

[1] http://www.twincityfellowship.com/cic/articles/issue84.htm Bob DeWaay, *Means of Grace* in *Critical Issues Commentary*, Issue 84.

[2] "Germany." Encyclopædia Britannica. 2004. Encyclopædia Britannica Premium Service.

3 Dec. 2004 http://www.britannica.com/eb/article?tocId=58088.

[3] Justo L. Gonzalez, *The Story of Christianity* Vol. 1, (San Francisco: HarperCollins, 1984) 267.

[4] Ibid. 266.

[5] http://www.newadvent.org/cathen/14741b.htm

[6] Donald McGavran, *Understanding Church Growth*; (Grand Rapids: Eerdmans, 1970, 3rd edition, 1990) Revised and edited by C. Peter Wagner, 28.

[7] Ibid. 29.

[8] Ibid. ix, x.

[9] Ibid. 29.

[10] Rick Warren, *The Purpose Driven Church*, (Grand Rapids: Zondervan, 1995).

[11] Ibid. 100.

[12] Rick Warren's website, Pastors.com, explains how "synergy of energy" is important in his type of church:

http://www.pastors.com/articles/SevenTransformation.asp Peter Drucker, the business guru is mentioned favorably.

[13] Warren, *Church*, 107.

[14] Ibid. 101.

[15] Ibid. 226.

[16] Ibid.

[17] Ibid. 227.

[18] Ibid. 230.

[19] See the entirety of John chapter 6. The gospels disprove Warren's theory.

[20] John 18:37.

[21] Warren, *Purpose Driven Church*, 130, 131.

[22] Ibid. 112.

[23] Warren, *The Purpose Driven Life*, (Grand Rapids: Zondervan, 2002) 167. Also, Rick Warren requires people to sign a "growth covenant" which requires tithing for those who are committing to his church; Warren, *Purpose Driven Church*, 54.

[24] Warren, *Purpose Driven Church*, 130.

[25] Warren, *Purpose Driven Life*, 166.

Chapter 3

[1] Dan Southerland, *Transitioning; Leading Your Church Through Change* (Zondervan: Grand Rapids, 2000).

[2] Ibid. 115.

[3] Rick Warren, *The Purpose Driven Life*, (Zondervan: Grand Rapids, 2002) 167.

[4] Southerland never admits that the church used to be a Bible church. Previous churches are called "program driven" by Rick Warren in the foreword, *Transitioning*, 9.

[5] Ibid.

[6] Ibid. 13.

[7] Ibid. 14.

[8] Ibid. 14, 15.

[9] Ibid. 15.

[10] Robert Schuller, Self-Esteem: The New Reformation, (Waco, Word Books, 1982).

[11] Warren lately is distancing himself from Schuller and likely would object to being linked to Schuller's reformation. However, the rationale that Schuller offers is very much the same as Warren's. Says Schuller, "However, I have seen my calling as one that communicates spiritual reality to the unchurched who may not be ready to believe in God. . . . As

a missionary, I find hope of respectful contact is based on a 'human-need' approach rather than a theological attack." Schuller, *Self-Esteem*, 12. Schuller, like Warren, uses the apparent lack of growth of the church as justification for a new reformation: "For decades now we have watched the church in Western Europe and in America decline in power, membership, and influence. I believe that this decline is the result of our placing theocentric communications [gospel preaching and Bible teaching] above the meeting of the deeper emotional and spiritual needs of humanity." Ibid. Unless Rick Warren somehow shows how his "reformation" is different than Schuller's, I must assume that Warren is of the same ilk as Schuller.

12 http://www.globalharvestministries.org/index.asp?action=apostolic

13 Martha Sawyer Allen, *The Divine Redefined – From female theologians come the stirrings of a new Reformation*; in *Minneapolis Star Tribune*, November 3, 1993. The article states, "They are exploring the sensual and sexual side of the divine, rooting around in contemplative and introspective interplay with God, and talking about women's daily experiences of the divine in every culture as central to theology today," Ibid.

14 Ironically, if these "reformations" actually succeed, there will be so much wrong with the church that we will need a reformation to get back to the principles of the first Reformation.

15 This passage is cited as proof that the service should be designed for unbelievers: "If therefore the whole church should assemble together and all speak in tongues, and ungifted men or unbelievers enter, will they not say that you are mad?" (1Corinthians 14:23) This passage, however, falls into the category of not giving needless offense, not designing a service to appeal to the sensibilities of the unregenerate. It describes the undesirable results of a hypothetical situation, not a meeting designed to appeal to the typical unsaved Corinthian.

16 Southerland, *Transitioning*, 12.

17 Ibid. 20.

18 Ibid. 21.

19 The Definition of equivocation is, "The same word used with two different meanings." http://www.datanation.com/fallacies/equiv.htm; This example is given: Criminal actions are illegal, and all murder trials

are criminal actions, thus all murder trials are illegal. (Here the term "criminal actions" is used with two different meanings). Here is another use of the term equivocation: "falsification by means of vague or ambiguous language."
http://www.hyperdictionary.com/search.aspx?define=equivocation

[20] Southerland, *Transitioning*, 21.

[21] Ibid.

[22] Ibid. 26.

[23] Ibid. italics in original.

[24] Ibid. 117.

[25] Ibid. 117.

[26] Ibid. 49.

[27] Ibid. 51.

[28] Rick Warren, *The Purpose Driven Church*, (Grand Rapids: Zondervan, 1995) 170.

[29] Ibid.

[30] Southerland, *Transitioning*, 118.

Chapter 4

[1] The Roman Catholic Church teaches what is called works of supererogation. These were works above the call of duty that certain people bound themselves to. I will explain them further later in this chapter. The Reformers rejected these forthrightly. Even the Arminian Wesley rejected supererogation: "Voluntary works, besides, over and above Gods commandments, which they call works of supererogation, cannot be taught without arrogance and impiety. For by them men do declare, that they do not only render unto God as much as they are bound to do, but that they do more for His sake than of bounden duty is required; whereas, Christ saith plainly, 'When ye have done all that is commanded you, say 'we are unprofitable servants.'" From 25 Articles of Religion – Methodist; cited from
http://www.imarc.cc/br/br2/wesley25ar11.html

[2] Rick Warren, *The Purpose Driven Life*, (Zondervan: Grand Rapids, 2002) 297-299.

[3] http://www.pastors.com/RWMT/default.asp?id=203&artid=8205&expand=1

4 http://www.purposedriven.com/en-US/AboutUs/SaddlebackAnniversary.htm

5 http://www.assistnews.net/stories/s05040087.htm

6 "This article is printed from the website www.Pastors.com. Copyright 2005 by Rick Warren. Used by permission. All rights reserved."

7 The LXX in passages like Ezra 10:5 uses the same Greek work for taking an oath that Jesus uses in forbidding oaths.

8 This means, "Argumentation that is specious or excessively subtle and intended to be misleading." http://www.hyperdictionary.com s.v. casuistry.

9 Rick Warren, *The Purpose Driven Church*, (Grand Rapids: Zondervan, 1995) 331-382.

10 Rick Warren, *The Purpose Driven Life*, 167; and Warren *The Purpose Driven Church* 321.

11 Warren, *Church* 321.

12 William Hendriksen, *The Gospel of Matthew in New Testament Commentary* (Grand Rapids, Baker, 1973) 309.

13 Warren, *Church* 320.

14 Martin Luther, *The Judgment of Martin Luther on Monastic Vows* from *55-Volume American Edition Luther's Works on CD-ROM* (Fortress Press, Concordia Publishing: Minneapolis, 2001) Vol. 44, page 243.

15 Ibid. 260.

16 Ibid. 262.

17 Ibid. 273.

18 Ibid. *Pastors.com*

19 Luther, 277.

20 Ibid. 278.

21 Ibid. 280.

22 Ibid. 285.

23 http://plato.stanford.edu/entries/supererogation/

24 Ibid.

25 Luther 384, 385.

26 Ibid. 297.

27 Ibid. 309.

28 Ibid. 311.

29 Warren, *Church*, 349.

[30] Ibid.

[31] Ibid. 350.

[32] Ibid. 349.

[33] Gordon J. Wenham, *Genesis 1-15 in Word Biblical Commentary* (Word: Milton Keynes, England, 1991) 317.

[34] Rick Warren, *Life*, 297-299.

[35] Warren, *Church*, 345.

Chapter 5

[1] Rick Warren, *The Purpose Driven Life*, (Zondervan: Grand Rapids, 2002).

[2] Warren, *Life*, 5.

[3] Ibid. 20.

[4] Ibid. 9.

[5] Ibid, 20.

[6] Ibid. 21.

[7] Ibid. 20.

[8] Ibid.

[9] Ibid. 27-30.

[10] Ibid. 30.

[11] Ibid. 30-33.

[12] Ibid. 34.

[13] Ibid.

[14] Ibid.

[15] Since the blood atonement is never explained, Warren's readers are supposed to accept what Jesus did for them. But the significance of what Jesus did in satisfying God's wrath against sin is unknown to them. So Warren expects them to "accept" what they do not know and understand.

[16] see http://www.probe.org/docs/mormon-jesus.html for a good description of how the Mormon doctrine of Christ deviates from the Bible.

[17] Comfort discusses this in his video "Hell's Best Kept Secret"; http://www.crosstv.com/ video wp0017.

[18] Warren, *Purpose*, 37.

[19] Ibid. 58

20 Warren, *Life*, 58.

21 Ibid.

22 Ibid.

23 Ibid.

24 Ibid.

25 Ibid. 59.

26 Ibid. 79.

27 Ibid. 78, 79 Warren sites the NRSV which gets this passage right.

28 John MacArthur, *Hard to Believe – The High Cost and Infinite Value of Following Jesus*; (Thomas Nelson: Nashville, 2003) I highly recommend MacArthur's book for anyone who wants to understand what the offense of the gospel is, and what terms it presents to sinners.

29 Warren, *Life*, 124. All four times Warren mentions doctrine he downplays its importance; pages 34, 124, 183, 186.

Chapter 6

1 Rick Warren, *The Purpose Driven Life*, (Grand Rapids: Zondervan, 2002) 9.

2 ibid.

3 I am not claiming that Warren's motive is money; it probably is not. It appears that his motive is to have massive, worldwide clout, favor with the world, and pull off his "reformation" to alleviate world problems.

4 ibid 5.

5 Ibid.

6 The citation by Warren actually includes Ephesians 1:11 and 12 from *The Message*. *The Message* translation makes the last part of verse 11 into verse 12, and does not translate Ephesians 1:12 at all, leaving it out. Leaving out verse 12 keeps us from knowing the important purpose that God has in working all things after the counsel of His will: "to the end that we who were the first to hope in Christ should be to the praise of His glory" (Ephesians 1:12). This makes the passage parallel to the thought of Romans 8:28-30.

7 There are many people who like that idea theologically, but it is an abuse of the Scripture to mistranslate the Bible to advance one's theological preference.

[8] Merriam Webster online dictionary; http://www.m-w.com/; s.v. "para-phrase."

[9] From the Preface of *The Living Bible* (Wheaton: Tyndale, 1971)

[10] Warren, *Life*, 17.

[11] Ibid. 19.

[12] Ibid. 18, 19.

[13] Ibid. citing *The Message* version of Matthew 16:25.

[14] Ibid. 325.

[15] Ibid. 20 This is how Warren cites it, which is a partial citation.

[16] See Gordon Fee, *The First Epistle to the Corinthians in The New International Commentary on The New Testament*, (Grand Rapids: Eerdmans, 1987) 105. Fee says this about "mystery," "In the singular the term 'mystery' ordinarily refers to something formerly hidden in God from *all* human eyes but now revealed in history through Christ and made understandable to his people through the Spirit."

[17] Warren, *Life*, 20.

[18] Ibid.

[19] Ibid. 24.

[20] Ibid.

[21] Allen P. Ross, *Creation and Blessing A Guide to the Study and Exposition of Genesis* (Grand Rapids, Baker, 1988) 185.

[22] Gordon J. Wenham *Genesis 1-15 in Word Biblical Commentary* (Dallas: Word, 1987) 145.

[23] Warren, *Life*, 69.

[24] Ibid.

[25] Ibid. 70-74.

[26] Ibid. 70.

[27] Ibid. 195, 196.

Chapter 7

[1] Rick Warren, *The Purpose Driven Life*, (Zondervan: Grand Rapids, 2002) 30.

[2] Ibid. 30-33.

[3] Ibid 41 (a partial citation of James 4:14b from the NIV).

[4] Ibid. Nin's writings are so sensual and perverse that the Web site con-

taining them has this disclaimer: "This is not a pornographic website; The following selections of "literary erotica" & unexpurgated Diary entries are for ADULT EYES and require PARENTAL PERMISSION for readers under the age of 18 in the United States." http://dreamlike.org/erotica.html I do not recommend going to the site unless you feel the need to verify that Nin is indeed an erotic author.

[5] Warren, *The Purpose Driven Life*, 41.

[6] Ibid.

[7] Ibid. 42.

[8] Ibid.

[9] Ibid.

[10] dokimazo_

[11] Warren, *The Purpose Driven Life*, 42.

[12] Ibid. 32.

[13] Ibid.

[14] Ibid. 33.

[15] Ibid. 119.

[16] Ibid. 33. Shaw cited by Warren.

[17] Ibid. 87.

[18] This is endorsed by Warren on page 88.

[19] Ibid. 89.

[20] Ibid.

[21] Ibid. 93, citing Job 42:7 from *The Message*.

[22] Ibid. 108, 269.

[23] Ibid.

[24] Ibid. 221.

[25] Ibid. 323, 324.

[26] Ibid. 91.

[27] Ibid. 20.

[28] Ibid.

Chapter 8

[1] http://saddlebackchurch.com/flash/believe.html (as of 4/13/2005)

[2] Rick Warren, *Learn to Love Yourself*, Ladies Home Journal, March 2005, 36.

3 All citations from Ibid. 36.

4 http://www.biblebb.com/files/MAC/mac-lkl.htm

5 http://transcripts.cnn.com/TRANSCRIPTS/0411/22/lkl.01.html

6 Ibid.

7 Ibid.

8 Ibid.

9 Ibid.

10 http://www.religioustolerance.org/resurrec8.htm ; Jeffrey Hadden, results of a survey of 7,441 Protestant ministers published in PrayerNet Newsletter, 1998-NOV-13, Page 1. Cited in Current Thoughts & Trends, 1999-MAR, Page 19.

Chapter 9

1 See http://www.achievement.org/autodoc/page/sch2bio-1 for a biography of Schuller and his achievements. It is interesting to me that he grew up 20 miles from the farm where I was raised. Schuller is from the town of Newkirk, Iowa that now is nothing more than a couple of houses on the intersection of two rural roads. He was married there in June 1950, six months before I was born.

2 http://www.purposedriven.com/en-US/AboutUs/WhoWeAre/Vision+and+Mission.htm this statement was current as of 3/25/05.

3 Rick Warren, The Purpose Driven Church, (Grand Rapids: Zondervan, 1995) 107.

4 Ibid. 101.

5 http://www.purposedriven.com/en-US/AboutUs/About_PD_Homepage.htm 3/25/05.

6 http://www.purposedriven.com/en-US/Resources/Purpose+Driven+Resources.htm?PageNumber=5

7 http://whatis.techtarget.com/definition/0,,sid9_gci347744,00.html

8 http://www.purposedriven.com/en-US/AboutUs/WhatIsPD/PD_Articles/Church_Health.htm

9 Ibid.

10 Warren, The Purpose Driven Life, 236.

11 Warren, Purpose Driven Church, 86.

[12] Ibid. 112.

[13] Ibid.

[14] Ibid. 117.

[15] See Robert Schuller, *The Be Happy Attitudes* (Word: Waco, 1985); I purchased a copy of Schuller's book as part of my research. The amazing thing is how much it reads like Warren. There are aphorisms and pithy sayings on nearly every page. For example, "What is the cross? It is a minus turned into a plus" with a cross symbol under the saying. 56. Whether Warren copied Schuller or not cannot be proven, but they surely have the same approach.

[16] http://www.forbes.com/management/2004/11/19/cz_rk_1119drucker.html

[17] Ibid.

[18] Business format franchising, which is the dominant mode of franchising today came onto the economic scene after World War II with the return of the millions of U.S. servicemen and servicewomen and the subsequent baby boom. The baby boom is still driving the economy and will continue to do so into the next century. There was an overwhelming need for all types of products and services, and franchising was the ideal business model for the rapid expansion of the hotel/motel and fast food industries. http://www.franinfo.com/history.html
"One of the unique features of franchising is how it has evolved with time over the years," says MBE's Amos. "It's been around in its present form for only about 50 years and is now a trillion-dollar business, where nearly half of every retail dollar spent in the United States is on a retail concept. Franchising is malleable and changes rapidly to meet the needs of the consumer."
http://www.franchising.com/library/a_theamevariation.shtml

[19] http://pewforum.org/events/index.php?EventID=80 as of 7/18/2005. The terminology "in a box" means to create a reproducible package, i.e. a franchise.

[20] http://www.activeenergy.net/templates/cusactiveenergy/details.asp?id=29646&PID=251005&mast

[21] From 40 Days of Purpose sales advertisement sent to me unsolicited by Purpose Driven.

[22] Rick Warren, The Purpose Driven Life, (Zondervan: Grand Rapids,

2002); 307.

23 Ibid.

24 Ibid. 323.

25 http://www.pastors.com/pcom/subscriptions/

26 http://www.pastors.com/pcom/conferences/pdcconference.asp The DVD set costs $299.

27 http://www.purposedriven.com/en-US/AboutUs/WhatIsPD/7+Myths+of+PD.htm Purpose Driven claims to work in any denomination like a computer chip that would work in any computer. I have heard from people from many denominations whose churches have been infiltrated by the Purpose Driven philosophy.

28 There are a series of articles on Warren's pastors.com Web site that detail how to change a church to Purpose Driven: http://www.pastors.com/article.asp?ArtID=4702 You can follow links from the first article to the next four.

29 http://www.challies.com/archives/000479.php This site has a copy of the original newspaper story and commentary.

30 Ibid.

31 Warren, *Purpose Driven Life*, 167.

32 Ibid. 166.

Chapter 10

1 http://www.purposedriven.com/en-US/AboutUs/WhoWeAre/Welcome.htm

2 ibid.

3 ibid.

4 John F. Walvoord, *The Revelation of Jesus Christ* (Chicago: Moody, 1966) 51.

5 R. C. H. Lenski, *Revelation in Commentary on the New Testament* (Peabody: Hendrickson, 1998 originally published 1943, Augsburg Publishing) 82.

6 This phrase is found at the conclusion of the message to each of the seven churches. It is a call to listen to God who is speaking authoritatively to His people.

7 See Rev. 2:7; 2:11; 2:17; 2:26; 3:5; 3:12; 3:21.

8 See Heb. 9:12.

9 Consider Revelation 6:17: *"and they said to the mountains and to the rocks,
'Fall on us and hide us from the presence of Him who sits on the throne, and from
the wrath of the Lamb'"*

10 Ephesians 4:15.

11 One church that received this award tells about it on this Web site:
http://www.northway.org/nwccweb/pages/PurposeDrivenChurchAward
/PurposeDrivenChurchAward.asp They got the award by following Rick
Warren's processes and principle. Evidently a "healthy" church is one
that most perfectly replicates Rick Warren's ideas.

12 Rick Warren, *The Purpose Driven Life*, (Zondervan: Grand Rapids,
2002) 34.

13 http://pewforum.org/events/index.php?EventID=80

14 James Sundquist, *Who's Driving the Purpose Driven Church?*; (Bethany,
OK: Bible Belt Publishing, 2004) 149-171 establishes the connection
between SHAPE and Carl Jung.

15 Warren, 89.

16 http://www.lighthousetrailsresearch.com/blanchard.htm

Conclusion

1 http://www.purposedriven.com/en-
US/AboutUs/WhatIsPD/PD_Articles/New+York+Times+Best+Seller.htm

2 http://www.assistnews.net/Stories/s05050056.htm

3 Darrell Dorr, "The P.E.A.C.E. plan: Are You Ready for Purpose Driven
Mission?" in *Mission Frontiers*; (Vol. 27, No. 3, May – June 2005) 16.

4 http://pewforum.org/events/index.php?EventID=80 page 16.

5 Ibid.

6 Dorr, 16.

7 Charles Finney; *Lectures on Revival, Lecture 1 section 1 – A Revival is not a
Miracle*. 9. from, *AGES Software, version 8.0* [CD-ROM] (Rio, WI: The
Master Christian Library Series, 2000)

8 Ibid. section 15, 292. Finney wrote: "If the whole Church, as a body,
had gone to work ten years ago, and continued it as a few individuals,
whom I could name, have done, there might not now have been an
impenitent sinner in the land. The millennium would have fully come
into the United States before this day."

Appendix 1

1 Louis Berkof, *Systematic Theology*, (Grand Rapids: Eerdmans, 1938, 1996 edition) 565.

2 Ibid. 565, 566.

3 Ibid. 566.

4 Berkof, 566.

5 Martin Luther as cited by C. F. W. Walther, Church and Ministry, (Saint Louis: Concordia, 1987 edition) 94.

Appendix 2

1 George Eldon Ladd, *Commentary on the Revelation of John* (Grand Rapids: Eerdmans, 1972) 39.

2 John F. Walvoord, *The Revelation of Jesus Christ* (Chicago: Moody 1966) 59.

3 Ibid. 61.

4 Ladd, 45.

5 Ibid. 46.

6 Walvoord, 67.

7 See Ladd, 48.

8 Ibid.

9 Walvoord, 71.

10 Ladd, 50.

11 Ibid.

12 Ibid. 52.

13 Ibid. 55.

14 Everett Ferguson, *Backgrounds of Early Christianity* (Grand Rapids: Eerdmans, 1987) 225-229 describes the Cybele and Attis mystery cult and the celebrations and practices associated with it.

15 Ibid. 399, 400. Ferguson includes a picture of the synagogue as it is now. It likely dates from 270 ad.

16 Ladd, 56.

17 Ibid. 60.

18 Ibid. 59.

19 Ibid. 66.

[20] http://www.ourfatherlutheran.net/biblehomelands/sevenchurches/laodicea/l aodictxt.htm

[21] See Ryan Habbena's article published in CIC issue 59: http://www.twincityfellowship.com/cic/articles/issue59.pdf; Habbena corrects this misinterpretation.

[22] Robert H. Mounce, *The Book of Revelation in The New International Commentary on the New Testament* (Grand Rapids: Eerdmans revised edition, 1998) 109.

[23] Ibid.

[24]

http://www.ourfatherlutheran.net/biblehomelands/sevenchurches/laodicea/laodictxt.htm

[25] See Malachi 3:3 and 1Peter 1:7. Genuine faith will stand the test of fire that burns up dead works and leaves only that which is pure.

[26] Mounce, 111.

[27] Ibid. 113.

More Information

Bob DeWaay has written over 90 articles on numerous topics.. You can find these critical issues commentaries at :

http://www.cicministry.org/articles.php

Forty, easy read pdf files called the discernment tool for *The Purpose Driven Life* are available for free download at:

http://www.cicministry.org/berean.php

Many of Bob DeWaay's sermons and Bible teachings can be found at his church website:

http://www.twincityfellowship.com

Bob DeWaay can be reached by mail at:

Pastor Bob DeWaay
Twin City Fellowship
P.O. Box 8068
Minneapolis, MN 55408

Phone: 612-874-7484

or email at:
pastorbob@cicminstry.org